Marie Dorval
France's Theatrical

Chiasma 21

General Editor

Michael Bishop

Editorial Committee

Adelaide Russo, Michael Sheringham,
Steven Winspur, Sonya Stephens,
Michael Brophy, Anja Pearre

Amsterdam - New York, NY 2007

Marie Dorval:
France's Theatrical Wonder

A Book for Actors

Bettina Knapp

Cover illustration: engraving by Vigneron, 1829.

Cover design: Pier Post

The paper on which this book is printed meets the requirements of
'ISO 9706: 1994, Information and documentation - Paper for documents -
Requirements for permanence'.

Le papier sur lequel le présent ouvrage est imprimé remplit les prescriptions
de "ISO 9706:1994, Information et documentation - Papier pour documents -
Prescriptions pour la permanence".

ISBN-10: 90-420-2132-2
ISBN-13: 978-90-420-2132-7
©Editions Rodopi B.V., Amsterdam - New York, NY 2007
Printed in The Netherlands

EDITOR'S PREFACE

Chiasma seeks to foster urgent critical assessments focusing upon joinings and criss-crossings, single, triangular, multiple, in the realm of modern French literature. Studies may be of an interdisciplinary nature, developing connections with art, philosophy, linguistics and beyond, or display intertextual or other plurivocal concerns of varying order.

*

To trace the life of Marie Dorval through the turbulences and exhilarations of her epoch is to engage not just with the genesis and the full flowering of a rare theatrical genius but also with the teeming literary, emotional, economic and material dramas in which such a genius is implacably embroiled. Dumas, Vigny, Hugo, Sand, Gautier and many others mingle their creative and affective energies with Dorval's in a ceaseless dynamic interplay. But to read Bettina Knapp's exceptional story is to realize too the so easily overlooked backcloth to life in Marie Dorval's times: poverty, the need to will one's survival, unimaginably trying circumstances in which theatre is performed, whether in the provinces or in Paris. And the account that follows further seeks, upon this at once intimate and societal canvas, to give us some real insight into the uniqueness of Dorval's acting techniques, simultaneously instinctive, viscerally natural, and learned, studied, though more from life than instruction. A book for actors, indeed; but a book, too, for lovers of the theatre and, beyond that, of the sheer improbable drama of existence.

Michael Bishop
and
Anja Pearre
Halifax, Nova Scotia
Canada
June 2006

CONTENTS

FOREWORD

Illusion has always been implicit in the human lot. It was and is a way of life. Instrumental in war and in peace, it is crucial to the arts and to the sciences as well. It drives people to achieve and to sorrow, to dream and to create, to love and to hate. It is the byword of the actor, the dramatist, and the audience!

Paris: 1820. Melodrama is the rage. While official theaters remain virtually empty, crowds flood Paris' left bank Théâtre de L'Ambigu and Théâtre Porte Saint-Martin, where blood-curdling melodramas, replete with comedy farce, mime, burlesque, opera, as well as unidentifiable extravaganzas, assuage the appetites of the famished.

Paris: 1945. The film director Marcel Carné creates one of France's screen greats, *The Children of Paradise,* featuring such outstanding actors as Arletty, Jean-Louis Barrault, Pierre Brasseur, Maria Casarès, and Pierre Renoir. Arletty plays the role of the seductive and brilliant actress, Garance, whose wiles, be they on or off stage, magnetize those around her. This mysterious stage personality was none other than Marie Dorval, whose real life dramas we are about to unravel.

CHAPTER 1

Our tale begins on an icy cold, and blusteringly windy day in Vannes, Brittany, a city on the northwest coast of France. Members of Ambroise Bourdais' itinerant acting company are safely snuggled in a large covered horse and wagon plodding its way into town. Their trajectory is not unusual for the times. Itinerant theater groups, mounte-banks, clowns, monks, and other types of entertainers had been performing throughout France since the Middle Ages. Whether they did so for educational or religious purposes, to sell some kind of miraculous elixir of healing, or simply to entertain passers-by, their goals, for the most part, were both artistic and remunerative.

Some companies and families of actors took to improvising their scenarios, parodies, satires, and/or joyous escapades. Others committed entire plays to memory, be they popular ones of the day, classical, or religious in thrust. Their sets usually consisted of a single large décor, with several specific locales – a seascape, an inn, a prison, a house, a church, a log cabin – painted or smudged on to wood or canvas, depending on the program of the day. Some traveling companies were handed down from father to son. Others, were created on the spot, to fulfill some inner need, love, rage, or poetic outburst.

A storm had broken out on this evening of January 7, 1798. As the clouds advanced, the setting sun dimmed, inviting an eerie yet brilliant light to pervade the area. The rain poured. The air was icy. The dozen or so performers and stage hands inside the van were huddled around a small wood stove. A mood of confidence reigned, now that the sets, costumes, decors, and accessories had been safely packed away in the back of the large covered wagon, although the troupers were still quite a distance from their destination, the flourishing city of Lorient, which had been home to France's royal navy since 1690. The citizens of this commercial city were proud of its international flavor. Not only were wares from every part of the globe sold and purchased here, but Lorient could also boast of being one of the four ship-building centers in France. Itinerant acting companies performing in this intriguing city usually had no cause to worry about attracting audiences. Nonetheless, while they believed they could count on the patronage of its citizens, an element of doubt, uneasiness, fear, and expectation still permeated the hearts of the performers.

After the passing of several somewhat tedious hours, replete with squalls of rain and wind, the huge covered wagon suddenly stopped. One of the actors jumped to the ground, unbridled the dripping and exhausted horses, then led them to a sheltered area to rest and to feed. After a brief waiting period, the animals were harnessed and the troupe continued on its way. A note of urgency marked this last lap of the journey. The eighteen year-old Marie Bourdais, daughter of the troupe's manager, Ambroise Bourdais by his deceased wife, Françoise Barrière, was experiencing her first labor pains. The thought of giving birth in the covered wagon horrified her. She recoiled at the memory of other actresses having done so.

Her father sensed her anguish and tried to speed up the journey. A hard-working man who had always earned pitifully little during his on and off engagements in Paris and elsewhere, he supplemented his income every now and then by organizing itinerant road shows with his new wife, Marie Delfèvre. Although a singer at the Paris Opera, her badly paid work was insufficient to pay her share of the couple's expenses. In time, she settled into the job of *ouvreuse* at the opera (Francis Ambrière, *Mademoiselle Mars et Marie Dorval,* 60).

Since childhood Marie Bourdais had been inured to the instability of her peripatetic existence. The constant packing and unpacking, the changes of habitats in no way disoriented her. On the contrary, she had come to enjoy the excitement involved with each displacement. Having learned to sing, dance, and act in infancy, playing small and large roles, even walk-ons, whatever was called for in the drama or opera the company was giving on a specific day or night, she was a natural on stage. As an adolescent, she dreamed, as did many a young girl, of meeting a prince charming – a handsome man who would fulfill her emotionally barren life in a long-standing marital love relationship. When at age sixteen, some say seventeen, Marie Bourdais chanced upon the handsome twenty-seven, in reality thirty-one, year-old Joseph-Charles Delaunay, she fell head over heels in love with him (Ambrière, 61).

Impermanence seemed to have been one of Delaunay's most attractive characteristics: the drama of not knowing where he stood vis-à-vis his many lady friends left young girls gasping for want of him. As an actor, he had usually been called upon to play stock male leads in the various traveling acting companies that had hired him. Indeed, he had performed in Orléans, Blois, Bordeaux, Limoges, Paris, to mention but a few cities he knew well. To the chagrin of the many girls he had attracted to his orbit, he refused to settle down in any one area, or with any one girl, including Marie Bourdais. So blinded had she been by her love for him, that she believed herself to be the exception to the rule: that he loved her and her alone. Her father had warned her over and over, back in 1796, prior to the onset of her relationship with Delaunay, to resist his advances until the marriage documents had been signed. These warnings redoubled after the two had been seen together at Lorient in spring of 1797. By the time their names appeared as performers on a poster advertising *Mélomanie*, an opera by Champein, it was too late (Ambrière, 61).

Since the highly emotional Marie Bourdais failed to heed the words of wisdom offered by her father and others in the troupe, the age-old scenario was again lived out. She and Delaunay became lovers and, alas, pregnancy was sure to follow. Although she performed on stage until virtually the last days of her ninth month, it was on the cold blustery night of January 7, that Marie Bourdais lay anxiously on a makeshift bed in her father's covered wagon that the onset of her labor suddenly began. Sensitive to his daughter's fear that the infant would be born *en route,* he ordered the caravan to stop on the outskirts of the city of Lorient, where she and the other troupers would settle into a family style inn. Minutes later, the midwife was called.

The following day, on January 8, 1798, a healthy baby girl, Marie-Thomase Amélie was born out of wedlock in a hotel on the Rue de la Comédie. The following morning, Delaunay went to city hall and declared the newborn infant to be his daughter. She would bear his name. In due course Marie Delaunay was baptised. Despite her mother's entreaties, however, Delaunay refused to marry her. Indeed, after some months he left Ambroise Bourdais' troupe, never again to see either mother or daughter. A wanderer to a fault, Delaunay left for the Antilles on a singing tour and died of yellow fever on July 15, 1802 (Ambrière, 62). After the birth of her baby,

Marie Bourdais had no choice but to remain in Lorient. It went without saying that she would have to provide for herself and for her newborn by finding acting or singing jobs.

These were unsettling and precarious times. France had been through a bloodthirsty revolution which had begun officially on July 14, 1789, with the storming of the Bastille, her fortress and state prison. The decapitation of King Louis XVI on January 21, 1793 and that of his wife, Marie Antoinette, on October 16 of that same year, was followed by Robespierre's sanguinary reign of terror. The death penalty meted out to him in 1794, neither alleviated shortages of food, pillagings, burnings, nor mayhem in the land. During the rule of the new French government known as the Directory, Napoleon, fired by his visions of grandeur and conquest, led military campaigns, one of the most moving for many a French soldier being the one waged in Egypt against England in 1798. At the sight of the Egyptian Pyramids, the future Emperor Napoleon, lapsing into high dramatic style, cried out to his troops "Forty centuries have their eyes upon you," predicting, as it were, the glories that would henceforth be theirs (Durant, *The Story of Civilization,* 108, 110).

Napoleon's enthusiasm for conquest and, understandably, England's need to protect itself via retaliation, served to endanger the lives of the citizens of Lorient. The French ship *Hercules*, only twenty-four hours after having left the safety of Lorient's port, had been captured along with its crew by the English. Indeed, it could be said that the entire French coast was dangerous at this time, particularly that of Brittany, Normandy, and the Vendée region. The peasants of the latter area, known as the Chouans – meaning "owls" in Norman French – had risen up against the French Revolutionary government in 1793. Using the hoot of the owl to signal their friends, these peasants had become such masters of guerilla tactics in warfare that even Napoleon's troops had difficulty putting them down. In fact, in 1815 he was forced to withdraw some of his troops from Waterloo to stem further Chouan uprisings. Understandably the citizens of the area lived in constant dread (Ambrière, 63).

While Marie Bourdais agonized over her own and her baby's safety, she also feared that as a single mother she might be unable to support a child, particularly since well-paying acting and singing jobs were at a premium. Nor could she count on her father for support, since he could himself barely eke out a living. Her strange life style, paradoxically, attuned as it was to the insecurities of a performing career, gave her the strength needed to face her problems squarely. After all, she was of sound stock!

The Bourdais name may be traced back to sixteenth century Angers, a picturesque city 360 kilometers west of Paris. This cathedral town with its exquisite stained glass windows, and seven tower castle, had produced such greats as Jean Bodin, the political philosopher, Gilles Ménage, the grammarian and etymologist, and the sculptor and medalist, David d'Angers. This municipality was known for its inns as well. Most exceptional, was that of the "Cheval Blanc," owned by the Bourdais family and catering to the high and mighty. As centuries passed, Paris, the artistic center of France, beckoned to aspiring actors and singers. Some of the Bourdais trudged to the big city, others refined their talents in Belgium, the Low countries, Germany, Poland, and far away Guadeloupe.

The young at heart, aspiring to make a name for themselves in theater and opera or both, lusted for that perfect elsewhere, dreamed of that unequalled paradise – the Paris stage – where fame and fortune could be achieved. Ambroise Bourdais, the "black sheep of the family," entertained such dreams when he left home at fifteen to join an itinerant theatrical troupe. Soon thereafter he married the actress Françoise Barrière, four years older than he. The couple settled in Marseille where they barely earned a living. Upon receipt in February of 1772 of an incredible acting and directing post at Lubéron, the two were convinced that God had blessed them. They happily settled in the castle of Lacoste and began directing plays for a private audience. The stipend was an unheard of 800 francs. The contract was signed on 1 April, 1772. Only one caveat emerged: Bourdais' future employer was none other than the Marquis de Sade, who, soon after their arrival, fled the area when facing imprisonment for having flagellated and sodomized four prostitutes. That Ambroise Bourdais' name was, henceforth, associated with the Marquis de Sade implicated him in the scandal. While disenchantment cast a pall over the would-be director for years to come, tenacity and the comfort of a large family helped him through his ordeals. He faced his daughter's pregnancy and delivery in the same imperturbable manner.

The constant political and military perils facing Marie Bourdais during her stay at Lorient were compounded by her anticipated financial plight. Ironically, its citizens, seeking solace and a change of atmosphere, flocked to the theater during these unsteady times. To find work as an actress would not be Marie Bourdais' problem. What she had not counted on was the drastic lowering of salaries in the performing arts. It had become virtually impossible for a single mother to support a child. Despite her penny-pinching, she soon found herself in debt. She had no choice but to join another touring company. Life, while far from simple, could be, she hoped, up-beat in the company of her new family of actors. There were moments when she did appreciate their humor and inventiveness. She failed, however, to condone their frequently quarrelsome ways.

Little Marie was different from other children. No sooner had she learned to walk than she reveled in being the center of attention. At three, this bright child started to mimic the antics of those around her – acting out moments of anger, instances of great passion, and/or loving and quarrelsome sequences to which she had been privy, either during rehearsals or at other times. What stunned her was her mother's seeming wretchedness. While she did not understand the reasons behind the frustrations involved, she reacted with sadness, and at times, with surprise, when her mother took out her dissatisfactions on her. Although Marie Bourdais loved her daughter deeply, there were times when, either fatigued, or out of sorts, she could not help but harass the child. "Your birth was a mistake," she told her repeatedly. "You have tripled my workload."

Certainly, Marie Bourdais was overworked and under stress. She spent a good deal of time memorizing her lines for what seemed to her an ever-changing repertoire of plays to be put on. Nor were rehearsals a simple matter. Costumes were even more worrisome to her. In those times performers had to pay for their gowns no matter their vintage. If faded, worn, or torn, funds had to be found to refurbish them. When need be, Marie Bourdais, along with other members of the cast was expected to cook, clean, do the wash, market, whatever was needed to keep their mobile home in good order. On top of it all, she had to care for her young child.

Traveling continuously from one town or city to another was arduous, particularly in the heat of summer and the cold of winter. It may have been far more than Marie Bourdais could stand. But she had no choice. She loved her daughter as she could love no one else. Sensitive to her mother's mood swings, the child reacted to her pain, though rarely, if ever, overtly. She almost always interiorized her feelings, sensing, perhaps, that she might one day draw upon them for one reason or another.

Marie's childhood years posed no real problems. She ate so well, in fact, that the members of the earliest traveling companies with which Marie Bourdais was associated, nicknamed her *Boulotte* (little ball). She was delightful in every sense of the word – smiling, glowing, and responsive to her large and fluid theatrical family. Inquisitive to a fault, she sometimes stood in the wings of the theater during rehearsals, agog at everything that was going on around her. She also loved to hide amid the stock of costumes available to her, fingering each of them in turn, fantasizing about the people wearing them. The painted decors – off and on the stage – captured her attention as well. The variously colored creams, however, posed a problem for her. Why, she used to ask herself did performers smear their faces with so many creams? Why red? black? brown? blue? There were times when she must surely have applied some on her own face in secret – ever discreetly, to be sure. Wigs also drew her attention. They were fanciful. But why wear a wig when you had hair of your own? She asked herself many questions. Why, for example, did her extended family of actors continuously repeat the same words, then abandon them only to repeat new ones? Life for Boulotte spelled mystery. It enthralled her (Françoise Moser, *Marie Dorval,* 4).

In 1802, at the age of four, Marie was called upon to play children's roles. She appeared alone on stage dressed in a white apron, a cotton bonnet, a Nanking-like vest, and rouged cheeks. She curtsied, then spoke a few words, and disappeared behind the curtain (*Marie Dorval. Documents inédits, 27*). At times she held someone's hand on stage. Not only was she adorable, she was an apt pupil. Nor was her education neglected. She was not only schooled in writing and reading, but in elocution, singing, dancing, walking, everything pertaining to the art of acting. At seven, Marie was called upon to play a variety of different roles, from Spanish dancer, to small parts in the *Magic Flute* and *Camille,* to mention but a few. Marie was learning how to fare in the real world as well.

When on their own, mother and daughter traveled to Nancy, Strasbourg, Nantes, and Bayonne in search of acting jobs. Though perhaps no great actress, Marie Bourdais was certainly a competent one.

The vagaries of fortune, like the throw of dice spell mystery! The wealthy and good-hearted Marseillais, Bathélemy Maurin, who had been running a successful second-hand furniture store, suddenly decided to give it up and fulfill his life-long dream of founding an itinerant theater company. Astute and kind, he decided to teach his wife the business and have her direct all surplus money to his future theatre company. All went as planned. Maurin bought a van large enough to house his performers, costumes, decors and whatever else was needed for his touring company. His novel idea of having his troupe perform regularly in three different cities – Lorient, Vannes, and Quimper – proved financially viable.

Maurin's vision and integrity saved many a performer in the area from destitution, including Marie Bourdais. Indeed, so successful had his theatrical company become that Marie wrote to her father, who had been playing bit parts in Paris, to join the troupe. He did so. An unfortunate altercation between him and Maurin followed, earning the former a ten-day prison sentence, after which he returned to Paris (Moser, 64).

While Marie Bourdais fared relatively well at this time, she again became pregnant. The young man in question this time did not even see fit to lend his name to the birth certificate. Nonetheless, the demise of the infant boy a few months later caused her grief. Under the circumstances, however, it may have been a blessing.

Hard times were again in the offing. Roles suitable to Marie Bourdais grew fewer and fewer, particularly since premature aging had begun to impress itself on her features. Whether in Lorient, in Paris, or elsewhere, acting jobs were at a premium. Her only solace was her daughter, to whom she told of her fears, grief, and pain. The two were inseparable. It was to her, now five years old, that she confided, always in overly dramatic terms, her mishaps and sorrows, and her unrequited loves. She had no one else she could trust.

By January 1804, mother and child moved to Lausanne, Switzerland. Although this Protestant land did not "tolerate" theater, which its citizens considered immoral, they awarded special favor to the newly arrived "theatrical dynasty of comics," directed by Pierre-Joseph Chevalier (Moser, 65). That Marie and her daughter had participated in this enterprise seemed a stroke of fortune. As fate would have it, however, the director died only months later, leaving his nineteen year-old son, Charles-Henri in charge.

Marie Bourdais' solitude and despair for her future thrust her into the arms of the bereft and equally terrified young Charles-Henri. They consoled each other at first. Then became lovers. Another pregnancy resulted. She was obliged to hide her "immoral" act from the puritanical citizens of Lausanne, or suffer the consequences. Disaster upon disaster now befell mother and daughter. Charles-Henri left. Marie Bourdais' new-born died in 1804, the acting company failed, and some of its members were subsequently expelled from Switzerland. The whereabouts of Marie Bourdais and her daughter are unknown for the next year. Some believe she became a street singer and that a kind soul sheltered mother and daughter in secret (Moser, 66). Mysterious, as well, are the means they used to flee Lausanne and make their way to Lille (Flanders), eighteen months later, in July of 1806.

The now twenty-seven year-old Marie Bourdais had aged gravely during these painfully arduous times. Few directors had work for her. If they did, she was relegated to playing small parts, mostly those of duennas. Neither her voice nor her acting were praised in the reviews she received. Jobs were so scarce it is thought that she and her daughter might have simply become wanderers, working briefly in one Flemish city after another – Gand, Anvers, Louvain, Malines. Whatever their conditions throughout these ordeal-filled years, mother and daughter were inseparable. Marie was her mother's mainstay, her confidant, listening attentively to her sorrows, litanies, outbursts of hysterical tears, pouring out her ever-continuing sense of abandonment and aloneness. George Sand described the mother/daughter relationship years later:

> Her mother was one of those excitable people who excite the sensibilities of their children at too early an age. At Marie's slightest infraction, she would say to her: *you are killing me! You are making me die of sorrow!* And the little girl who took her exaggerated words seriously, spent entire nights in tears, painfully remorseful, ardently praying, and repenting, asking God to return her mother to her, accusing herself of having

assassinated her – the entire incident, having been provoked by a torn dress or a lost handkerchief.

Traumatized since earliest infancy, her emotional life had been intensely developed, inexhaustible, to some extent, necessary. (Moser, 65)

While mother and daughter were intimate, their personalities were poles apart. Marie was charming and delightful. More importantly, she had a beautiful voice. She needed training, to be sure. On the other hand, she already knew the nitty-gritty of her *métier*. She had played walk-ons, bit parts, even full length roles. Her slightly hoarse, but mellifluous voice, unique in its way, enhanced her vocal appeal. She sang both solos and in choruses, including one of Etienne Méhul's comic operas. Marie was handy as well. Having been in theater since her earliest days, she knew just how to fix and restore broken and outmoded sets, costumes, and had a flair for designing them. Gifted with a fine memory – virtually photographic – she was capable of learning all types of parts in several hours. Although one cannot be certain, it is believed that Marie began her theatrical career between 1806 and 1809.

By 1810, mother and daughter had returned to Brittany and began touring its cities – Brest, Laval, Saint-Malo, Rennes, Mans, Alençon, among others. Two years later, they were still touring. Their stops included Pau, Bagnères, and Tarbes. While Marie Bourdais had been playing older women and "noble mother" types, the fourteen year-old Marie was growing in charm and as an artist, impressing her audiences with her versatility and her stage presence.

Following a brief visit to Paris in March of 1813, and thanks to the Bourdais family connections, mother and daughter joined the just forming itinerant acting troupes of Johann Ross. As impresario, he chose to direct the more important comedy troupe. The handsome thirty-five year-old Louis-Etienne Allan Dorval was put in charge of opera performances (Moser, 71). Marie and her mother were assigned to the second troupe.

Their comfortable covered wagon left for Laval in May of 1813, where they performed for a while, returning to Rennes in October. By this time, Marie had tired of working for Ross, whom she now looked upon as overly domineering. After contacting a certain Maurin in Lorient and asking him to become director of the operatic troupe, agreement was forthcoming. Mother and daughter continued on with Dorval to Lorient.

This city held unpleasant memories for Marie Bourdais. It had been the seat of her first pregnancy. The devastating humiliation after the father of her child refused to marry her, still ached. She was adamant that history would not repeat itself. Marie Bourdais had good cause to be vigilant after Dorval cut his ties with Ross and became associated with Barthélemy Maurin's acting company. Having until now led a rather checkered career, including womanizing and imprisonment for draft dodging, this itenerant theater director and impresario of sorts, excelled as a tenor and in other areas as well, namely that of a Don Juan. When he began eyeing the fifteen year-old Marie, her mother grew worried. Not only was he mesmerized by her daughter's singing, but she sensed he responded viscerally to her young, sensual, and untouched body.

Within a few months, it became quite evident that the thirty-six year-old Allan Dorval, was interested in the fifteen year-old Marie not merely as a performer, but as a woman. She, on the other hand, intent upon meeting his stage expectations, felt honored by the attentions he accorded her. As his advances became increasingly persistent, her mother's wise words of advice – marriage first, sexual relations afterward – reverberated in her ear. She surely empathized with the years of suffering and humiliations her mother had experienced. It must not happen to her, the mother affirmed. It was already too late. Marie was pregnant. When the perceptive Mme Bourdais discovered the unfortunate turn of events, she immediately planned an official wedding ceremony which took place in Vannes on Feb. 12, 1814. Only following the event was she assured that her daughter would not suffer the searing cruelties known to unwed mothers with bastard children.

With the birth of Marie-Louise-Désiré six months later, joy was written over the face of the new and utterly relieved grandmother. So too did the kind and protective godfather, Bathélemy Maurin, who had taken it upon himself to look out for the couple's welfare, rejoice over the event.

Not only had the thoughtful and creative Maurin organized an acting company with the goal of touring Vannes, Lorient, Quimper, Morlaix, and Saint-Brieuc, but he had designed special cars seating twelve people, each provided with benches and drawers in which the actors' costumes and accessories could be stored. He spent long hours training Marie Dorval for the stage as well. He warned her to beware of easy success, to study her roles in depth and not to allow only instinct to prevail. As for Dorval, he seemed to glory in his new wife, at least for now. Perhaps he sensed her glowing future, and took pleasure in advising his wife, along with the other actors. Wherever they performed, from the North Coast to Saint-Brieuc or elsewhere, audiences thrilled to his productions. Marie earned praise for her performances, no matter the melodrama in which she starred. It could be said that Allan Dorval was a happy man.

Not only was history being made in the theatrical domain, but in the battlefield as well. March 31, 1814 marked the fall of Napoleon's Empire, bringing his dream world to a sorrowful conclusion. That factions for and against Napoleon added to the tumult throughout the land understandably preoccupied the French. Theater also suffered. Stage drama was being replaced by street drama. People were arguing their points of view in the open, in stores, alleyways, theaters, in any and all areas. Without a written scenario, young and old expressed their illusions, fancies, and distresses.

So few tickets were sold during this cataclysmic period that Maurin found himself ruined, and the bands of roving actors that had also taken to the streets presented stiff competition to the legitimate troupes. There were times when Dorval accused his own managers of financial malfeasance. They in turn, charged him with spying on itinerant actors. Soon Dorval's meager earnings were further depleted. During this turbulent period, he and his wife knew but one joy: the birth of their second daughter, Catherine-Françoise-Sophie-Gabrielle born in 1815 in Lorient. But even this pleasure was short-lived.

Dorval's faith in the future, and in his own abilities, had come to a sad and sudden conclusion. One may presume that he was suffering from deep depression, or having a nervous breakdown. By 1816 he had lost interest in his work, his babies, in everything, even in his beautiful and gifted wife.

Marie was stunned by her husband's changing comportment and outlook on life. This once handsome, pleasant, and delightful man had turned inward, becoming morose and unreachable. Marie and her two daughters were locked out of his life. Whatever attraction she might have felt toward Dorval had now vanished. As she confessed: "I became the protector of [my] protector" (Ambrière, 80). Despite her legal marriage, ironically, she, like her mother, would have to fend for herself and for her two daughters.

They had not counted on the storms, floods, and high winds assailing the coast of Normandy and Brittany on this, their latest journey in quest of acting jobs. Although accustomed to life's problems, these natural catastrophes seemed to accentuate the negative vibrations constellated within the family complex. Dorval's condition had grown so unstable during this latest sojourn, that he left his family at Saint-Brieuc without saying goodbye. Catering to her husband had grown worrisome and tiresome, and she did not have time to spend consoling him. Money was at a premium. The ten month-old Gabrielle and the two year-old Louise had to be cared for. By 1816 mother and daughter, relieved of the constrictive atmosphere Dorval's presence had imposed on them, decided that Marie would travel to Strasbourg in search of acting jobs, thereby recouping family finances, while her mother would tend to the children.

Although the wiry and graceful Marie Dorval might not have been considered a classical beauty, her large forehead, expressive face, and twinkling blue eyes were arresting. She would set these attributes – and her talent – to work. As fate would have it, Nicolas Desprez, the director of the Théâtre de Strasbourg, happened to be at his wits end. Unable to tolerate his lead actress, Mlle Fleury, Marie was immediately hired to replace the disruptive star. Forever sensitive to mood changes and personalities, the diplomatic Dorval, while agreeing to play certain roles, refused to enter into the director's political machinations which had led to Fleury's dismissal. Marie handled herself with such sensitivity, that she not once alienated the disgraced Mlle Fleury. For her efforts, she won the admiration of the entire cast, even supplementing her income in the process by performing in such comic operas and comedies as *Aline, Queen of Golconde, Richard the Lion-Hearted, Le Calif de Baghdad, My Aunt Aurore,* concluding her stint by the spring of 1817.

That same spring, fate again intervened on Marie's behalf. She had always felt that attending theater could be a learning experience. In this regard, she anxiously awaited Desprez' new production, *The Culpable Mother* by Augustin Caron de Beaumarchais, starring the relatively unknown younger sister of the celebrated Mlle George. Only hours prior to curtain time, however, the star slipped and broke her leg. Aware of the cost of cancelled shows to theater companies, Dorval, in all innocence, suggested she replace the star in the role of the Countess Almaviva. As an itinerant performer most of her life, she had learned from Maurin to anticipate cancellations and sicknesses on the road. To allay replacement problems, she had taken to memorizing the roles of the plays performed, and continued to do so instinctively throughout her life. While Desprez was dubious as to her mastery of such an important part, he had no choice, and agreed.

By intertwining patheticism and imbroglio, as well as movement and excitement, *The Culpable Mother* took on the allure of a "drama of intrigue." Replete with escapades, sardonic humor, and bravura, it burrowed deeply into the human heart as well. Beaumarchais, whose parents had asked their teenage son to leave home temporarily because they could no longer tolerate his continuous stunts and antics, knew better than anyone how to play up the unexpected, the thrilling, the exciting and the titillating in a stage production. Once on his own – but only temporarily, since his parents took him back – the wayward youth had already learned to earn his daily bread by performing vaudeville acts on street corners. Later, Beaumarchais the writer understood the importance, breadth, humor, scope, dynamism, and the power which could be harnessed though the interaction of multiple escapades.

Like his highly successful *Marriage of Figaro*, Beaumarchais' *Culpable Mother* also featured stock characters – Count and Countess Almaviva, Figaro, and Suzanne, among others. This time, however, the creatures of his fancy were older, more divisive, nonetheless repentant. The action was swift, accounting in part for the pyramid construction of dovetailing scenes, serving to accentuate the play's humor and brio, while also adding momentum to its inherently melodramatic aspects. *The Culpable Mother* revolves around an important moral lesson: – youthful passions have diminished, the joy of fatherhood is experienced, even an evil person can turn into a good one.

With the bravura of youth, and the incredible advantage of being sure of herself, Marie made her character – the deeply unhappy, notably pious, and frequently weeping Countess Almaviva – her own that night. To express emotions subtly, be they anguish, disappointment, tears, or joyous banter, she at times had recourse to the art of mime. A brief smile, a subtle rolling of the eyes, a delicate turn of the head, allowed her to wipe away a tear, thereby revealing heartbreak. She stilled her body movements when seeking to dissimulate her feeling world. Marie held her audience in thrall. The applause was deafening. She had won the hearts of the Strasbourgeois. The director Desprez showed his appreciation of her talent by awarding her other parts. She knew she had a future. She glowed inwardly at the thought.

Nonetheless, for some odd reason, the image of Marie's own mother kept emerging and reemerging in her mind's eye. Despite her heavy schedule, she had noticed on occasion a slowing down of her mother's pace. At times, she had difficulty bending down. She even hesitated when walking. She seemed able to perform fewer and fewer tasks. Apologetically, she would tell her daughter that some days she was simply not up to doing anything. Few if any secrets existed between mother and daughter. Despite her utter fatigue, the former still took care of the home, saw to the education of her grandchildren, and, rehearsed theater choirs to earn a few extra *sous*. She was adamant about paying her share of household expenses, no matter how modest it was.

Marie, however, was uneasy. She sensed that something was awry. Predictably, only weeks later, on February 18, 1818, Marie Bourdais died in her sleep in Strasbourg. She was only thirty-eight years old. Thus ended a life of exhaustion and disappointment, but one of great love for her daughter and for her grandchildren. The thought that her daughter was on her way to stardom reassured her in the end.

That a vacuum now existed in Marie's life is an understatement. Nonetheless, she had little time to mourn. The little money she had saved, if wisely spent, could possibly see the family through a few weeks, but no more. She would have to find work and she did, accepting as many acting jobs as possible. Unlike her mother, she was ambitious and had confidence in her talent and will to succeed. The lure of Paris had become so great, that nothing but the city of lights, theater, mime, and artistry could assuage her appetite. By September 1818, she and her daughters were on their way.

No sooner had Marie begun treading the streets of Paris than she understood that she would have vast amounts to learn. Neither intimidated nor fearful of the difficulties facing her, on the contrary, she felt invigorated.

Young, strong, and determined, Marie was ready for the fight of her life!

CHAPTER 2

Marie was twenty, ambitious, and newly arrived in Paris, the epicenter of the performing arts. The sun was shining on this late April day. Her face glowed with anticipation. She couldn't help but feel thrilled as she strolled along the boulevards, lined as they were with cafes, theaters, restaurants, and brightly decorated *fiacres.* The Boulevard du Temple, the entertainment district *par excellence,* was of particular interest to her. Although relatively calm in the morning or even at midday, by evening crowds gathered to observe the many attractions offered. Its circus, marionette artists, acrobats, midgets, the much lauded Mme Saqui, the tight-rope dancer, automatons, peddlers, freak shows, street vendors, wax museum, fairgrounds, and merchants, were a continuous source of fascination to her. Theaters were everywhere. Among them, the well known Funambules, the Variétés amusantes, the Gaîté, the Folies Dramatiques, the Théâtre Montparnasse, the Cirque-Olympique, and, of course, the Porte Saint-Martin Theater. She made her way to the last named. She had been told that so many melodramas had been performed in this theater, that it had come to be referred to as "The People's Opera."

Melodramas were the rage in Paris. While they glorified the good and punished the evil, they were replete with violence, stabbings, kidnappings, poisonings, and other nefarious and virtually unthinkable deeds. Marie chuckled inwardly at the thought that melodrama had taken such a hold on audiences that the Boulevard du Temple, the area in which they were performed, was now referred to as the *Boulevard du Crime.*

These cloak and dagger plays, where villainy and the vindication of virtue were offered nightly, had been popular in Lorient and all over France. Marie had seen quite a few of them: innocence, righteousness, and virtue, forever pitted against evil, the latter always punished for the crimes committed. If only such were the case in the world of reality, she thought. She admired Guilbert de Pixérécourt in particular, for he had been the dramatist who had helped put innocence, rage, and murder on the theatrical map. Although not the creator of melodrama, he had given impetus to plays of this genre. His *Coeolina* or *The Child of Mystery* (1800), labeled a *"pantomime dialoguée,"* was one of his most popular ever. His monologues at times depicted such heart-rending images and situations, that sobs could be heard throughout the house. The background music – the tremolos of a violin, the pathos of piano tones, frightening drum rolls, clanging bells, among other jarring tonalities – were used to enhance the shrieks of the innocent and accentuate love, hate, rage, jealousy, joy, and laughter. Mood changes were frequently ushered in with the help of sequences of ballet, comedy, mime, monologues, each art form aiming to teach pathetic, mysterious, and elusive lessons in morality. So incredibly successful was Pixérécourt, the author of sixty melodramas, that he came to be referred to as the *"Corneille des Boulevards."* His friend, the *bibliophile*, Charles Nodier, used to call him Shakespérécourt. (*Le Mélodrame,* J.M.Thomasseau, 48)

Melodrama which had been flourishing in Paris since 1797, and would remain popular until 1835, took its name from seventeenth-century Italian *melodrama* which was sung. Many of its stock characters, such as he famous Harlequin, were adapted from Italian *commedia dell' arte* to suit French taste. Its Parisian counterpart, which included pantomime, dialogue, song, and all types of action, was, nonetheless, considered a new art form (Thomasseau, 8).

Nightly audiences at the Ambigu Comique, the Gaîté, the Théâtre de la Porte Saint-Martin, sat at at the edge of their seats watching evil-doers being punished, and the good rewarded. After sequences of harrowing incidents, fate forever intervened on the side of the good. Complex decors and stage effects, featuring earthquakes, peals of thunder, floods, tempests, fires, flamboyant reconciliations and love scenes of all types, added gusto to the sometimes excruciating climaxes, forever welcomed by spectators greedy for entertainment (M.P. Le Hir, *Le Romantisme aux enchères,* 4).

Marie was neither fearful nor intimidated by the many theaters she saw in Paris and the vast amounts she had to learn, including the uncertainties of life in the big city. To the contrary, she felt impassioned by the novelty of it all. Parisians were sophisticated. Provincials, on the other hand, enjoyed a relatively simple life style. Parisians longed for the here and now and not the redundant, archaic, and incomprehensible historical classical dramatizations to which many could no longer relate. Only present realities spoke to them.

Pixérécourt's dramatizations of faithlessness, rancor, adversity, crime, love, and generosity played to packed houses.

Upon her arrival in the big city Marie moved into a furnished room for herself and her daughters on Rue des Vinaigriers, then moved in with a friend for a bit, and hired a pleasant and trustworthy woman to care for her daughters. She judged the area, not far from the open air markets of the Boulevard Saint-Martin, to be convenient, at least for the time being. While the crowds in this popular and deafeningly noisy commercial area were baffling at first, she knew she would grow accustomed to the cacophonies of the hawkers and merchants shouting and plying their wares. In fact, such clamor could even become music to her ears. Haggling was a way of life which she knew well. Although markets were far from new to her, having seen so many in Strasbourg and Lorient, among other cities, this Parisian commercial center seemed unique – gigantic and so colorful in comparison with the provincial ones. The variety of foods and novelties from different lands, not to speak of the aromas filling the air, piqued both her curiosity and her senses. The hustle and bustle in virtually every section of the market intrigued her as well. As she walked on, she could not help but think back to the privations she had known as a child, her mother's continuous penury, her relentless search for acting jobs, her willingness to struggle so long as her daughter was with her. Rarely had a mother and daughter bonded so strongly. The memory of her mother's incredible delight as she, Marie, took her first steps on stage at age four, and then bowed so charmingly, had retained its vividness.

Although Marie had two daughters to support, and life would be far from simple, strangely enough a sense of relief and release came over her, in part because her continuously morose husband had ceased plaguing her existence. No sooner had his mother died – two weeks after her own – than he left for Paris to claim his inheritance. That Marie had not seen him since did not surprise her, given his depressed frame of mind. Furthermore, hadn't her mother taught her to count only on herself for support? She had heeded the advice. Unlike her mother, however, she was determined to succeed in her art. Enough Boulevard-strutting in the provinces, Marie said to herself. It was time to tend to her Parisian career. While she had originally counted on her mother to help her settle in, fate had willed it otherwise. She was not one to brood over the irrevocable.

Could one call Marie a conniver? Or simply clever? Her thoughts clustered around her new, still secret, beau, the forty year-old Alexandre Piccini. They had seen each other quite a bit in Strasbourg. Not even her mother had guessed of his existence. He was a kind and caring man who lived and breathed music. As head pianist at the Royal Chapel and music director, *chef de chant,* at the Opera, he knew the right people. She smiled at the thought. He was a composer as well. His songs and incidental music for popular comedies, melodramas, and ballets were sought after. Most significantly, he had been conductor of the orchestra at the prestigious Porte Saint-Martin Theater, which meant that he had good contacts.

Piccini's rise to fame had been unusually rapid. That he was the grandson of the famous Italian composer, Nicolas Piccini (1728-1800), known for having invested his operas with high drama, had certainly helped further his reputation. Everyone in Paris had heard of the rivalry between his father and the famous German operatic composer, Christoph Gluck.. Admirers of one or the other elevated their favorite to great heights while spewing venom on their enemy. She smiled at the thought of the continuous vilifications of both men during the famous "quarrel between the Gluckists and the Piccinists" in the 1770's. As of necessity, the intelligentsia took sides. In time, the enmity between the factions died down. Serendipitously, Marie's lover, the gifted Alexandre Piccini had benefited from the publicity!

As she walked on, her thoughts reverted to Strasbourg, where she and Piccini had met. A sentimentalist at heart, no sooner had he learned that Marie was the second cousin of his friend, the celebrated comic actor François Bourdais, he took to her even more kindly. They seemed to answer each other's needs, at least for the present. Nonetheless, Piccini was a strange man, she thought. Although a talented musician and composer, he had never been able to find himself. That he was married was of no import to Marie. She too was married. She had heard that he was a womanizer. No matter; at this point, their personalities worked in perfect harmony. The knowledge that he was generous to a fault helped soothe her anxieties about supporting her children and herself. Competition in theater was fierce. Although she had confidence in her ability, she knew talent to be widespread. Piccini, nonetheless, had promised to help her. He would keep his word, of this she was certain. She had found her man – her protector – at least for the time being.

Prior to her move to Paris, Piccini had introduced her to his good friend, the well-known comic actor, Charles Potier, who had been performing at Paris' prestigious Variétés Theater, attracting untold crowds in the process. When he left in April 1818 to seek greener pastures at the more important Porte Saint-Martin Theater, his enormous following went with him.

Whether by luck or design, planned on Marie's part, her Parisian acting career began at this very theater on May 12, 1818. She was cast in the role of Pamela, in *Pamela Married,* by the popular melodramatist, Pelletier-Volméranges. While enormously talented, to have been given the lead in such a popular play would have been virtually impossible had not someone interceded on Marie's behalf. That person was most certainly Piccini. A word to Potier from Piccini had undoubtedly helped her gain entry to the prestigious Porte Saint-Martin Theater. On the other hand, had she not been a fine singer and actress, no matter what Piccini's connections, she most probably would not have been hired.

Marie could not help but feel taut and ill at ease on opening night, May 24, 1818. Was she aiming too high by accepting the lead? According to the *Journal de Paris*, although she was well-proportioned, her acting was dismal, dull, uninteresting. More unfortunate, she spoke with a burr. But hadn't Potier and Piccini noticed this speech characteristic when she tried out for the part, Marie asked herself? She had always trilled her *r*'s, whether on or off stage. No one had as yet made derogatory comments about it. Some considered her pronunciation rough, others mannered. To be sure, it mirrored the accent of the masses and not that of the upper crust. Although her delivery was pleasant and her words well spoken, the critic added, her speech was "cold." Her facial features were less than animated, at odds with the "sentimental character she [was] portraying" (Ambrière, 104).

Not one to linger on disappointments, she accepted the fact that her acting had been strained and that she had been a prey to nerves. She knew from experience that one has to *feel into* roles. She would improve her performance next time by accentuating the emotional side of her character and, if need be, heightening the accruing sensations. Self-taught for the most part, Marie relied on the truth of her instincts to guide her on stage. It was in her blood, she sensed. She knew just how to assuage the audience's appetite for high-voltage talk! She blamed her deficiencies on her nerves.

Far from arrogant, however, Marie understood her need for practice, training, and experience. Parisian audiences were far more sophisticated and demanding than those of Lorient and Strasbourg. Unlike many performers at the Porte Saint-Martin Theater, she had not enjoyed the prestige of those who had enrolled in the classes of Paris' Conservatoire, the teaching organ of the Comédie-Française, founded by Louis XIV in 1680. She had, however, benefited from the fame attached to the Bourdais name. Several members of her family had not only studied at the Conservatoire, but had earned teaching chairs in this august institution.

To improve her acting techniques and, perhaps, remedy her feelings of inferiority caused by lack of official training in the dramatic arts, Piccini again intervened on Marie's behalf. Only days later, on November 6, 1818, and much to her joy, she was not only miraculously accepted at the Conservatoire, but would study with the celebrated tragedian, Pierre Lafon. Piccini also obtained a monthly pension for her of 75 francs, which permitted her and her family to move to better rooms on 3 rue de Bondy (Ambrière, 104). Marie felt honored at the thought of attending this renowned age-old institution. She was positive it would broaden and structure her acting technique. Her imagination soared at the thought of entering the sacred portals of the Conservatoire. Parading before her mind's eye were the names of the great performers of past eras whose luster still filled those sacred portals – Lekain, Mlle Clairon, Adrienne Lecouvreur – and present day stars – Mlle Mars, Mlle George, and the magnificent Talma, the latter having been Napoleon's favorite actor. Marie felt buoyed at the thought of them.

Of immense help to Marie at this stage in her career was the kindness bestowed on her by Saint-Romain, the director of the Porte Saint-Martin Theater. First and foremost, he understood her predicament. He believed she had been ill-suited for the role of Pamela. With this in mind, he gave her other parts to play, even one night stands, and in so doing, was in a position to discover where her talents lay, and perhaps to increase her understanding of how to play up certain facets of human nature. Practice and experience were essential. As soon as Saint-Romain considered her sufficiently prepared to face a first night, he offered her a premium role, that of Amélie, in Victor Ducange's melodrama, *La Cabane du Montagnard* (*Montagnard's Cabin*), scheduled to open on September 25, 1818.

The liberal social ideas voiced by Ducange in this and in his other plays were implicit in his life experience. As the son of a secretary of the Dutch Embassy, he had been overheard voicing revolutionary ideas, resulting, at times, in his imprisonment or exile to Belgium. A perfect medium of expression for revolutionaries, theater allowed him not only to voice his opinions, but to please audiences by working them up to a frenzy of suspense and delight. Last, but not least, it gave him the means of earning money, for which he was ever wanting. Audiences loved him "for his insolent verve," wrote Jules Janin, "for his disdain of those seated in stalls" (Jules Janin, *Histoire de la littérature dramatique,* III, 302).

Ducange's action-packed melodrama focused on moral issues: vice as opposed to virtue, weakness and pathos in conflict with brute strength, hate in contradiction with love. Modalities of family relationships were forever heightened on stage, drawing audiences ever more deeply into their dramatic polarities. How these jarred with the well-being of its individual members was at the root of Ducange's theater piece.

La Cabane du Montagnard exploited the evil father image in Baron de Leirac, a wealthy lord who posed as the essence of kindness when, in fact, he was evil incarnate. The Baron's duplicitous cruelty toward his gentle, loving, and unsuspecting daughter (Amélie) is at the heart of this melodrama. The pathos invested in the role Marie was to play could not have been better suited to her own life experience. Hadn't her father forsaken her and her mother? Sugar and cream when he courted her, abandon when it came to dealing with the responsibilities of fatherhood. How Marie must have cringed when facing her stage father. Evil to the core, this immensely wealthy and powerful individual masquerading as ultra kind and generous to those in need was in fact the arch hypocrite, particularly vis-à-vis his daughter who loved him dearly for what she believed to be his altruism.

The Baron's goal in life could not have been more nefarious: to kill his dead sister's son, Charles, in order to take over his fortune. Outwardly generous, he invites the lad and his tutor to his home following a serious avalanche accident that nearly killed them both. Unaware that Charles is being protected by his real father, Dolzan, who had also been the butt of the Baron's persecution mania, audiences listen in shocked disbelief as the Baron maps out plans for his murderous deeds. The plot thickens the moment Charles, who has succeeded in avoiding his persecutor, finally confesses his love to Amélie, and she, hers for him. Her moment of trauma occurs upon learning that her beloved father, while giving the impression of being kind and gentle is, in reality, anything but. The play concludes in a mountain retreat to which the persecuted lovers have fled to safely, thanks to Providence, in the form of the heroic old soldier, Labrèche. As in all good melodrama, the villain is punished for his murderous deeds and the Baron is swept to his death by an avalanche. All ends well. Charles retains his fortune and will marry his beloved Amélie.

More than a mere theatrical spectacle, *La Cabane du Montagnard* may be viewed as a social commentary attempting to grant women a modicum of stature by questioning the validity and worship of the ideal father image, so popular in theaters of the day (Le Hir, *Romantisme aux enchères,* 26). Ducange cleverly transferred the good father image to a soldier who worked for a living rather than one who worked on unearned increment, as was the case of the play's evil father.

Marie believed she was at her best as the gentle, giving, and loving Amélie. Rather than libidinous attraction, virtue reigned. Admiration was the lovers' common denominator. Ethics motivated Amélie. The grace of her dialogue and the moral goodness and integrity of her behavior contrasted sharply with the baseness of her father's tones and ways. The emotional extremes underscored in the play were just what audiences sought.

Virtuous in every way, Amélie's strength of character emerged overtly in the scene featuring her escape from the clutches of the evil-doer by seeking shelter in a mountain cabin. Amélie/Marie could have run the gamut of affects upon realization of her plight. Instead, the text called for wisdom to protect her future. Her restraint in this regard not only augured well for herself and for her beloved, but for society in general. To transform evil by means of an individual's action was the only way society as a whole could benefit.

Understandably, the audience howled with glee the moment the murderous baron met his fate and the joyous couple the fulfillment of their love. Isn't it a wonder how, for centuries, audiences have projected their rage on evil-doers, salivating at their punishments, and in so doing, believe themselves to be cleansed of guilt! These so-called innocents, thus cleared of all malevolence, consider themselves superior to others. Audiences thrilled – and still thrill, as punishers!

Marie felt more herself in the role of Amélie, less tense than at her opening, in *Pamela Married*. This time audiences neither whistled nor heckled. They applauded instead. The critics, while favorably disposed, were, nonetheless, not lavish with praise. Marie, the realist, although confident of her abilities and stirred by her desire to work into future roles and strive for greater perfection, was prepared to forge ahead. Thinking back to her mother's career, she realized that good intents and only a little talent did not make for a great artist. She also knew that she had far more talent than her mother. The willingness to work, the determination to succeed, augured well for this budding star.

Good news does come at times in small bundles. Marie gave birth to Piccini's baby Alexandrine-Thérèse on July 13, 1819, and was thrilled. Since she was still legally married to Dorval, although she had not seen him in over a year, she declared him the father of her child, at the baptismal font, and Piccini, the godfather. So too did she proceed for her next child, Victorine Alexandrine, born on November 20, 1820. Joy was short-lived, however, as both infants died at an early age.

Circumstances and the chance factor again intervened for Marie, but in negative ways. The wonderfully patient and understanding Saint-Romain, having recently lost his wife, was broken in spirit. No longer interested in anything, not even in theater, he gave up his directorship of the Porte Saint-Martin Theater to withdraw into a world of his own. The day Antoine Lefeuve was appointed to succeed Saint-Romain, as director of the Porte Saint-Martin Theater, Marie felt that her future there was in question.

Avaricious, impatient, dictatorial, lacking in understanding and warmth, Lefeuve summarily deprived Marie of the heretofore joyous rehearsals that she had not only looked upon as a learning experience, but had come to treasure. Gone was the positive cast of Saint-Romain's presence and directorship. Banished as well were his humorous and tender asides. Under Lefeuve's lead, art and acting were no longer primary concerns. With this in mind, he not only reduced Marie's salary, but refused to invest in the proper costumes for his performers. Nor would he spend the money to have them cleaned.

What gnawed at Marie and could not be dealt with via levity was Lefeuve's ultra Spartan misdirectorship of the Porte Saint-Martin Theater. For spite, she thoughtlessly accepted an offer to perform in July at the Grand Théâtre de Bordeaux. Not vindictive by nature, her intent behind her acceptance had been two-fold at the time: to leave Paris, thereby punishing Lefeuve who would be rehearsing at that time. Conveniently or not, she completely forgot about her contract with the Bordeaux theater and remained in Paris to be with her lover, Piccini. When she failed to appear in Bordeaux at Easter, 1820, a non-suit was served. Marie lost the case and was obliged to pay (Le Hir, 106).

Not to worry, the birth of Philippine-Caroline Allan, came along on December 11, 1820. While also of Piccini's manufacture, their third child was more robust than the first two and survived. It would, however, be the last time that Marie would be able to claim her husband as the father of her child. Allan Dorval died on May 30, 1820, in St. Petersburg from a high fever brought on by the rigors of the climate. His death did not overly pain Marie since the two had been separated for so long. But then, she might have caustically claimed, he had served a purpose.

Marie's diligent work habits had convinced her that she would be capable of handling all of her commitments. Apt and well organized though she was, she had overlooked the time element when assessing her abilities to fulfill her obligations. Caring for Gabrielle and Louise, her two daughters, fathered by Allan Dorval, in addition to Philippine Caroline, Piccini's offspring, attending rehearsals, memorizing roles, and performing at the Porte Saint-Martin Theater so encroached on the time she had allotted to her classes at the

Conservatoire, that after more than a year of desultory appearances, and much to her dismay, she was summarily dismissed from this august teaching institution for non-attendance.

So dissatisfied had Marie become with Lefeuve's directorship, that she finally sent a letter to the *Journal des Théâtres* (July 2, 1821), accusing the director in ironically clever terms of altering the colors of the costumes she was to wear. Instead of a snow-white dress, for which the text called, she was given an off grey one to wear and a dirty one at that (Ambrière, 106). The repercussions of Marie's satiric verbal thrust not only liberated her from the rancor of this parsimonious being, but vindicated her right to have the theater pay for the cleaning of her costumes.

Better directing under the aegis of both Jean-Pierre Deserre and Jean Toussaint Merle would usher in a far less avaricious approach to theater. Actors would not only enjoy higher salaries, but more attention would be paid to decors and costumes. Once the dual directorship of the Porte Saint-Martin Theater was set into place, new and exciting plays, along with a panoply of increasingly varied characters, were to be offered to greedy audiences. The administrative change included a physical revamping of virtually every corner of the theater as well. Such modernization not only enhanced Marie's status, but her self-esteem, gusto, and enthusiasm for her art.

One could hardly accuse Marie of laziness. To the contrary, in October 1822, she appeared as Elizabeth in the Gothic drama, *The Castle of Kenilworth*. The plentiful applause served to bolster her spirits. In fact, she was so up-beat that she even fantasized about pursuing an acting career at the prestigious Comédie-Française. Marie again persuaded Piccini to intervene on her behalf. Her wish was granted and on July 30, 1822, she was readmitted to the class of declamation at the Conservatoire, only to be dismissed on February 4, 1823, for having again missed so many classes (Ambrière, 109).

For Marie, any administrative alteration at the Porte Saint-Martin Theater meant a reworking of relationships, be it with her two new managers, Jean-Pierre Deserre, whose function revolved around money management aspects of theater, or Jean Toussaint Merle, a southerner, a royalist, who despised anything and everything related to the Empire. The latter seemed to intrigue Marie. That he was a bohemian, melding perfectly the theatrical and artistic domains, gave her hope of a future *entente* between them. His enjoyment of lengthy, leisurely, and provocative conversations at cafés, his love for gourmet foods, and his fascination for the world of letters attracted Marie's attention. His reputation of shying away from imbroglios, quarrels, and rivalries added even more allure to his personality. He had spent most of his youth awaiting the inheritance his grand uncle had promised him. To survive, however, he worked as editor in publishing houses, whipped up comedies and vaudevilles for production at the Gaîté Theater, and spent the rest of his time enjoying life. That he was subsequently disinherited for failing to meet his grand uncle's expectations shocked him. Even more deleterious was his next mindless act. In anticipation of his future wealth, he had borrowed 500 francs from his grand uncle. The time had come for him to return the sum to the estate. In order to avoid repaying monies he did not possess Merle decided to hide. In the end, he somehow availed himself of the sum owed to the estate (Ambrière, 112). By 1817 he began writing for *La Quotidienne,* a French version of the English *Morning Herald.* Although he had few funds, Merle knew everybody and anybody in many walks of life, most particularly in theater. When, in 1821, he learned that the Vaudeville, Odéon, Gymnase, and Lefeuve's Porte Saint-Martin Theater were prospering, he decided the time was ripe to try his hand at theater directing. A master manipulator, Merle finally reached his goal in 1822, upon assuming the co-directorship of the Porte Saint-Martin with Jean-Pierre Deserre. The two worked well together and in less than five months they had not only succeeded in redecorating the house, but in revamping its finances as well.

This cultured, suave, industrious, well-mannered, well-dressed, and well-spoken lady's man fascinated Marie. That he was creative and kind added to his luster. He would be a perfect addition, she thought, to the Porte Saint-Martin Theater. Her assessment proved justified, at least at the outset.

The Boulevard du Temple with its theaters, acrobats, vaudevilles, melodramas, marionette shows, even classical productions, was as usual, crackling with excitement, but even more so, since the bohemian-born clown, Jean Gaspard Deburau, only two years older than Marie, was drawing crowds to the Funambules Theater. He was sixteen when he and his family first arrived in Paris. Although Marie had seen him many times, she looked upon each of his performances as unique. She marveled at the manner in which he used his body to convey subtle emotional changes – usually sorrowful – but on rare occasions, a mitigating smile could be seen on his face.

In performance, Deburau's face was painted white. His loose white tunic with large buttons, balloon sleeves, and large pantaloons was white as well. She knew him to have been born into a family of strolling acrobats touring Europe. That his father, Jan Dvorjak, had been a severe and unrelenting perfectionist, and that his children were expected to follow his lead, was evident in Deburau's expert economy of movement – pointing up an emotion, a feeling, a sudden change in mood with the twist of the wrist, eye movements, or a crease of the brow. Although Gaspard had obeyed his father's orders, and practiced tight-rope walking, he did not take to this precarious stunt. One slight miscalculation could wreak havoc with his back and paralyze him forever! Deburau was fortunate, he did not suffer a broken back, only severe bruises, when he miscalculated and fell to the ground after performing his tight-rope walking stunt (Kozik, 7). Worse, his brothers and his parents ignored him. He was a stranger amidst his family. By the age of fifteen, he was on his own. He wandered about in search of work. He sorrowed in loneliness and poverty, many a day going without food. As the months and years passed, the emotionally scarred Deburau worked at perfecting a circus routine: somersaults, cartwheels, back somersaults, among other stunts. Although poverty, rejection, and physical discomforts were his daily fare, one great happening comforted the despondent Deburau. During the course of his peregrinations, he not only met Emperor Napoleon, but had been invited by him to ride in his carriage. He, who rarely talked, told the Emperor he liked pantomime, or dumbshow, as they called it then, better than tragedies. When Napoleon asked him where he performed his art, he replied, "sire, on the rue du Temple,' adding, 'perhaps they'd do better to write pantomimes instead of tragedies,' whereupon Napoleon smiled with pleasure" (Kozik, 35).

What made for Deburau's genius were his extraordinary powers of observation and imagination. These enabled him to mimic odd, grotesque, mean, cantankerous, hateful, gentle, tender, and loving people. As he spun his mimed story, every segment of his body moved, breathed, impersonated, or remained immobile in stilled silence, under-scoring specific aspects of the dramatized narration. His gestural art inspired Marie, as it had the throngs watching him mime his most complex and popular role, that of Pierrot, the clown. Although presented in an interpretation of his own, this stock character not only dated back to Greek and Roman times, but had been popular in medieval France and later, in Italian *commedia dell'arte* productions. It was the forever sad mute mime Deburau who introduced the character Pierrot – an ignorant, fumbling, foolish, silent clown – to audiences at the Funambules Theater. His ability to transform facial and bodily gestures into subtle mood tones, ranging from joy through sorrow to dispair, was unique. His face, painted white, while enhancing its spiritual cast at one moment, altered seconds later to one of mischief, with a wink of the eye, a twist of the wrist, the crinkling of the brow or cheek. His subtle body and facial movements conveyed Pierrot's love, hurt, anger, jealousy, sorrow, compassion, tragedy, and so much more. At times, the mime's eyes brimmed with sadness for a lost love. Moments later, when recalling happy times, nostalgia dominated and a tear ran down his cheek. Unexpectedly, when alerted by a mood of fun, a smile invaded his features. Deburau's unique art inspired writers, such as Charles Nodier, to compose pantomimes for him, namely, his *Le Songe d'O*, which became one of Paris' favorites. They also inspired Louis Daguerre, the physicist, and illusionist stage set painter, to create his *daguerreo types*, photographs produced on a silver-coated copper plate. Such illusionistic painted sets were crucial for Marie and for other stage performers.

Each time Marie attended one of Deburau's performances, she returned home stunned by his remarkable insights into human nature and his ability to translate these not into words, but rather into body language, tonal modulations, and/or vibrations. His genius not only revealed the extent, depth, and profound understanding of his feeling, as manifested in facial expressions, but their translation into sign, action, and movement. Marie had come to realize that, whether the part she performed on stage called for weeping, anger, jealousy, sorrow, or other feelings, rather than being an involuntary act, it had to be constructed and manipulated by the artist. Muscular changes, when throwing the body's weight in a certain manner, were the result of concerted analysis and work on the part of the artist to give the impression of being natural. Practice and direction served to underscore feeling and mood. To add mime to her performances would surely broaden and deepen her acting techniques. She understood that in addition to words enunciated on stage, gesture, finger action, eye activity, facial figurations, must be added to convey the sought for emotions on stage. Deburau, as Pierrot, among other creatures of his fantasy, came to Marie's rescue. Mime would henceforth contribute to the grip she held over her audiences.

Merle nourished the dream of transforming the Saint-Martin Theater's tried and true, but at times banal, repertory with higher quality plays and programs. He was convinced that foreign influences should and would intensify and deepen the landscape of French theater. During one of his frequent trips to England he became so fascinated with the productions of Shakespeare's plays and with the complexities of the stage machinery that made them work, that he invited the English actor and entrepreneur Penley and his troupe to perform some of the works of Shakespeare and of Sheridan at the Porte Saint-Martin. To make certain both that his efforts would be remunerated and that the French would react positively to the English bard's genius, he had posters splattered all over Paris. Merle was, nonetheless, very much aware that French audiences still smarted from their military defeats at the hands of Wellington in the Spanish Peninsula war of 1809 and again, in 1814, at Waterloo (Carlson, 57). Such memories are not so easily forgotten.

Opening night on July 31, 1822 at the Porte Saint-Martin Theater was destined to make theatrical history. But not the kind Merle had anticipated. Although the curtains parted on *Othello* without mishap, and continued on without raucous intrusions, by the time Othello began strangling his wife, Desdemona, deafening barrages of catcalls and hooting were unleashed in every corner of the theater. (Let us note that the act of murder on the French stage was considered indecent, vulgar, and barbaric, and had been banned since the seventeenth century. Any violation of this and other theatrical laws of decorum were considered reprehensible). Since the damage had already been done on-stage, audience reaction to what was considered base and vulgar comportment was instantaneous. The performance of such staged indecencies had to be stopped in any way possible.

Not one to bow to old and what he considered, retrograde ideas, the unstoppable Merle made a point of introducing audiences of the Porte Saint-Martin Theater to more British imports, namely, Sheridan's *School for Scandal.* The curtains parted on August 2, with high expectations. Soon, however, audience rage broke out with such virulence that a frenzied spectator took it into his head to throw a coin on stage. He did so with such force that it hit one of the actresses in the temple, causing her to drop to the stage floor in a faint. More than sixty policemen were needed to quell the riot that had broken out. Flapseats, benches, potatoes, and eggs were thrown onto the stage. The theater had to be evacuated. Never having been exposed to such behavior prior to this incident, the English troupe was advised to use a secret exit to escape the crowds awaiting them outside. Although newspapers had informed their readers of the possibility of just such outrageous comportment, the government disclaimed any and all complicity in the affair (Ambrière, 116).

Nor did Marie appreciate Merle's behavior – or non-behavior – toward her when he unwillingly agreed to her performing in two slight comedies of his own manufacture – *The Sandbar (Le Banc de Sable) and Jean-Jacques' Tailor (Le Tailleur de Jean-Jacques).* Soon thereafter, she took umbrage with him for refusing to cast her as Mary Stuart in a French imitation of Schiller's play by the same name. Even worse, after a few rehearsals, he withdrew the role entirely, considering it far beyond her capacities.

Still smarting over the catastrophic reception accorded his English troupe, Merle decided to trudge the safe and narrow path, which led him to finally begin to understand Marie's many-tiered depths as an actress. Sensitive to what she considered to be his limited, albeit negative, opinion of her talents, she concluded that he intended to let her contract lapse. In reality, this well-mannered and deeply-feeling man had no intentions of doing so. He had, however, sensed that her very special talents had not yet peaked. Other factors worked on Merle as well. He warmed to her charm, poise, and feline ways. All this was well and good, but Marie was impatient for success. Despite some fine reviews, she had not yet made a name for herself at the Porte Saint- Martin. In fact, she considered the little crumbs Merle had handed her insulting. Rather than flare up, she quieted down. Patience, she told herself, solves many a problem. Moreover, she reasoned, life's uncertainties must not always be considered in the negative. Still, she had to face the fact that the celebrated critic, Jules Janin, had deprecated her acting in *The Young Werther, Scottish Chiefs, The Vampire, The Castle of Kenilworth* and other hair-raising, lurid, and passion-streaked love dramas in which she had performed.

In early October 1822 and much to Marie's surprise, Merle offered her the opportunity to play in *Les deux forçats* by J.B.E. Boirie. Not that the play was a masterpiece, far from that. Nonetheless, this melodrama was lively, thrilling and attracted large crowds. Cast as Thérèse, her acting brought her lavish commendations from *Le Courrier des Spectacles*.

> This interesting actress deploys a soul, a sensibility which wrenches tears from all spectators. And what assigns her a very distinguished rank among actresses in our theaters, is the flexibility of her talent which lends itself to roles which her age would seemingly exclude, but which she can perform with ease. How many actresses of the Porte Saint-Martin can even perform their roles competently? (Ambrière, 18)

Nonetheless, the well known critic, Jules Janin conveyed his opinion in true to form negations. Not only did he consider *The Two Convicts* a "foolish" play, but he looked down on the manner in which "the little Dorval" spoke her "idiotic lines." Merle was prepared to close the play down. The following day however, something odd occurred. No sooner had Dorval spoken her opening lines, than the audience began reacting in "stunned" disbelief to the tenor of her voice. They marveled as well at her sensitivity and at her ability to "shudder." They not only listened "passionately" to her every word, they applauded! They screamed! They sensed they had "witnessed the birth of a true *comédienne*" (Marie Dorval. *Documents inédits*, 35. J.Janin, *Histoire de la littérature dramatique,* vol. VI, p. 155).

Moved to tears by the wild applause, Marie intuited that she was finally *en route* to stardom. As a realist, she was aware that the road ahead would be treacherous – filled as it was with pitfalls. If success were to be preserved, perseverance was implicit in the process. The thought that she was learning comforted her. After all, she reasoned, wasn't life one grand and continuous exploration? She admitted that while she had a long way to go, she was deeply encouraged by some, but not all, of the overtly positive reactions to her performance. That fighting instinct so deeply ingrained in her being propelled her on.

There was no doubt in Merle's mind that a star had been born. The reviews warmed his heart. Never had he dreamed that the unassuming Marie was capable of projecting such depths of feeling onto the mediocre character she was portraying. He was determined to play up her dramatic style – her rough, and tumble, at moments, coarse speech in contrast to the posed, cerebral, and studied lucubrations of the forty-five year-old Mlle Mars, France's celebrated actress of the prestigious Comédie-Française.

Coincidentally, Mlle Mars had won accolades at the opening on December 21, 1822 of *Valérie*, a play by the German dramatist August von Kotzebue, adapted by Scribe and Mellesville to suit the star's needs (Ambrière, 119). Four months later, on April 17, 1823, *Valérien* opened at the Porte Saint-Martin starring Marie, in a different adaptation of the same play by Carrion-Nisas and Thomas Sauvage.

In keeping with the original text, Marie was cast as a fifteen year-old boy. Under no circumstances could Mlle Mars, given her age, play such a part. Hence her transformation of Valérien into a girl, Valérie.

Merle's gamble proved to have been astute from both an artistic as well as a financial perspective. Kotzebue's play, be it *Valérie* or *Valérien*, was "an actors' play;" that is, everything depended on the acting. Since the plot revolved around a blind boy or girl recovering his or her sight, the love motif became secondary, depending on the actor who played the blind child. Of prime import, then, was the emphasis placed on the protagonist's feelings. How did these sensations manifest themselves? What did each protagonist see? How did each convey her or his joys, fears, anxieties? Did they grope, hesitate, or glance here and there when taking their first steps following their ability to see? Did they hold on to someone or to pieces of furniture to steady themselves? Did they stumble as they attempted to leave their cloistered environment and make their way into the real world? How was their breathing affected during their progressive steps leading into the world of sight? These and other acting techniques were crucial to the creation of mood, tempo, and the heightening of suspense. Marie's subtle head and body movements, each acting in consort with the other senses, such as hearing, conveyed the anguish suffered by those incarcerated in a sightless world, attempting to structure imaginary routes for themselves.

Certainly Merle had taken a chance. The critics were virtually unanimous in their praise for Mlle Mars's performance. While the older actress reigned supreme in this acting competition, the article appearing in the *Courrier des Spectacles* underscored Marie's "depth of understanding", "delicacy", and profound "sensitivity" in bringing her character to life. He urged audiences to see not one but both plays (Ambrière).

Marie Dorval owed a great deal to Merle for having put her name in the limelight. He, in turn, was grateful to her for not only filling the coffers of the Porte Saint-Martin, but for the prestige she brought the house. He and Deserre showed their appreciation by both extending her contract to 1830 and increasing her salary to 500 francs a month. Ironically, it would be twice that of a *pensionnaire* at the Comédie-Française.

Questions arose as to why Merle organized a giant benefit for Marie on May 22, 1824. That he invited such popular "Boulevard artists" as Potier, Bernard Léon, Léontine Fay, and the unique acrobat, Valentin-le-Désossé, is still a mystery. Most likely, Marie, who had no sense of money, must have suddenly run out of funds.

Marie always took her work seriously. When, on one occasion she failed to show up for a dress rehearsal, Merle grew annoyed. Moments later, the stage manager ran into his office, shouting, "Mme Dorval has just tried to asphyxiate herself." Astounded by such news, Merle rushed to her dressing to find her livid and feverish. He immediately thought that she had attempted suicide because of her tragic disappointment over a break with Piccini. With utmost care, he told her to take her time, to get over her trauma, assuring her he would not seek a replacement. Upon detecting a bit of jealousy in Merle's voice, she burst out laughing, confessing that she had not the slightest intent of committing suicide.

On the contrary, she wanted to stun future audiences. To do so, she had to discover the exact gestures, tone of voice, called for in cases of asphyxiation. Try as she might, she had not yet succeeded. Imagination yielded few answers to her dilemma. Reality alone could serve her purpose, she thought. While she lit her wood heater, she neglected to open the window. As she studied her part, she was experiencing the effects of asphyxiation and growing weaker and weaker by the minute. When her neighbor heard what seemed to her to be a death rattle, she rushed into the room to find the semi-conscious Marie. She had just come to when Merle entered her dressing room.

To his angry words, berating her for going to such lengths to underscore the reality of a role she was to play, she retorted proudly that she had finally "grasped" her part (Moser, 17). She knew how to roll her eyes, to experience facial pallor, to rigidify her gestures, to speak not with false inflections, but with true to life tonalities. Merle was stunned by her dedication to theater. He understood her determination to create real people onstage, not just wooden effigies. The visceral Marie had to go through the spasms and agonies of her characters in order to play them out on stage. To Marie's delight, Merle offered her a contract in the winter of 1825 for the melodrama, *The Musician's Daughter*, by Crosnier and Ferrières, which opened on December 10, 1825. It included the famous asphyxiation scene she had been practicing. Her sequences of mimed gestures, and facial expressions conveying defiance, scorn, and pride, were so astoundingly real that audiences remained riveted to their seats. Some sobbed. Acclamation followed.

Later that night, when the celebrated comic, Charles Potier, came to her dressing room all smiles, he congratulated her, and then told her outright that she had finally found her real self. To think, he told her, that he had been the one to sense her talents as a teenager when attending one of her performances in Strasbourg (Moser, 17)!

Nonetheless, she was still unconvinced of her great success. Serendipitously, when she arrived at the theater the following day, she noticed crowds in front of the ticket bureau. She thought someone had taken ill and the show had been canceled. No! She was told that crowds of people were standing in line to buy tickets; whereupon, she shrugged her shoulders in disbelief. Moments later a worker happened to recognize her on the street and took his cap off, saluted her and screamed out "Vive Marie Dorval! Vive la grande Dorval!" No sooner had others heard his words than they shouted, giddy with rapture, "It's Dorval!" (Moser, 18). Moments later, Merle told her that the Saint-Martin Theater had been sold out for the entire week. Marie exploded into tears (Moser, 18).

New plays were always in the offing for Merle, who not only wrote them, but adapted them for the stage. To suggest that he was compulsive would be an understatement. He worked hard to maintain the elegance of the Porte Saint-Martin. When need be, he took it upon himself to not only refurbish the theater, but to overhaul its complex stage machinery. He availed himself of trick photography to create the illusion of enlarging stage space, of creating sliding doors in the wings and behind the scenes. The famous photographer Jacques Daguerre was involved as well. As the inventor of the diorama, he had devoted many long hours to creating sub-frames, which would give the illusion of extending stage space both in depth and width. Decors, he mused, had made a tremendous leap forward in the early nineteenth century (Allévy, 41).

It was important as well that the the famous chemist Lavoisier discovered a means of not only brightening street lights, but of adapting and directing light emanating from certain lighting fixtures able to shine on specific areas of the stage during special scenes. Fire, floods, and gruesome effects of all types were crucial for catering to the audience's greed for the macabre.

Merle, the anglophile, knew just how to put fiendish behavior to good use. Since an adaptation of Mary Shelley's *Frankenstein* had enjoyed a successful run in London, why not produce a French version of it in Paris? This tale about a student of the occult who had built a creature and given it life would surely attract crowds. Since the subject of monsters, robots, and the creation of life via scientific means was in the air in Paris, Merle and Antony Béraud set to work on The *Monster and the Magician,* which opened at the Porte Saint-Martin on June 10, 1826. This gruesome work which dramatized the nefarious deeds perpetrated by the scientist, Zametti, and his young and beautiful infernal geni, involved incredible staged disasters. The extraordinarily complex stage machinery this play required obliged Merle to import the equipment involved from London, along with the English machinist, Tomkins, who was to set it up at the Saint-Martin.

The famous English mime, T.P. Cooke was invited to impersonate Zametti, the scientist who, with the help of his infernal geni, enacted by Dorval, produced unparalleled catastrophes on stage, namely, drowning, cascading waters, floods, abysses, a giant monster capable of swallowing entire ships, of setting villages aflame, and of creating tempests, replete with incendiary lightning and peels of thunder – the quintessence of horror.

As the monster/scientist Zametti, Cook's sleight of hand enabled him to pass through walls, to disappear, and seconds later to reappear to a captivated audience (Marie Dorval, *Souvenirs dramatiques,* 213) Each time he passed through walls Cooke's suavely insidious gestures, revealing the pleasures and satisfactions he took in carrying out his sadistic scientific experiments, enabled him to perpetrate his cold-blooded crimes with *panache.*

Dorval, as Zametti's fiancée, played to the hilt her role of the terrified virgin, that is, in an overtly exaggerated melodramatic style. Her piercing screams, her howls, following the explosion of the scientist's laboratory, were, to say the least, blood-curdling. As for the ever greedy spectators, they too reached a state of fright-induced shock at the sight of countless innocents swallowed up by pounding waves, opening abysses, and endless whirlpools in a sea lusting for flesh and blood. Even the Marquis de Sade would have shuddered at the play's conclusion – the submersion by a monster of an entire ship and its passengers in the pounding seas (Carlson, 51).

Not only did *The Monster and the Magician* enjoy a huge financial success at the Porte Saint-Martin, but it received laudatory reviews as well. Marie's portrayal of Zametti's fiancée and Cook's impersonation of the monster, replete with his staged contortions in the enactment of his insidious scientific experiments, were memorable. Despite the praise awarded Dorval, she deplored her role as the continuously terrified archetypal virgin. That her talents had been restricted to screams and yelps diminished the pride she might have taken in her performance. Few realized how much ingenuity was required of Merle and of his technicians to simulate gigantic natural horrors. So expertly had they succeeded in their task, that when the stage shook, audiences trembled, fear raged, and terror reigned. As for Merle, the efforts expended in creating and in seeing to the continuous functioning of the complex stage machinery led to such extreme exhaustion on his part that he resigned as administrator of the Porte Saint-Martin, fearing that overwork and stress would lead to a nervous breakdown. Henceforth, his time and talents would be devoted to literary endeavors rather than administration.

Nontheless, the play's success allowed Marie and her three daughters to move out of the rue des Vinaigriers into rooms on the Boulevard Saint-Martin. She believed she was finally on her way!

That Merle's admiration of Marie's acting capabilities had risen a hundred-fold during the past months and that her own self-esteem had grown contributed to the birth of a new and closer relationship between the two. Other factors intervened as well. By the fall of 1826, the twenty-eight year-old Marie had abruptly broken with Piccini. A man she had once admired and in whom she had the utmost confidence, who had received the Legion of Honor among other testimonials to his talents, had turned into a libidinous middle-aged man. Unable to control his eyeing and pawing of young girls, be they members of the choir he directed or of some other artistic group with whom he had contacts, had led to his summary dismissal on October 26, 1826. No longer singing director of the royal Academy of Music, he found himself destitute and alone (Ambrière, 123). In Piccini's riposte to Dorval, he not only denied the allegations, but asked her how she could play the prude? Merle had already inserted himself into her life!

Jean Toussaint Merle, both handsome and distinguished, succumbed to her charms. He was called "Le Merle Blanc," the white flag having always been that of the monarchy. When he asked her to marry him, although hesitant at first – he was sixteen years her senior – she soon realized it would be to her advantage to accept. He was generous, kind, and traveled in all societies. He knew the right people. More importantly, he was deeply attached to her.

The best way to win Marie's graces was to endear himself to her three beautiful daughters. The older ones had always proved to be more difficult, even for Marie. However, the fifteen year-old Louise and the thirteen year-old Gabrielle, while aware of his manipulations, reacted with pleasure to small gifts designed to embellish their hair, and to his attentions. Young Caroline, her mother's favorite, was frankly delighted. Merle charmed them all in the warmest and most diplomatic way with his gentle small talk. He was even comforting when need be.

There was no question that Merle was deeply attracted to the slim, seductive, and feline Marie. He was cognizant as well of her proclivity for men. When she wanted a man, she got what she wanted! He knew this and would respect her privacy.

Marie took her time about accepting his marriage proposal. She would first have to taste of him in the flesh. They became lovers. She was satisfied. This did not mean that she would give up other lovers. She was free to do as she wished.

They would be married on October 17, 1829 (Moser, 28).

CHAPTER 3

Theatrical history was made on June 19, 1827. The Porte Saint-Martin was buzzing with excitement. Crowds had gathered long before curtain time to see Marie Dorval and Frédérick Lemaître play opposite one another for the first time. Nor would they be performing in a run-of-the-mill melodrama. The one chosen for the occasion, *Thirty Years or A Gambler's Life,* had been authored by the celebrated Victor Ducange, whose plays had been performed at the Porte Saint-Martin, L'Ambigu-Comique, and the Gaîté since 1813 (Le Hir, 15).

The very thought of a successful run buoyed Dorval's somewhat negative outlook on life. 1826 had been an unpleasant year for her. After Merle's resignation as director of the Porte Saint-Martin, and the appointment of a new co-director, the baron Mongenêt, who cast his mistress in the best roles, Dorval's future looked dismal. Not one to refrain from expressing her feelings whenever she felt an injustice had been perpetrated, she spoke out forcefully on the subject to Montgenêt. While artistry should have reigned at the Porte Saint-Martin, volatility, anger, even rage corroded the atmosphere. Despite the intervention of the level-headed co-director, Deserre, little could be done to soothe the scalding tempers. Rancor had created such an impasse that by October 1826, the minister of the Interior was informed of the in-house deadlock. Days later he stepped in, transforming chaos into relative order.

The flamboyant Frédérick Lemaître, nicknamed "the Lion of the Boulevard," was born in 1800 at Le Havre. At fourteen, he chanced to attend a performance of the well- known actor, Jean-Baptiste-Bernard Joanny. Impassioned by what he had seen and felt, Lemaître became a devotee of the performing arts (Baldick, 17). Like so many other would-be greats, prior to turning dream into reality, the young Lemaître fulfilled his military obligations, after which he followed the well-trodden road of financial difficulties, partaking in several less than successful business ventures. Once he narrowed his field of activity to the performing arts – which included acrobatics and pantomime – he applied to, and was accepted at, les Variétés-

Amusantes, one of the smallest theaters on the Boulevard du Temple. Inventive, humorous, and given to making a spectacle of himself, Lemaître loved to indulge his on-stage fantasies. One of his earliest, seemingly unforgettable, pantomimic roles was that of a lion. He stood motionless on stage in his formidable lion's costume, when suddenly he wheeled about on all fours. Not knowing what to make of this human beast, audiences, particularly those in the front rows, grew fearful. Moments later, Lemaître emitted such a blood-curdling stage roar, that many in the audience cupped their ears in an unconscious attempt to protect themselves from this furious beast (Baldick, 27).

By 1816, Lemaître went on to greener pastures, namely to the Funambules, where Jean Gaspard Deburau, was to create his unique impersonation of the clown, Pierrot. To the joy of its performers, the management of the Funambules had just allowed the names of its actors to be posted outside the theater, an advertising boon particularly appreciated by young aspiring artists (Baldick, 28).

Lemaître had the knack of creating a fantasy world for his audiences, of exciting their imaginations via his side-splitting, shocking, and frequently terrifying facial gymnastics. When they expected tears of terror, he laughed loudly and boisterously. To add spice to his performances, he took to rolling his eyes at appropriate moments, to elongating or jerking his jaw, turning his head almost completely to one side, smiling sardonically, or indulging in other subtly focused facial contortions. Lemaître's ability to incorporate sadness, banter, and joy into his pantomimic forays, proved irresistible in *The Birth of Harlequin*. His gaze, at times fixed, at other moments replete with pathos, joy, hurt, resolve, anger, charm, admiration, desire, scorn, dread, love, and jealousy deeply impacted his audiences (Baldick, 30). His facial expressions and body movements said it all.

Not one to rest on his laurels, the enormously energetic Lemaître joined the Cirque-Olympique in 1818, rightly judging that training in acrobatics would be an invaluable asset to his aspirations as an actor. As if this were not sufficient, the hard-working and ambitious Lemaître enrolled at the Conservatoire in the course of the celebrated tragedian, Pierre Lafon. This teacher not only discovered Lemaître's aptitude for tragedy, but both recommended him to, and saw to his acceptance at, the prestigious Odéon Theater. After a three year stint at this theatrical institution, Lemaître's hopes of making a name for himself at the Odéon remained unrealized. Quick to size up situations, the virile twenty-three year-old Lemaître simply changed course. By 1823, he had left the Odéon to carve out a future on the Boulevard du Temple. Perhaps at the Porte Saint-Martin?

Nothing seemed impossible for Lemaître. The variety and brio of his acting technique, his innovative antics, zest, humor, stylized mannerisms, and gimmicks, be it on stage or in everyday life, attracted those with whom he came into contact. People would stop and stare at this odd young man strutting down the street ever so nimbly, sporting his proverbial cane at his side and his well-placed cigar stub dangling from his mouth. His inventive approaches to situations and characters and his novel asides injected laughter, fright, even tawdriness into his many impersonations. One of Lemaître's most extraordinary creations was that of Robert Macaire, the celebrated assassin he made famous in the melodrama, *L'Auberge des Adrets* in 1823. Not only did his characterization win him overnight fame, but it allowed him to indulge his creative bent as well. The inventive Lemaître transformed the sinister gangster Macaire into a punning and humorous, even ribald creature. Rather than terror, he inspired laughter; rather than hatred, compassion. Parisians were captivated by his vision and imagination, not to mention his gusto.

To refer to *The Auberge des Adrets* as simply an overnight success would fail to do justice to the innovative nature of Lemaître's acting technique. The rave reviews this melodrama received gave impetus to his stardom. In no time Lemaître was referred to as the grand master of suspense and the initiator of stage havoc. One word, one glance, and a prosaic stage play sent audiences into virtual frenzies of terror, tears, or laughter. Wherever and whenever this innovative, passionate, and visceral actor performed, he held his spectators in the palm of his hands. The combination of his pantomimic talents and his imaginative and instinctive approach to melodrama cast a spell on Lemaître's admirers who followed him as lord and master whenever they spied him on the street. To see him once was to remember him always.

The evening of June 19, 1827, was awaited with anticipation, reservations, and questions. How would Dorval react to Lemaître's innovative antics? His flare-ups, his capers? His scene stealing? Would Dorval's reactive powers and poise be sufficiently imaginative to help her deal with her stage partner's sporadic style? To face the unpredictable on stage would be difficult. To deal with someone known to be non-compliant would be even more hazardous. Would she stand a chance next to the imperious and daunting Robert Macaire type? That Dorval had seen Lemaître on stage many times was not the issue. Indeed, she lauded his imaginative and visceral acting style. Strangely enough, the more she thought about acting opposite this theatrical phenomenon, the less apprehensive she became. Indeed, the intuitive Dorval was excited at the prospect of acting with the unconscionable Lemaître. It would be a test of her own resiliency. She sensed the similarities of their innate approaches to theater. They would be well-suited to each other, she thought. Rather than cerebral, Lemaître, like Dorval, invited instinct to prevail.

Although the critic Jules Janin dubbed Lemaître's acting quixotic, he extolled his humor, spontaneity, and capacity to shock. In *L'Auberge des Adrets,* for example, he highlighted the scene in which Robert Macaire enters an elegant restaurant dressed in rags. Not only did he walk in and seat himself with bravura at the table of his choice, but he complained to the *maître d'hôtel* that he had neglected to give him a napkin. The dichotomy between Lemaître, the vagrant, dressed in ill-fitting black pants and jacket, wrinkled shirt, and misshapen hat, known to have had better days, and the poise with which he comported himself, brought down the house (J. Janin, *Histoire de la littérature dramatique*, III, 236).

There was no doubt in Dorval's mind that the extraordinary Lemaître had created a style of his own. He had an uncanny way of triggering laughter by playing up clichés (Carlson, 83). Rather than declaiming his lines, in keeping with French classical and melodramatic tradition, he spoke with sincerity, and, when need be, with true-to-life gusto. Never did he fail to dazzle beholders!

Although Dorval was fascinated by Lemaître's original and seemingly spur-of-the-moment actions and reactions, and was certain they would make great stage partners, she considered the unpredictability of his antics a challenge to her own creative powers. As a long-time trouper, Dorval was determined to look upon her disquietude as a positive experience. After all, hadn't she always been capable of dealing with uncertainty in the real world? In all modesty, she knew she would rise to the occasion. Important as well, she felt she could learn from this creative, much-solicited, very handsome, and highly volatile Lemaître. Young at heart, she had always been open to new ways. Moreover, Lemaître's scenic banter fascinated her. Not that her own ideas had not yet coalesced. They had to some degree. Fortunately, they had not become rigid. Her technique to a great extent consisted of personalizing and emotionalizing the characters she brought to life, by pointing up their foibles, failures, and fortes. She would continue along this path, adding new and pertinent elements to her personifications. Nuances of mood, namely, agitation, defiance, determination, anger, love, and a whole range of subtle passions had endowed her characters with depth and life.

Dorval stood slim, small, and slightly bent on stage on opening night of *Thirty Years or a Gambler's Life*. Her manner perfectly encapsulated the young, repressed, obsequious, soon-to-be married Amélie. According to the materialistic values of the day, she had the money, and her husband to be, the status. That her character was antipodal to her husband's, she being meek, and he, rash, would perhaps encourage him, if not to give up gambling, at least to diminish his proclivity for this "vice." Events did not fulfill expectations. Her unthinking, vacuous, weakly structured domineering gambler husband, Georges de Germany, played by Frédérick Lemaître, looked down with disdain upon his ever-cringing wife. She, the fearful virginal bride, considered her self-indulgent husband with fear and trepidation.

The play's suspenseful happenings are divided into three acts, each spaced at fifteen-year intervals. The incidental music, the hallmark of so many melodramas, was composed by none other than the talented and well-thought-of Alexandre Piccini, former director of the the Porte Saint-Martin orchestra.

At the beginning of Act 1 the year is 1790. The curtains part on Paris' brilliantly lit Palais Royal gambling hall. The sets by Lefebvre were so cleverly designed that they gave the impression of a series of endless rooms set in several different, yet connected, gambling parlors. The effects of this type of linear perspective suggests the all-consuming addiction of the dice players frequenting the establishment.

The gambling halls are astir with adventuresome risk-takers attempting to build castles in the air on what they erroneously consider solid games of chance. Attention is drawn to an upstage gambling table. Excited players seem to be holding forth. Outside of a few chairs and benches, downstage is empty (Le Hir, 81).

The bewitching hour of midnight has just sounded. The twenty-five year-old Georges de Germany strides on stage, ebullient and self-confident to the extreme. His friends, Warner and Rodolphe, are deeply engrossed in their risky ventures. While Warner has just won a bundle of money which he now seeks to double, the wise Rodolphe, who has lost a third of the fortune left him by his hardworking father, has decided to never again allow himself to be influenced by either Georges or Warner. Unlike them, he harbors no delusions of grandeur.

In contrast, the flamboyant Georges seems in no way bothered by the important sums of money he has lost, nor disconcerted by his mounting debts. With a twist of the wrist, Lemaître casts the whole idea to the winds. Indeed, he is in high spirits. And why not? His marriage to the wealthy Amélie the following day augurs well for him. In keeping with French law, upon her marriage, her fortune passes to Georges. The spoiled and virtually mindless Georges, forever encouraged by Warner to indulge his vice, is the perfect pawn for him. It is via Georges that Warner finds gratification in both his gambling disease – considered by Ducange to be a social sickness – and in the superiority he feels each time he encourages – or orders – the pusillanimous Georges to indulge his weakness. Both Warner, the manipulator, and Georges, the obsessive compulsive, may be considered partners in crime.

At ten the following morning, the curtains part on a summer drawing room which opens onto a beautiful garden. Arm chairs and tables are placed on either side of the stage. The servants are busy talking. They bemoan the fact that Georges, who is to be married in a few hours, has not yet returned from his previous evening's gambling venture. Should his ailing father hear of his unpardonable behavior, he would surely die of apoplexy. No matter, the flashy Georges feels no allegiance to him nor to anyone else, save to his partner in crime.

All eyes now focus on the sixteen year-old meek, tender, angelic, and all-giving Amélie (Dorval). Although she smiles demurely, as only Dorval knew how, her frequently tense facial expressions and subtle eye movements disclose a sense of urgency and concern over Georges' absence. Her silence is eloquent. As she stands motionless on stage, her every feeling, every impression, every judgment is transformed into the magic of sensation. How could he not show up on his his wedding day, she asks herself silently? Even the servants are surprised by Georges' unprincipled behavior. What remains hidden from the audience, and from Amélie as well, is the extent of the young man's singularly obsessive character.

Dorval plays the naive and compliant Amélie with absolute commitment. While utterly ignorant of the ways of the world – having been purposefully kept so throughout her adolescence – she is, nonetheless, aware of Georges' utter lack of interest in her. Dorval's on-stage silence, her frequently static poses, her deeply troubled physiognomy is forever operative in underscoring her subordinate position as future wife. They also predispose the audience to pity her, to identify with her sorrow, to empathize with her aloneness, against Georges' complete disregard and indifference to her. Her cloistered life until now has spelled gentility and total ignorance of the ways of the world. Having been orphaned at age ten, Amélie had been summarily invited to live in the Germany household. As such, she not only knew what to expect from her future husband, but had been taught to remain subservient in all matters and at all times to the male. Nonetheless, hope springs eternal for some, even in a society where women were given short shrift and marriages of convenience were not the exception but the rule. Inexplicable to her was Georges' gambling fixation and, the monies continually siphoned from her inheritance to fulfill his lust.

Dorval, standing motionless on stage at the outset of the drama, gives the impression of suffering in silence. Her stance, poise, and mannerisms are controlled to the extreme. Like the stoic that she is, all forms of emotion are lived inwardly. Repression is the rule of the day. Nonetheless, while Amélie remains virtually immobile, her subdued hand movements and questioning facial expressions reveal an interplay of complex inner modes – that of the self-abnegating young girl brought up to obey, to fit into a certain mold maintained throughout life. Although sensing that nothing augurs well for her, she is utterly naive, going so far as to harbor certain Pollyanna traits. She hopes that Georges will change, that he will woo her and love her.

To convey Amélie's vacillating expressions – the dread of being forgotten and the hope of being loved – Dorval's eye movements, most frequently cast toward the ground or to the side, disclose both suffering, strength and inner resolve. In accordance with the woman's inferior place in French society, Amélie had been trained since childhood, along with others of her class, to obey her future husband, to live under his aegis, and, perhaps, most importantly, to give up all power over her inheritance.

Moments later, Georges's ailing father, old M. de Germany, arrives on the scene and is helped into a chair. Clearly, he loves Amélie as a daughter and is understandably agitated when he learns that his son has not yet arrived. Minutes pass. Suspense grows. When Georges finally makes his appearance, rather than acknowledging his fiancée's presence, he asks for Warner. And well he might, since he had secretly requested that his friend pawn the diamond spray he was to give to Amélie on her wedding day. How else could he have paid his staggering gambling debts? Tension rises until Warner, who had been sent to redeem the diamond spray, finally appears, hands it to Georges, who in turn gives it to the delighted Amélie. No sooner are the marriage vows exchanged in an off-stage ceremony, than Dorval's facial traits take on an expression of sadness, revealing the deepest recesses of her heart. Only now, perhaps, does she begin to understand the fate of the unloved wife. Could she have expected otherwise? Dorval's face questions herself in the profoundest of visual languages. Sorrow appropriates her eyes. Pained lines invade the once smooth surface of her adolescent forehead. Dorval's eloquent gestures guide listeners and observers to increasingly complex areas of her being.

Georges' apathy toward his bride is evident in Lemaître's gestural language. He is not only perfectly at ease with his own passion for gambling, but has no qualms about a habit which has already caused so much disruption and turmoil in his home. More important in this macabre round is the strange influence Warner exercises over Georges. Well-spoken and handsome, Warner is, nonetheless, an avowed thief. He is a seductive fellow as well. His increasing power over the naive Georges leaves this perfectly poised manipulator master of life's play. Like the devil, he ushers the morally flaccid into temptation. What makes their relationship all the more intriguing is the strange emotional hold – possibly latent homosexual love – he exercises over his victim.

What perturbs both the audience and Georges' father are his son's continuous lies. Hadn't he sworn to him that he would never gamble again? If such were the case, then why did he spend his days and nights at the Palais Royal? Emotions heighten when Rodolphe, Georges' only honorable friend, delivers a letter to M. de Germany from Amélie's beloved uncle, M. Dermont, requesting that her marriage be called off. It is of course too late. So as to defray any possible anguish on Amélie's part, Dermont's letter will be kept from the bride.

Neither in love with Amélie nor with anyone else except perhaps Warner, Georges remains detached from everything save his vice. His only wish is to rush back to the gambling hall and, in all good conscience, to use his wife's money to further gratify his ever-consuming lust for the game of chance. Lemaître's coldness, reserve, and sardonic smile capture Georges' lack of tenderness and consideration for his wife. Matters come to a climax when the magistrate enters the Germany home and declares the theft of a diamond spray – the very one Amélie is wearing. No sooner does Georges hand this magnificent jewel to the magistrate, than Dorval's face is encapsulated in sorrow.

In typical melodramatic style, old M. Germany's outrage is such, that after cursing his son for his unconscionable behavior, he dies of humiliation and shock.

The rhythmic interplay between the controlled pain experienced by the increasingly withdrawn Dorval, in keeping with the comportment expected of a refined young girl of the time, and Georges' obvious maneuverings, amplified by his never-ending lies, dynamize the tragedy for both protagonists and audience.

Lemaître's utter indifference toward his wife is even made manifest each time he snuffs tobacco center stage, in the palpable enjoyment he derives from it. A subtle smile, a grin, a glance, even the raucous tones in which he addresses her at times measure the gamut of his apathy, perhaps even antipathy, for Amélie (Baldick, 59).

Dorval's pained responses, her ever increasing sense of humiliation, subtly rendered by her increasing predisposition to gesture as the language of the heart, let the viewer share in the further encroachment of her pain

Act 2 takes place in 1805. The curtains part on a small room in Georges de Germany's home. The passive and subservient Amélie is busy writing a letter to her beloved uncle, Dermont. Every now and then she wipes her eyes. The burned-down candle suggests she has been up all night. Nothing has changed in her life, save for the fact that Georges, who continues to spend his days and nights in the gambling parlors, is now heavily in debt. Most of the couple's furniture has been sold. Ethics, as always, prevail in Amélie's world. Despite her husband's utter disregard for her, as wife and mother, she now has but a single goal in life – to protect her beloved son.

Dorval's measured approach to Amélie's hopeless existence, is subtly conveyed in body language: her sense of determination may be measured by her steady, but small, strides across the stage. Her facial expression is stilled, as though routed by controlled despair. To help her cope with the hopeless disarray in the Germany home, Amélie summons her faithful and loving chamber maid, Louise. Upon entering, she finds her mistress disconsolate. She had been weeping. And Dorval wept as no one in French theater could weep. She wept real tears. Georges' equally caring butler, Valentin, takes center stage to disclose the deepening morass in the household.

Nor has the irascible George ceased to hound Amélie for money. On the contrary, his blatant insistence that his wife hand him more funds – her last *sous*, including her dowry – sets her trembling.

The scene is cleverly handled by Lemaître, who stands erect in his manly pride, a true caricature of the male's overblown dominance over the weak female he calls his wife. Lemaître becomes the living incarnation of the arrogant male bourgeois. To evince his power over her, his voice rises several decibel points.

> Madam, since when have you arrogated the right to bar my best friend Warner from entering my home? (II, 2, 13).
> [Obsequiously, yet cleverly, she replies:]
> I am not in the habit of receiving guests so early in the morning when you are not here (II, 2, 13).

Increasingly angry, Georges blurts out, "Your answer is frivolous" (II, 2, 13). He accuses her of hating his friend Warner. In no uncertain terms, he emphasizes the fact that he is master of the household, which allows him to broach the real reason for his visit: to demand more money. The brow-beaten Amélie once again yields to her husband's demands, justifying her acquiescence as a means of keeping him out of jail which would bring shame to the family, and thus harm their son (III, 15). The master/slave relationship imposed on wives by French law, comes to the fore as Amélie signs over her remaining funds to her husband. To play up Georges' satisfaction at his anticipated winnings to come, Lemaître again takes center stage to snuff tobacco, which he does with a twinkle in his eye (Baldick 59).

Nonetheless, altercations between husband and wife, be they over money or for barring Warner entry to their home, trigger Georges' volatile personality. At times, he even resorts to threats, particularly when he believes he sees through his wife's excuses, her asides, and sorrowful demeanor. The louder his rancor, the more commanding his attitude, the less forceful she becomes. At this juncture, he orders his wife to obey him at all times, totally and unconditionally.

Anguished to the extreme, the vanquished and abused Amélie kneels before her husband. She begs him to flee with her and their son to a distant land where they would be able to live in peace. Nor is the decisive "no" enunciated by her husband, surprising. He needs more money to keep him out of prison. In a moment of strength, or bravura, Amélie cries out her refusal to give him any more funds. To do so would be tantamount to disinheriting her son, to which she would never agree. In desperation she cries out:

> When your father cursed you he predicted you would end up by committing a crime! (III, 15)

Although aware that French law gives her husband complete power over her and her money, she has now built up sufficient strength to categorically refuse to comply with his command. While her stand is heroic, panic sets in moments later, when her manipulative husband threatens to kill himself right then and there. Think of the humiliation that such an act would bring on the family Lemaître unctuously opines, smiling coyly as he pronounces his words. Predictably, she again yields to her husband's insidious threats.

As fate would have it, Uncle Dermont arrives at the appropriate moment and speaks his gentle words of solace to Amélie.

> Tender and noble victim, take care not to yield under the weight of your chains. Remember at least that you have a father, and he watches over you (III, 18).

Amélie bursts into tears.

In these superbly moving scenes Dorval plays out Amélie's gratitude toward her uncle and faces her remaining options in refined, heartbreaking pauses, subtle hand gestures, and painfully moving vocal innuendoes.

Upon Georges' return that evening, fate seems to have interceded in his favor. Not only is he in a happy frame of mind, but he hands his valet a sum of money and orders him to arrange for a masked ball to be given at his home. One that must "astound all of Paris," he adds (II, 17) .

Upon sight of Dermont in his home, Lemaître, a master of mood swings, flips into a rage. Hadn't he barred him entry? Amélie enters the melee. Her shrill tones pierce all thought of amenable solutions. Rather than allowing Georges to subvert her intent, she sees fit to vent her spleen.

> Your ingratitude revolts my heart. .. I sacrificed everything to you. I have only one remaining friend on earth, your disinherited son has only one protector in the world, and you seek to wrench him from me? (II, 4, 18).

The splendid ball, typical of *à la mode* melodrama, opens onto a large hall aglow with candlesticks and excitement exuded by a mix of partygoers. Dancing, music, merriment, and pantomimic sequences, while underscoring the spectacle side of the production, also trigger emotional interaction between audience and stage personalities.

The noxious Warner, having succeeded in leading his disciple into a world of iniquity, will now attempt to seduce the "arrogant" Amélie, for whose body he longs (II, 4, 18).

Audiences view Amélie's richly decorated pentagon-shaped bedroom. Uncle Dermont who has arrived in secret remains long enough to inform Amélie of her husband's imminent arrest and the ruination of the family name. Seconds later, Warner, like the snake that he is, enters Amélie's room via a secret stairwell. His love for her is not only all-consuming, he tells her it will be her salvation. The horrified Amélie is beyond shock. "Leave," she orders peremptorily. "Never," he replies. His overly saccharine sweet talk, rather than entrancing Amélie, revolts her. The once restrained and outwardly passive wife, having taken on the allure of those strong and virago-like heroines of classical drama, grabs the sword lying on the table, and cries out: "Death rather than infamy" (II, IX, 23).

Remarkable was the manner in which Dorval, at times whispering, at other moments whimpering meekly, ran the affective gamut – from controlled determination to searing pain and despair, to conclude in attempted violence.

In keeping with the play's melodramatic pattern, Georges knocks at the door at this very moment. Warner flees. Should she ever divulge his presence in her room, he tells her, she would be dishonored (II, 4, 23). Amélie faints. Georges breaks down the door, peers stealthily about, sees Warner's sword, and Amélie, lying unconscious on an arm chair. "Amélie has a lover," he howls. She has betrayed him. The now conscious Amélie denies the accusation. Screams, yelps, tears, rage, and more fainting spells ensue.

When it is learned that Georges is to be imprisoned for debt and other misdemeanors, Uncle Dermont again comes to the rescue and provides the couple with a means of escape. Gunshots are heard. Mayhem. Soldiers rush in.

Act III, which takes place fifteen years later, opens on the courtyard of an inn on the main road to Munich. Its owners, Mr. and Mrs. Birmann, are setting up the rustic tables and benches for their customers. Mr. Birmann has good news for his wife. "The ugly man, that poor good-for-nothing, that pariah who arrived two years ago from Hungary, Bohemia, and a host of other countries with a wife and young daughter, and has been living in a ramshackle hut on Red Mountain, is to be evicted for non-payment of rent and taxes " (III, 2, 26). The townspeople avoid him like the plague.

The mood suddenly changes. Music and gaiety take over. Townspeople dressed in brashly colored clothes sweep onto the stage.

In sharp contrast to the festive surroundings is the presence of the pale, wan, albeit sinister man walking slowly toward the Birmanns' inn. He is Georges. Taken with pity for the starving man, the owners offer him bread and beer, enough for his wife and daughter as well.

A young captain in the military, who had been stopping at the Birmanns' inn, looks at Georges with compassion and invites him to have some wine. Georges accepts. The townspeople look on askance. The traveler offers Georges remuneration for indicating the quickest way to Munich. Music sounds in the square.

The sets change. The stage features the interior of a broken-down cabin on a mountain top surrounded on all sides by precipices. The weather is menacing. Streaks of lightning flash in the distance. Winds howl. Thunder rages. Amélie's and George's young daughter, Georgette, is hungry. While Amélie sews, her mind wanders back to her son, Albert. Moments later, Georges, whose face is contorted with horror, arrives with a basket filled with food and gold. Where did he find the gold, she asks. Where had he been all night? Be grateful, he tells her. Georgette notices blood on his hand. The smooth-talking Warner enters. He attempts to convince Georges to give him his gold. Georges balks. He must use it to pay his taxes, he replies righteously.

The presence of a young soldier becomes visible from the window. Suspense heightens. What happened to the voyager who had wanted to go to Munich? Some foul play seems to have occurred. Georges is terrified. He asks Warner to help him bury something. They leave. Some time later, the young military man who had offered Georges some wine at the inn, knocks at the door. "Does Georges live here?" he asks. Georgette replies in the affirmative and invites him in. Amélie arrives in short order. They talk. Not surprisingly, he identifies himself as Albert. The recognition scene between mother and son, so typical of melodrama, is more than heart-warming. Albert has a present for his parents: a million in gold, which he leaves on the table. Better still is the written permission, which he brings with him from the French government, allowing them to return to France. Albert is tired. His mother urges him to lie down and rest in the next room. He does so. Amélie leaves.

Georges and Warner return. Georges sees the gold on the table and covets it. Strangely enough, at that very moment, he lapses into some kind of reverie, during which he discloses that he has committed three murders. He then mentions his son nostalgically. "But you haven't seen him for fifteen years," Warner blurts out. With that, Georges' face takes on "a terrible expression" (III, 15, 39). "You want me to assassinate the stranger who is resting here?" (III, 15, 39). Yes, Warner tries to convince him to do so:

> "It's night, he is alone...A million. No one will ever know that this young man stopped here."
> [Georges:] "Amélie received him."
> [Warner:] "You will tell them that you sent him away. Thunder and lightning invade the mountain area. If lightning struck the cabin and all was consumed, would we be responsible?" (III, 15, 39)

In sequences of incredible stage effects, lightning and thunder renew their assault. The hut is struck. Fire rages. Its beams fall one by one. Warner wants to torch the hut so as to get rid of the traveler. Georges refuses to allow it. Warner asks: "Is he more frightening than the other traveler?" (III, 15, 39) With that, he grabs a knife and makes his way to the room where the stranger is sleeping. By this time, thunder and lightning have invaded the stage. Georgette rushes in. She is terrified. Georges grabs and hugs his daughter. "Stop...Warner...Stop!" he shouts (III, 15, 1). The hut is burning. Warner returns to the main room, throws a wallet at Georges' feet and closes the door. Seconds later, Amélie enters, followed by some peasants, and runs to Georges, announcing that there has been a murder in the area.

The soldiers have just discovered the corpse. "My son!!!," he admits. "Yes, our son, Albert is here!" Amélie intercedes. "Soldiers are coming to arrest you." With that Georges rushes into the flaming room and carries out his wounded son in his arms.

> "Here he is," Georges screeches, as he sets his son down in front of his wife.
> "I am returning your son to you. My time is up...I am..."

Whereupon, Albert blurts out:

> "Stop! mother! My father saved my life" (III, 15, 2).

Meanwhile Warner, who had fled, returns hoping to convince Georges to follow him. The villagers, however, are in hot pursuit. Degenerate to the extreme, Georges, in a raucous voice admits to his son that he had killed a traveler while attempting to rob him. Then he hugs his son. "You know the truth….spare your mother, goodbye." The hut has been evacuated.

Mortified by his crime, Georges grabs the now terrified Warner, and pushes his partner in crime toward the burning hut. "You will never leave me," he screeams, and with that, the two evil-doers fling themselves into the fire as Amélie and her son look on aghast. The soldiers rush to save them. Georges falls to the ground. His wife kneels before him and his children surround him.

The curtains come down to thunderous applause. Clearly, Dorval and Lemaître had revolutionized French theater. Gone were the squealings, bombast, roars, exaggerations, affectations, overblown emotions, and emphases, so habitual to melodrama. Simplicity, forthrightness, and reality not only lent special grace to Ducange's work, but empowered his every word with meaning and truth.

Audiences were spellbound. Some were outraged by society's cruelly outmoded treatment of women. Others attempted to justify such behavioral dispositions. Cheers mingled with tears were visible on the faces of many of those attempting to enter Dorval's and Lemaître's dressing rooms. They wanted to convey their awe for the pithily spaced tirades and dynamic dialogues with which they identified. Some wept and even wailed. Idealists felt comforted at the thought that marriage laws would one day change. Some daring individuals were prepared to agitate for divorce. Realists understood that it was much too early to expect the enactment of such broad legislation for women.

In keeping with the text, Dorval interiorized Amélie's gentle personality. Kindness, resilience, courtesy, generosity, and strength of character saw her through life's ordeals. Never did she allow her scruples or honor to yield to the machinations of her pusillanimous husband. Nor did she deviate from the ethical road inculcated in her as a child. Audiences yielded to Dorval's increasingly moving torment. Her uncomplaining, seemingly passive, facial expressions and the adamant stand she took to remain with her husband rather than abandon him – an act which would have, she believed, countermanded everything she had promised at the altar – were considered heroic at the time. While Dorval's Amélie had never verbalized the indignities she had suffered, they were engraved for all time in her glances, rhythmic breathing, and bodily movements. While she agonized in silence at the prospect of her husband's slow and inevitable doom, her silent grandeur was not only eloquent, but actively served to save the family. It requires little stretch of the imagination to say that Dorval's enactment of her protagonist's commitment to her marriage vows and to the suffering they provoked in her life, might have steadied Dorval in her own frequently helpless emotional wanderings.

Dorval's dramatic foray, lived as it were in an inner mode, gave evidence of the hold she had over her portrayed character. No matter the humiliation her husband's lack of feeling for her triggered in her heart, Amélie was contoured on Dorval's personality. Rather than whine and bewail her lot, she stood strong in her dignified sorrow. Nor did she grow angry. Her stoicism was memorable. As Georges' wife, she bore all ills and suffered all indignities in silence. Perhaps, in some morbid way, Dorval saw Amélie as having been grateful to her husband for offering her the possibility of bypassing facile solutions, of proving her worth, of proving woman's worth in general?

The economic subjugation and martyrdom of women by their frequently dictatorial and abusive husbands was well known in Dorval's day. A case in point was the ever-courteous Amélie, who had been taught since childhood to repress hurt and pain. Identifying completely with the non-life which some husbands inflicted on their wives, either through complete lack of interest or outright dislike of them, Amélie refrained from expressing her feelings. Only on two occasions did she meekly attempt to persuade her rogue husband to alter his ways. In contrast with some wives of the day, she abstained from tears, yelps, and bursts of anger to express her disapproval of her husband's unconscionable behavior. To avoid eye contact, she glanced at the floor, and turned away from him, thereby hiding the searing pain his actions and his complete detachment had caused her.

Most male intellectuals, be they philosophers, spiritual leaders, or government officials, were prone to intellectualize economic and emotional situations and in so doing, failed to understand the lot of the gentle and long-suffering, browbeaten mother and wife caught up in an unfortunate marriage. Life for such a one, and there were many at the time, kept her incarcerated in a world of unrelieved sorrow. Accolades go to Ducange, for having pointed the way – and pithily at that. Part idealist, part realist, and part social critic, he understood that while one could not change the evils of society in one fell swoop, one could try to allay their tragic consequences by pointing them out. In *Thirty Years or the Life of a Gambler,* Ducange proved himself to be a merciless theatrical master at fighting against France's prevailing legal system, with its arranged marriages and forceful deprivation of rights imposeded upon wives and women in general.

Ducange's pert dialogue and Lemaître's aggressively portrayed, vicious unawareness of the baseness of his character's actions, were played out in sharp contrast to Dorval's dilating sequences of docile martyrdom. Together, however, they profoundly stirred the spectators, instilling despair in those who identified with the pathos of Amélie's sadness, and distress for those who came to realize society's lack of involvement in helping, or even acknowledging, those in need. The case in point here focused on the gambler type. To refrain from coping with Georges' emotional illness which had led to the slow and relentless degradation of his being – from gambler to forger, to thief, to assassin – was an immoral and retrograde act.

With controlled determination, Lemaître, playing Georges over a thirty-year span, injected a sense of increasingly degenerative lust for gambling into his character, which he conveyed in part via his three articular centers – shoulder, elbow, and wrist. His dynamically focused vocal intonations, accompanied by body movements, revealed his protagonist's intent to dominate the chance factor. To point out Lemaître's extraordinary appeal as Georges, despite or perhaps because of his obsessive vice and his clearly indifferent feelings for his wife, may have been due in part to audience identification with his character. How many men in the audience would have unconsciously wished to gamble nightly on their own? Lemaître's use of gesture, timing, intonation, humor, in increasing stages of violence, disclosed his protagonist's potentially lethal acts in networks of prolonged asides, smiles, cover-ups, and lies. Georges' weak will had allowed his *penchant* to dominate his life, thus underscoring his patheticness, which manifested itself in his increasingly dictatorial attitude toward his wife. Unperturbed, Georges, believing himself in command, was in fact enslaved to his own weakly structured psyche. Rather than master of his destiny, as he thought of himself, he was its slave. The rash, ebullient, physically appealing Lemaître was unapproachable in the breadth and scope of his portrayal.

While the frail, self-effacing, and obedient Amélie, daughter of a well-to-do French bourgeois family, slipped ever more deeply into the morass of her own living pathos, Dorval's highly disciplined and rightfully placed emotive lamentations were never once uncontrolled. As the stronger of the two, Amélie, not Georges, was the survivor.

The play triumphed. Newspapers, such as *Le Globe*, *Le Corsaire* and *La Pandore*, commented on Dorval's nuanced interpretation of the self-effacing Amélie. Her performance was referred to as "admirable," and as "playing her role to perfection" (*Le Courrier des Théâtres* Oct. 3, A, 155). Dorval could hardly believe the critics, writing as they did about the "truth" of her impersonation, its "elegance," "its cutting pathos." Praised as well was the manner in which she conceived and executed such an extraordinarily painful role. "Let us admit, and in all sincerity, that without seeking to diminish the worthiness of other actresses of the time, not one among them would have been able to acquit themselves of such a nuanced role" (*Le Courrier des Théâtres* Oct. 3, A, 155). Critics began referring to Dorval as the "feminine Talma of the Boulevard" (Ambrière, 156). She was a revelation!

However, what became apparent at the conclusion of the *Thirty Years or a Gambler's Life,* was the remarkably innovative manner in which Dorval and Lemaître worked as a unit. Never did they play as two separate individuals. The two made for one.

Jules Janin considered the theatrical couple revolutionary in their approach to drama. The audience, used to the shrill tones of melodrama with its shouting and uproar, looked at one another in astonishment, moved and delighted by such simplicity and grace. Frédéderick Lemaître, a handsome young man at the time, was admirably suited for his part: fiery, passionate, violent and proud; while Mme Dorval, with her slightly stooped figure, had everything necessary to command the deepest compassion.

Victor Ducange had the honor of signaling the beginnings of these two newly inspired actors who, together, pointed up the drama's passions. They started on the same footing, intent in their search for astonishing, terrifying and charming conquests to come. Art nouveau poets will draw their nascent splendors from their work.

The new Frédérick Lemaître was a handsome young man, daringly built for his art, animated, audacious, violent, quick-tempered, superb! The new-born Mme Dorval revealed in her person the strongest justification for accolades. (Carlson, *The French Stage*, 1853-58 ,VI, 156)

Certainly, Victor Ducange may not have been a great poet. However, he opened a breach. And when he found it open, he enlarged it; and he was the first to discover the two interpreters, Frédérick Lemaître and Marie Dorval. Whatever false note might have been written into the text, Dorval and Lemaître played it with naturalness and credibility. Rather than emphasizing key words in the script, they spoke them naturally, attempting to feel and touch the listener. Nothing was hackneyed. All was a question of temperament and understanding. When Lemaître felt his character to be out of hand, he allowed brute force to take over on stage, sometimes breaking a chair in the process. Before indulging in such stage violence, he of course warned Dorval of his intent. The realistic decors added, too, to the physical, spiritual, psychological, and economic ravages of a family in the wake of uncontrolled vice and self-indulgence. But the urgency of the protagonists' plights came through, above all, in splendidly active tonal sonorities, gestures, and verbal modulations. They performed as one does in a tournament – each supporting the other, each playing against the other when the role demanded it. They were soul mates, existing beyond the written and spoken word. Naivete is not condoned. Amélie knows she is victimized. This timid wife knows her husband's weakness. Stoic in character, she is fully cognizant of her acts. Like the modern existentialist, Amélie was aware of every facet of her life. Yet, while adhering to her brand of morality, she, the desolate wife, wept marvelously on stage – "in spasms, a delirium to beat them all," yet able at all times to dominate her heartbreak, while vivifying the world of a *A Gambler's Life* (cf. Janin, *Marie Dorval, Documents inédits* 38).

Panegyrics for Ducange were elicited as well from Janin. "He was born to create drama". His "insolent verve" revealed his "profound disdain for the stalls" (Janin, *Histoire de la littérature dramatique*, III, 302).

M. Bouilly, author of The *Priest of the Sword,* was overwhelmed by Dorval's acting, but singled out her penetrating voice for praise:

> Mme Dorval made me rediscover what I had been searching to find for so long: I mean those clean blows emanating directly from the soul, that irresistible accent which penetrates all the more deeply into the heart, because it is devoid of artifice and without preparation. It is a mechanism which suddenly escapes, strikes you, carries you off before you have any time to think (*Dorval. Documents inédits*, 41).

Understandably, Montgenêt, the new director of the Porte Saint-Martin Theater was more than pleased at the play's enormous success. No longer did he begrudge Dorval and Lemaître the enormous salaries they commanded. Wise as well was the leeway, unheard of at the time, he accorded the two stars. He sensed that their ingrained talents and sensitivities would guide them along the right path.

In March of 1828 Paris' highly acclaimed acting couple appeared in *The Bride of Lammermoor,* based on the novel by Sir Walter Scott, and adapted for the theater by Ducange and Anicet-Bourgeois. Among the seven different stage sets constructed for this work was a ruined castle and a flood, each in its way destined to point up the suspenseful and macabre aspects of this Gothic drama. As Théophile Gautier noted, "The time had come of spectacles made purely for the eye" (T. Gautier, *Histoire de l'art dramatique,* II, 174 , Allévy, 61)

Scott's work revolved around historical happenings: those of the Ravenswood family which had backed the Stuart king James II rather than the Protestant William of Orange during the bloodless revolution of 1688-9. During the course of the events, the vindictive lawyer, Sir William Ashton, causes the Master of Ravenswood to lose his title and most of his property. The ominous Wolf's Crag Castle alone remains his. As fate would have it, Edgar Ravenswood saves the life of Sir William Ashton's beautiful daughter, Lucy. The two fall in love and become engaged. The horrific Lady Ashton, Lucy's mother, adamantly opposes the marriage. She has another candidate in mind for her daughter. Believing that her beloved Edgar no longer loves her, Lucy agrees to marry the suitor her mother has chosen for her. Edgar, who arrives at the conclusion of the wedding ceremony, challenges Lucy's brother and husband to combat. Instead of overcoming their traumatic destiny, the lovers drown in the "magnificently horrible concluding catastrophe" (Le Hir, 69).

What was outstanding in this otherwise run-of-the-mill melodrama, was the horrific concluding stage set designed by the gifted mechanic, Griffe. His terrifying construct of a rising tide slowly enveloping the vast scenic space of the Porte Saint-Martin, seemed utterly compelling. Not only were many spectators in tears, but the ever-rising water surrounding them was so realistic that many spectators virtually feared for their lives.

Dorval and Lemaître again received accolades:

> The beautiful scene of the wedding contract, which precedes the catastrophe, so beautifully depicted in the novel... was superbly played by Lemaître... and we only have compliments to give to this actor. But it's not only in the third act that Frederick rose to remarkable heights, he was applauded throughout the beautiful second scene when the lovers unite and face the heavens. Lucy's role so well understood by Mme Dorval, adds greatly to the reputation of this actress... (Le Hir, 69).

Breathtaking as the heroic Edgar Ravenswood, Lemaître in his ardent love scenes spoke to every female in the audience. Nor did Dorval's understanding of Lucy's passion and anguish pass unnoticed. Singled out for praise was the novel manner in which she combined passion and naturalness in her acting, and in so doing, accentuated the originality and reality of her protagonist's increasing suffering (Le Hir, 70). The review in *La Pandore* on March 23, 1828, praised Ducange's meticulous stage adaptation of Scott's work. Accolades went to Lemaître's "remarkable" talent and to the sensitivity, finesse, and charm of Dorval's portrayal of Lucy (Baldick, 63).

During the summer of 1828, the Théâtre Saint-Martin closed its doors to undergo significant renovations. Dorval left for Strasbourg to be with Merle. Lemaître visited them briefly during that time, taking the opportunity of performing with her as well. At the end of July, he returned to Paris post-haste for the birth of his second child. By October 29, 1828, the Théâtre Saint-Martin again opened its doors to the successful stage couple who astounded their audiences in a production of Goethe's *Faust*, adapted for the stage by Merle, Bérault, and Nodier. Not only were they praised for their acting, but for the complex stage machinery and the blood-curdling effects these elicited: i.e. in the apotheosis scene in *Faust,* when the stage was divided in half, showing "both hell and paradise" (Carlson, 51).

Dorval was ecstatic. Not only had she and Lemaître enjoyed immense success as an acting duo, but they were lovers, or so it was bandied around. If this be the truth, why then did Lemaître break his contract with the Théâtre Saint-Martin? His departure caused a severe blow to both the Porte Saint-Martin, and to Dorval, in particular. It was said that she loved him passionately and felt abandoned by him when he left so suddenly. No one, she sighed, could convey emotion as he did. This sensually arresting – and variously demure, authentic, and flamboyant Lemaître – was one of a kind.

Lemaître's departure from the Théâtre Saint-Matin was caused, so it has been claimed, by the serious problems which had arisen between himself and his wife, the sometime actress, Sophie Hallignier. So morbidly jealous had she become of her husband's relationship with Dorval, that to appease his beloved wife, who was expecting their second child, Lemaître assured her he would see less of Dorval. That was not sufficient. His wife demanded that an end be put to her husband's and Dorval's theatrical partnership. The hours they spent together having become untenable to her, Lemaître's wife caused him to break – at least in part – his contract with the Théâtre Saint-Martin (Ambrière, 157). On the other hand, perhaps Lemaître was looking for greener fields, to branch out and perform at more prestigious theaters. He had reached the stage of being able to call his own cards as actor and director. And he did!

The sometime romantic dramatist, Casimir de la Vigne, who had written for both the Comédie-française and the Odéon, was anxious for Dorval to play the lead in his latest theater piece, *Marino Faliero*. It opened at the Porte Saint-Martin on May 30, 1829, unfortunately without Lemaître, who had bid Dorval adieu. Successful from the outset, this blood and thunder historical tragedy, focusing on a conspiracy by the Venetian doge to murder patricians and declare himself king, included illicit love scenes, necessary to assure its success. Although far from great art, it was a perfect vehicle for Dorval and would have been for Lemaître as well. The mix of his brio and brutality and her suave, and highly emotional outcries, would have complemented each other. It was not to be. Dorval missed him at her side, and wrote him the day after the opening.

> The more the moment approached, the more I felt that I had lost a good part of myself. (Ambrière, 167).

Although the actor Ligier had replaced Lemaître, Dorval, as Eléna, won accolades. The *Courrier des Théâtres* praised her diction as "so choice and so charming." Charles Nodier, writing in the *Revue de Paris* underscored his thoughts on the subject. Unlike some classicists in the audience who were shocked at the manner in which Dorval sounded the twelve-syllable alexandrine verse, Nodier was impressed.

> I heard that Mme.Dorval did not meet the public's expectations when reciting verse. This is a good omen because our theories of diction leave much to be desired. Mme Dorval's diction, like her talent, is perfect. It is not her fault if certain verses in her role are impregnated with old-fashioned rhythmic notions. (Ambrière, 167)

Despite the success, old times and old relationships could not be recaptured. Together, Dorval and Lemaître had inspired a revolution in dramatic arts. They had stunned audiences by the timber of their voices – at times strident, at other moments mellifluous. The two had worked as one, in simplicity and truth. The former, given to unbridled passions and violence, the latter, to words which astonished and charmed by their tremulous resonances. Both knew how to cry with abandon when need be, with ardor at other times, forever transforming their play, their persona, their poetics of gesture and stance.

Jules Janin conveyed his sorrow for this tragic artistic "divorce", the cutting in twain of two by a "grievous hand." Like twin stars, they "left their resplendent traces of romantic theater in the heavens" (Moser, 21). Janin bemoaned their separation. Possessing the the swashbuckler's vitality, his self-assurance, rarely if ever losing his footing in his theatrical impersonations, Frédérick Lemaître possessed as well the qualities necessary to turn Dorval's faults into brilliant theatrical moments, accomplishing such feats at times by the willed, even exaggerated absurdity of his antics. "Theirs was a single soul divided into two bodies; they were compelled by the same idea and imbued with the same passions" (Janin, *Littérature dramatique*, 158 V). Thanks to Lemaître, Mme Dorval had defined her art, tightened her inspiration, and complemented her performance.

Dorval, nonetheless, had little time for sadness. She and Merle, particularly the latter, had virtually no business acumen, and forever suffered under the weight of mounting debts. Such a precarious financial situation was nothing new in Dorval's life. She had always lived on the edge of bankruptcy and continued to do so. No matter how hard she worked, how adulated she was, she was almost never solvent.

More importantly, her fame was growing. She was in the limelight. The stylish portraitist Vigneron had even asked her to pose for him. She agreed to two one-hour sittings. The forthcoming lithograph was more than satisfying to her (Ambrière, 160).

Times were changing. French theatrical taste was broadening. In 1822, when the enterprising Merle had invited an English touring company to perform Shakespeare at the Porte Saint-Martin, his efforts had earned him untold humiliations. Understandably so, perhaps, as we have noted, since England had been France's historical enemy and Napoleon's adversary. For the most part, only avant-gardists in the audience were impressed by what they saw.

The climate in Paris vis-à-vis Shakespeare had so altered, that by 1827, when Emile Laurent, the new director of the Porte Saint-Martin, invited an English theatrical group to perform *Hamlet*, *Romeo and Juliet*, and *Othello* in Paris, they were received at the elegant Odéon Theater not with cat calls, but with ovations. French audiences thrilled to the stage happenings and to the great names making their appearance in Paris: the statuesque Charles Kemble and his partner, Harriet Smithson. Their performances triggered wild bravos. Smithson was revered in the role of Ophelia. Her mad scene was unforgettable. So startlingly realistic had her performance been considered by French audiences that the celebrated actress returned many times to Paris to direct her own English theater. In 1833, she married Hector Berlioz (Carlson, 59).

Shakespearemania prevailed in 1828. Only one year later, another English troupe arrived in Paris featuring William Macready in Macbeth, and some months later, still another exciting visitor, the renowned Edmund Kean, performed in *Richard III, The Merchant of Venice,* and *King Lear*. In July, Macready returned to Paris, with *Hamlet, Othello,* and more (Carlson, 60). Shakespeare had clearly taken hold of Parisians.

The innovative, violent, even bloodthirsty nature of Shakespeare's works had so impressed Stendhal, that the future author of the celebrated novel, *The Red and the Black*, went to London to attend performances of his plays. In his celebrated work, *Racine and Shakespeare,* he shocked many a French classicist by advocating that tragedies be written in prose and not, as required by the French, in the twelve-foot alexandrine verse that had ruled French theater since the seventeenth century. This young whipper-snapper reformer had also had the audacity to label the sacrosanct alexandrine verse a *cache-sottise*. As a defender of Romanticism, he advocated banishing the outworn rules of French stage, and invited "theatrical illusion" and Romanticism to reign on the proscenium instead. About Romanticism he wrote:

> The art of presenting literary works to the people, in keeping with their habits and beliefs, may give them the greatest possible pleasure.
> Classicism, on the contrary, presents literature which gave the greatest pleasure to their grandparents. (Stendhal, 71)

Stendhal cried modernism, reform, and open-mindedness for the theater.

Other reformers, namely the young Victor Hugo, born in 1802, also reacted powerfully to the unleashing of Shakespearean violence and sanguinary passions on stage. While preparing the preface to his drama *Cromwell* in 1827, he wrote brazenly:

> We have now reached the summit of modern times in poetry. Shakespeare is drama; a drama which blends in the same breath the grotesque and the sublime, the terrible and the buffoonish, tragedy and comedy. Drama takes on the true character of the third period of poetry in contemporary literature. (*Préface de Cromwell*, Hugo, 423)

The critic and author Charles Nodier had also been influenced by the British giant. In his gentle way, he held forth on the innovative nature of Shakespeare's dramas at many of the Sunday evening open-house suppers, which he hosted as curator of Paris' Arsenal Library. Visitors such as Hugo, Dumas, Musset, Lamartine,

Gérard de Nerval, Vigny, Sophie Gay and her beautiful daughter, Delphine, who had their own salons, also sparked lively conversations centered on the work of Shakespeare.

When time permitted, Marie Dorval attended Nodier's *cénacle*, honing in on the latest pros and cons of France's complicated stage politics revolving now, in large measure, about Shakespeare.

On those occasions, all attention centered on her exquisite diction and the alluring throatiness of her voice that so attracted her audiences.

Guests always felt at home at Nodier's *cénacle*. His was a happy *ménage* which included his beloved wife, who ran the gatherings and dinners offered on Sunday with such expertise, and his beautiful daughter, Marie, an excellent pianist, who was the apple of his eye.

Clearly French theater was in a state of turmoil. The new was pitted against the old! Stalwart, enterprising, and ambitious, Dorval sensed the catalyzing impact of creativity, the burgeoning of a different way. She was at a turning point in her career.

Chance intervenes in strange ways. It did so for Dorval on a moonlit March night at one o'clock in the morning. The year was 1830. After attending a performance of Alexandre Dumas' play *Christine* at the Odéon Theater, she hailed a *fiacre* and stepped inside. No sooner was she comfortably ensconced then she looked out of the window and happened to catch sight of Alexander Dumas walking in her direction. She asked the driver to stop.

"Monsieur Dumas," she called out. Her ultra seductive, slightly raspy voice, which she manipulated to her advantage, drew his attention and he approached her *fiacre*. "Step in," she said. He did so, happily. She complimented him on his latest play, *Christine,* based on Sweden's mysterious and reclusive seventeenth-century queen. The *fiacre* moved on. In case he did not remember her name, she introduced herself to him with utmost modesty as Marie Dorval, "just a minor actress at the Porte Saint-Martin" (Moser, 22).

"A minor actress?" he countered in his thunderous voice. "You're making fun of me...You're a genius," he added, kissing and hugging her effusively. Not surprisingly, since Dumas was a lady's man *par excellence.*

"Vile flattery," she responded, is "unworthy of a man of your intellect" (Moser, 23). Assuming a more moderate tone, he confessed to having sobbed when attending *Thirty Years or the Life of a Gambler*. He continued lauding her talents, as only Dumas knew how. His mastery of flattery and seduction was well known. Although Dorval saw through Dumas' ways, she enjoyed hearing him spell out his admiration for her qualities as an actress. His sentences, she mused, were so well constructed, his melodious voice so enticing, his physique unparalleled. That he had found *The Vampire*, written by his friend Nodier, in which she had starred, stunningly terrifying, was music to her ears. Thanks to the generosity of the playwright Casimir Delavigne, he added, he had been able to attend *Marino Faliero,* Dorval's latest sold-out performance (Moser, 23).

Given Dumas' detailed descriptions of the plays in which she had appeared, it was her turn to convey her admiration for his talents. Not only did she admire Dumas' extraordinary imagination, and his feel for words, but, too, his virtually overnight success as a playwright. Making the most of the opportunity, she vented her spleen against her rival, the mean-spirited Mlle Mars, a star at the Comédie-Française. Demurely, she told Dumas that "Mlle Mars must have been deeply grateful to you for choosing her to act in "your masterpiece, *Henri III and his Court.*"

"Mlle Mars, grateful!" Dumas responded contentiously, after which he proceeded to list the problems she had caused him once he had proposed his play *Christine* to the Comédie-Française. "Authoritarian, aggressive, and jealous," she had threatened multiple times to withdraw from the play if the role of the page, given to the "charming Despréaux," were not cut and the actress fired. A man of principle, at least in this regard, Dumas had stood firm. Despréaux remained in the cast and the play was very well received.

To further bolster Dumas' morale – were it to need any – Dorval flattered him on the excellent reviews *Henri III and his Court* had received.

Taking over the conversation as was his wont, he discoursed in detail on the accolades journalists had awarded his play on its final dress rehearsal – on February 11, 1829. Everyone of note had been invited to this event – from the Duke of Orléans and his family, seated in boxes, to Victor Hugo and Alfred de Vigny, among other aspiring Romantic writers, settling for the ground floor. Needless to say, they were part of the *claque* – or applauders – whose function it was to signal the audience when to manifest their delight or their ire!

The more excited Dumas grew while relating the events surrounding the production of *Henri III and his Court,* the more enticing Dorval considered him as a man. She was fully aware, as were many others, of his ever-increasing number of mistresses, including his favorite, Mélanie Waldor. She knew him to have a slew of illegitimate children as well. No matter, she thought, to each his own. As the two talked on, Dumas mentioned the enormous inroads Shakespeare had made in his life, singling out the courageous English acting troupe for praise. "They crossed the English Channel, arrived in France, only to be reviled by the French. Despite unfavorable odds, they made theatrical history." It was "the first time," he whispered, "that I have ever seen real passions on the stage; inspirational men and women of real flesh and blood" (Dumas, *Mémoirs, Paris, 1888, IV,* 280).

Dorval and Dumas began making plans. Dumas would write a play, he said, expressly for her. As he began laying out his ideas, he was suddenly aroused to passion, grabbed Dorval and drew her toward him. Not so fast, she cried out. "First the play," It was a question of pride. She refused to be one of many. Besides, she had just broken her on-stage partnership with Lemaître. Severing a love, a friendship or love-bond was a difficult affair for Dorval. She shuddered at the thought of a repeat performance. Sexual encounters were one thing, love was quite another.

As the *fiacre* slowed down, Dumas again tried to take her in his arms. It was useless. The empathetic Dumas understood her feelings. Indeed, he may have shared them. No sooner had the *fiacre* stopped than, gentleman that he was when he so chose, he helped her out. He had the feeling, he whispered to her, that in time their lives would be interlinked (Dumas, 25).

Was it braggadocio, charm, physicality, a way with people, tremendous ambition, and/or an immense inborn talent for story-telling that paved Dumas' entry into both the theatrical world and into Dorval's as well? Or was it simply his desperate need for money and his compulsive writing habits? Surely it was a combination of all these factors. The future author of *The Three Musketeers, The Count of Monte Cristo,* and so many other riveting works, had started out as a playwight. Self-taught, self-promoting, immensely strong, garrulous, and handsome, Dumas, like his father, had an instinctive way with women. They clustered around him and he around them.

Dumas' father, the illegitimate son of the Marquis de la Pailleterie, the owner of an estate in Santo Domingo, and of a black slave, Marie Cessette Dumas, was born and baptized Thomas Alexandre in 1762. The Marquis was fond of both the mother and their bright, brown-skinned lad. By 1780, eight years following her death, the Marquis re-turned to France with his son. Not only was the eighteen year-old Alexandre handsome, but he was immensely strong, and immensely ingenious. He was so massive that upon first sight of him, strangers took him for a giant. It was said that after a musketeer had insulted him one evening when seated in his box at the opera, Alexandre was so outraged that he "lifted [the musketeer] off his feet and pitched him over the front of the box on to the spectators beneath" (André Maurois, *The Titans*, 20). That a duel followed in which Dumas "ran his sword through his adversary's body" was not surprising, given his expertise in swordsmanship. A born Hercules, in 1786 he joined the Queen's Dragoons during the Revolution, and became commander-in-chief of the Army of the Western Pyrenees. During Napoleon's Egyptian campaign, the Mamelukes looked upon him as "the avenging Angel" (Dumas, 28). Dumas' relationship with Napoleon was, nonetheless, stormy, and resulted in Dumas being refused a pension. In 1792 Dumas married Marie-Louise-Elizabeth Labouret of Villers-Cotterêts. The writer, Alexandre Dumas was the fruit of this union. Following his father's death at the age of forty, the family lived in ever-worsening financial distress, accounting in part for the writer's lack of formal education.

As a youth Dumas spent a good deal of time roaming and hunting in the forest of Villers-Cotterêts. His bravura, self-confidence, lively conversation, and engaging smile were compelling. He was a born story-teller, excellent dancer, witty talker, provocative, and donjuanesque. After attending a performance of Jean François Ducis' translation of *Hamlet,* at Villers-Cotterêts, Dumas was overwhelmed by what he had seen and heard. A new world was opening up for him. He went to Paris and attended performances at the Comédie-Française. His well-placed friend, Adolphe de Leuven, invited him to see the superstar, Talma, in *Sylla* by Etienne de Jouy. Needless to say, Dumas was stunned by it all. Zeal, determination, and talent conspired to make a playwright of this young man. His persuasive charm, his evocative writing, his will of iron, and his enthusiasm brought about a theatrical miracle. Dumas' historical drama, *Henri III and his Court*, was not only accepted by the Comédie-Française, but featured both the celebrated Mlle Mars and the equally illustrious, Firmin, who had been playing romantic heroes since the death of Talma. Its final dress rehearsal took place on February 11, 1829. While the play was a triumph, the censors ordered it closed. Why? Because France's King Charles X, for some strange reason had convinced himself that the protagonists – Henri III and Henri the Scarface – were caricatures of him and of his cousin, the Duke d'Orléans. Fortunately, the honorable Duke interceded, rectified the king's errors of judgment, allowing the play to proceed on course (Maurois, *A Great Life in Brief*, 49). Dumas summed up this terrifying theatrical experience as follows:

> Few men had witnessed such speedy operational changes in their lives as I had on opening night during the four hours it took *Henri III* to be performed. While totally unknown in the evening, for better or for worse, I had become the talk of Paris by the following one. (Dumas *Mémoires*, I. p. 383)

The lion-hearted Dumas focused mainly on plot and suspense in his plays. Understandably, he was forever lusting for exciting events to feature on stage. He identified with English drama, rejecting in so doing all thought of following French classical theatrical tradition, steeped as it was in staid, cerebral, and rule-abiding drama.

It was Dumas' friend, Victor Hugo, the son of an army general, who developed the knack of manipulating and whipping up crowds and causes. Not surprisingly, he was declared head of the Romantic movement in 1827. In keeping with the Romantic tenor, both the poet Alfred de Vigny and Dumas also exalted and magnified emotional nuance. Each proceeded in keeping with his temperament: Hugo, flamboyantly, Vigny in a far more restrained and cerebral manner, and Dumas spontaneously and seductively. Emotional restraint in art and in life was *passé*.

CHAPTER 4

A new and important political and artistic battle was brewing in Paris. Romanticism was exploding into being in France, thanks in part to the highly articulate, imaginative, and energetic Victor Hugo and to the more subdued and restrained Alfred de Vigny. Hugo toppled the rigid and outworn classical rules regulating French theater and poetry in the outspoken *Préface* to his drama *Cromwell (1827)*. Not only did he make short shrift of France's moth-eaten classical theatrical agenda, but introduced sweeping new literary concepts of his own. Art must be realistic, he maintained. It must be "a copy of nature," for "everything that exists in nature exists in art." Since nothing is static, he further maintained, language, like the human spirit, is fluid and continuously on the march. Almost overnight, Hugo's *Preface* became the new school's manifesto.

The young Alphonse de Lamartine joined the Romantics on the move. While form-wise nothing was really new in his volume of poetic *Méditations* (1823), everything about it was different. Bereft of old guard dicta, his poignant, fluid, and incantatory voice stirred his readers deeply. He spoke to the heart, to emotions, to feelings. The more symbolic and philosophical *Poèmes antiques et modernes* (1826) by the reticent and highly introverted Alfred de Vigny, made their mark as well on readers of the day.

Hugo had met Vigny in 1820 (Ernest Dupuy, *Alfred de Vigny, et Victor Hugo,* 226). He was impressed by his poetic talents, most particularly his translation into French of Shakespeare's *Romeo and Juliet*. He even defended his new friend's work against an ever deprecating press (Dupuy, 229). During one of Vigny's visits to Hugo and his wife, Adèle, it is believed that the leader of the Romantics read him his as yet unpublished volume of poems, *Les Orientales,* and fragments of his forthcoming drama, *Marion Delorme* (Dupuy, 271).

Another Romantic, the handsome lady's man, Alfred de Musset, recited his love poems unrestrainedly to the world at large. Many were directed to George Sand. The prolific novelist, Honoré de Balzac, was of a different ilk, offering his readers networks of types, ranging from the violently passionate, to the prudishly restrained, the delight-fully kind and generous, to the insidiously evil. The poet, writer, and ballet librettist, Théophile Gautier, disclosed his penchant for the macabre and the fantastic in his short stories. As for Gérard de Nerval, the reticent poet, mystic, and future author of the otherworldly tale, *Aurélia,* he was more of a subtle listener. The flamboyant composer, Hector Berlioz, inspired by Scott, Shakespeare, Goethe, and Heine, among others, set the world of French music aflame with his tone poems, *Waverley, Les Francs Juges,* and *King Lear.* The painter Eugène Delacroix, foremost exponent of Romantic art, spoke poignantly, imagistically, and dramatically through his powerful subjects and colorations in *The Massacre at Chios,* which was so brutally attacked by classicists labeling it "monstrous, ugly, ignoble." He was nothing but a "barbarian," an "enraged maniac, who did not even know how to draw" (Gautier, *Histoire du romantisme*, 201).

Romantics had faith in the future as they saw it. Each in his or her own way believed he would and could change the world. They cried out in unison, "Liberate the written word," be it in the novel, theater, poetry, painting, or music, from its stodgy, restrictive, innocuous rules. "Speak your feelings!" "Let imagination and freedom of purpose reign!" These creative youths were only in the planning stage when a new battle began brewing in Paris. Censors took it upon themselves to close down plays. Freedom of expression was crushed. Young idealists began agitating. The ambiance in theatrical circles had become deleterious to innovation. Was the monarchy reverting to pre-Revolutionary antics, they asked?

Victor Hugo's new play, *Hernani,* starring Mlle Mars and Firmin, was scheduled to open at the Comédie-Française on the night of February 25, 1830. Few in the administration realized the degree of discontent and violence that was to strike the state-run theater on this occasion.

Enraged by the changes and corrections the censors forced Hugo to make prior to allowing *Hernani* to be performed, the volatile author took up the cudgel. Hugo felt secure in the thought that his friends would not only side with him, but would come to the theater *en masse* to back him up. His growing reputation as poet and as the author of *Cromwell* gave him the courage to declare open warfare on the classicists. As chief proponent of the Romantic movement, he was determined to use all available means against those who sought to smother his ideas. Inspired by the powerful mood tones and ideals encountered in the works of Shakespeare, Schiller, and Goethe among others, Hugo and his followers demanded that the dusty rules of French theater – the unities of time, place, and action, and of decorum, adopted in the seventeenth century - be abrogated. Equally outmoded was the banning of simulated killings on stage. Only reference to such acts had been acceptable. Nor should plays be written only in twelve-beat alexandrine verse. Prose should be allowed as well. Dramatists should be invited to deal frankly with contemporary subjects, situations, and realities. Plays must speak to this generation, and not simply to past ones.

The opening of *Hernani* was a mob scene. As leader of the Romantics, Hugo and his followers, referred to as "long hairs," planned to announce their revolutionary agenda on this historical evening. Words, which they believed were insufficient to dislodge France's antiquated theatrical ways, were to be replaced by acts. Agitation and shocking behavior on the part of these young creative spirits were aimed at their antagonists – classicists and ultra reactionaries. Freedom of artistic expression was demanded by Hugo and his crew. Promulgation of their literary ideals was their motivating force.

The old guard, the censors, and some members of the press were prepared to use whatever means at their disposal, to counter the fervor and the agenda of these young idealists, modernists and dreamers. On this night of nights, the twenty-eight year-old Hugo had taken it upon himself to reject not only the classicists' theatrical rules, but another retrograde custom, that of the *claque* made up of people actually paid to clap or hiss performers, their lines, or whatever else their employer favored or hated, including the work being performed. In this matter, Hugo was not motivated solely by artistic reasons. He feared the anti-Hugo factions in the audience. Their *claqueurs* could easily bring down his play *Hernani* before his very eyes if they chose. Courage, brashness, as well as self-confidence spurred him on to act overtly.

Like a general, Hugo mounted his army of passionate followers, beginning what has been referred to throughout the years, as *"La bataille d'Hernani"*. Shock techniques, organizational acumen, and incredible imagination for creating havoc amid theatergoers set the tumultuous and sometimes outrageously behaved Romantics apart from the *ultras*, as the reactionaries and stodgy bourgeois were labeled.

To prepare their strategy, Hugo and his cohorts – Gérard de Nerval, Théophile Gautier, Vigny, among others, arrived at the Comédie-Française at three in the afternoon, just as the doors to the theater were opening. Some young men brought chocolate and rolls with them to wile away the long hours until curtain time. Others carried the smelliest of salamis with garlic into the theater. Most offensive were the young men who chose to convey their anger at the old guard by urinating in one or another corner of the theater.

In lieu of distributing author's tickets to friends, Hugo's supporters passed out small red cards on which the Spanish word *Hierro* (iron) – beginning with an H and concluding with an O (like Hugo) – had been stamped. Thus did they indicate their aggressive determination to conquer by the sword.

When audiences began arriving at the witching hour in evening dress, some of them smiled at what they considered to be the "long hairs'" garish and riotous gear. Others chuckled at the pseudo rags they had wrapped around themselves. The most imaginatively dressed of the Romantics was Gautier, who wore an outrageously colorful red satin vest and water-green pants bordered in black. Everyone agreed that his outrageous garb had broken all previous conventions of avant-garde dress worn at a Comédie-Française opening. Forty years later Gautier mused nostalgically about this magic night of Feruary 25, 1830:

> The red waistcoat! ...people still speak of it, and will go on speaking of it in days to come, so deep did that flash of color penetrate the public's eye...

> February 25, 1830! That date – the first performance of *Hernani* – stands out in my past in letters of fire...That one evening molded my whole life. It was then that I felt the impulse which still drives me on, despite the passing of so many years...moments that will keep me going to the end of my career. ...I still feel the sensation of dazzling beauty; the enthusiasm of youth, which has in no way waned...and whenever I hear the magic sound of the horn, my ears perk up, like those of an old war-horse ready to rush into battle again. (Gautier, 137)

> Meantime the great chandelier with its triple row of gas-jets and its prismatic scintillations, was slowly being lowered from the ceiling. The

footlights were being lighted and drew a luminous line of demarcation between the world of reality and the world of fiction...The doors to the boxes opened and closed noisily. The ladies, seating themselves...,laid their bouquets and glasses on the velvet-covered rail.

The orchestra stalls and the balcony were filled with the bald heads of academics and of Classicists. Angry murmurings could be heard throughout the theater. The hour had struck. The curtain went up. So great was the animosity between the old and the young groups, that the possibility of their coming to blows prior to the opening of the play could not be ruled out. (Gautier, 147)

The *tout Paris* was there in full regalia. Dorval and her husband, Vigny, Berlioz, Dumas, Balzac, Lemaître, Sainte-Beuve, Hugo's wife, Adèle, Marie Nodier, Pétrus Borel, Mme de Récamier, Mme de Girardin, Delphine Gay, to mention but a few amid the excited crowd. Present as well was the celebrated Chateaubriand, author of such ground-breaking works as *Atala* and *René* – writings that had changed the face of nineteenth-century literature. Indeed, Chateaubriand was responsible for the burgeoning of the Romantic movement. Hugo had always idolized him. In fact, when he was only fourteen years old, he had written prophetically in his diary, "I want to be Chateaubriand or nothing."

Once the theatergoers had taken their seats, the three celebrated knocks announcing the rise of the curtain were heard. Gautier called the audience to silence.

A small sixteenth-century bed-chamber, lighted by a small lamp was visible on stage. Audiences could make out the elderly Dona Josefa Duarte, dressed in black. The bodice of her dress was embroidered with jet, as was the fashion in the time of Isabelle the Catholic. She closes the crimson curtains...Someone taps on the secret door. She listens. The tapping is again heard.

Could it be her mistress's lover? she wonders (Hernani, 1, i). With that, the handsome knight, Don Carlos enters. His coat covers his nose, his hat, and his eyes. "Hello, handsome knight," she says (Hernani, 1, i).

Hernani's opening line, "Bonjour, beau cavalier," severely defied decorum. It enraged the old timers (Gautier, 147). When Don Carlos began talking like a commoner, then hid in a cupboard like a thief, a virtual stampede broke out at the Comédie-Française. The classicists raged and hooted. Each time their sacred rules were breached, they were ready to challenge their enemies to a duel. The number of angry listeners filling the Comédie-Française on this night of nights was staggering.

At *Hernani's* conclusion Hugo and his cohorts had not only won the battle, but had made history as well.

These revolutionaries, Gautier wrote, "were not Atilla's dirty, ferocious bristling Huns encamped in front of the Théâtre-Français, but knights of the future; champions of the idea, defenders of free art; and they were handsome, free, and young" (Gautier, *Histoire du romantisme*, 101). They had made their statement. It reverberated throughout Paris!

Dumas had spoken with Dorval on several occasions following the *fiacre* episode: among these, at Nodier's home and at the opening of Hernani. Each time he broached the subject of a new play, her heart leaped at the thought of such a possibility. She knew talk to be cheap. Inwardly, she wondered whether he – an opportunist at heart – would invite her to star in his latest play, *Antony*. Although stalwart and enterprising, she realized that when dealing with the quixotic Dumas, the suspense factor might be inordinately great. She would do well, she reasoned, to control her anxieties. To do so was nonetheless difficult for her. Moreover, she feared for herself and her family's economic future. Her debts and Merle's kept mounting. But, even if Dumas were to give her his *Antony*, she reasoned, would it be a success? Whatever the outcome, she needed a hit. The empathetic Dumas sensed her fears about him, even mentioned them in a letter he wrote her on April 20, 1831.

> How could you not see into the man who has admired you for six years and who wished to know you, who succeeds in meeting you, who reaches you through your feelings and your words, only to discover his own words and feelings through you; who, when near you, discovers the soul of your acting in you, forgets when listening to you that there are prejudices in this world that do not permit thought to emerge after the first full and complete meeting, returns home, his head aflame, believing he is continuing the conversation that he had started, and in his folly, pursues his dream because it was delicious. This man, Madame, may be mad, but on my honor, he is not smug. (Ambrière 186)

> How could you not have sensed the nature of the man who has admired and wished to know you and finally meets you and finds that you mirror his feelings and dreams... (Ambrière,186).

And to how many other women had Dumas written similar letters, Dorval questioned. Was she jealous of his seemingly infinite swarm of mistresses? Could she be in love with Dumas, or was she simply eager for sexual play with a master, or was it simply a new play she was after? No matter the answer, she would have to bide her time.

Meanwhile, she would keep abreast of the latest literary and theatrical trends. What better way to fulfill these needs than to drop in on Nodier's *salon*. She admired his very special pen, his subtle humor, and his way with words. Even the eeriness of some of his works captivated her. She understood fully why he was drawn to the macabre. His father had presided for a short period over the criminal tribunal of Besançon during Robespierre's Reign of Terror. It was even said that as a child Nodier had witnessed some particularly excoriating spectacles: rolling heads, pathetic cries, blood flowing into the gutters. Memories of horrific experiences had remained fresh in his mind. Try as he could, he was never able to cleanse his thoughts of these harrowing images. In one way or another, they peppered the eerie tales he had written – including *The Vampire,* and adaptations for the theater such as Schiller's *Brigands* – achieving in the process popularity for Nodier as a melodramatist.

Minutes later, Marie's thoughts turned from Nodier, back to the tempestuous Dumas, the great lover, as he was called. His drama, *Christine*, had made such a stir in Parisian circles. Some considered it too daring, based as it was on certain intriguing episodes in the life of this eccentric Queen of Sweden. The accolades Dumas' *Henri III* had received yet doubled her admiration for him.

Intent on achieving fame, Dumas unhesitatingly marched over to the Comédie Française, where he hoped to place his latest play, *Antony*. And why not? *Henri III and his Court* had, after all, received resounding ovations. A born optimist, he rushed over to see Mlle Mars. She would be just perfect as the love-filled, but restrained female lead. The well-known classical actor Firmin would be ideal as Antony. The intuitive Dumas proved to have chosen well. Mlle Mars was indeed smitten with the role of Adèle, which she promptly recommended to the reading committee of the Comédie-Française. A few days later it was accepted.

Meanwhile, Dorval had heard nothing from Dumas. Not that she was unoccupied. On the contrary; unexpectedly, Lemaître, who happened to be changing course at this juncture, had not only become stage director of the popular Ambigu Theater, but had invited Marie to co-star with him in *Pablo,* a melodrama by Saint-Amant and Jules Delong, based on a Nodier short story. She accepted, certain that her audiences at the Theater Saint-Martin, faithful as they had been all these years, would continue to be so and follow her to the Ambigu. Unforeseeable events – the July Revolution of 1830 – broke out in Paris. *Pablo* was put on hold. Theaters were closed.

The July Revolution was a minor rumbling in comparison with the great French Revolution of 1789. Nonetheless, the noises of discontent were instigated by middle-class liberals and Romantics. Their goal was to defeat the ultra-reactionary royalists, notably King Charles X, who sought to reestablish the *ancien régime*'s regressive values. To allow such retrograde tactics would have paved the way to the reinstating of the tithe, changing voting requirements in favor of land-owners, and abolishing freedom of the press. To yield to such reversals would suggest that the bloodshed in 1789 had been in vain.

When Charles X insisted on having himself crowned at Reims, in keeping with monarchical tradition and demonstrating his belief in the divine right of kings, moderates and liberals began to balk. The government took steps to further censor and establish rigid controls of the press, thus restricting still further the hard-won freedoms accorded the people following the great Revolution. The forward-looking middle class, liberals and Romantics fought back. Fed up with the continuous discord and conflagrations, Charles X dissolved the Chamber and called for new elections in July 1830, the intent being to destroy freedom of the press. The people had a choice. The easy way out of the present quagmire would have been to remain aloof, look the other way, opt for pacifism. But events were to speak for themselves.

Dramatic battles in the political arena were to be constellated on life's stage. The July Revolution started. Parisians began by refusing to adhere to the king's latest edicts. Indeed, they fought them. Insurrections mounted. Some of the arms used in the great Revolution were taken out of storage. People poured into the streets. Liberals, students, and bourgeois joined in building barricades. They fought together and well, for what came to be called the "The three glorious days." On July 26, the day after the king issued his Ordinance, putting an end to the freedom of the press, the stock market fell. Panic struck. People took to the streets, breaking street lamps, overturning carriages, looting gunsmith shops. Shooting was heard at the Palais Royal. Insurgents were making their statement. Crowds gathered at Notre-Dame. The tricolor flag was hoisted there and elsewhere in the city. On to the Louvre, the Tuileries, the Place Vendôme. The insurgents were taking over. To the Arsenal, City Hall, Place de l'Odéon. Drums were pounded in celebration. "Long Live the Republic." The singing of the Marseillaise brought tears to those who remembered the sacrifices their fathers and grandfathers had made in the name of liberty. The insurrection spread like wildfire. The conservatives were rapidly losing ground. On to the Boulevard Saint-Martin. Frédérick Lemaître – great lover on stage – had become a real-life defender of human rights. Lafayette, so helpful to the Americans during their Revolution, now commanded the National Guard. Dumas, forever ready for a struggle, armed himself with a rifle and actively joined in the fighting. His immense strength enabled him to both participate in barricade building, taking pliers in hand to rip up parts of the rue de l'Université, and then helping the wounded and the dying. To say that he was heroic would be an understatement (Moser, 37).

Charles X abdicated on August 2. Two days later he left as an exile for England. The Duke d'Orléans, proclaimed as King Louis–Philippe, would reign as constitutional monarch. It had been a victory for the liberals. The tricolor French flag was raised and the white one, representing the monarchies of the past, was dropped. Theaters were opening again. Dumas, who had already begun to make a name for himself in the theater, had now won fame as a fighter as well! Would Dorval be part of his new theatrical plans, she still wondered?

CHAPTER 5

Shakespeare lovers, intent upon attending Dorval's triumph as Lady Mabeth, packed the Porte Saint-Martin theater on a tepid November evening in 1829. The handsome and distinguished contemplative poet Alfred de Vigny was present as well. The experience changed his life forever.

The journalist, Augustin Soulié, had invited Vigny to the Porte Saint-Martin. His anglophile friend would surely appreciate *Macbeth,* he reasoned. Not only did he know and admire Shakespeare, but he had translated *Othello,* which had been successfully produced at the Comédie Française. Soulié was correct in his assertion, even more than he realized. Moments after the curtains had parted on that fateful November night, Vigny sat transfixed as he watched the small and slim Dorval step on stage and rise before him as the great Lady Macbeth, whose capacity for murderous deeds in Scotland's eleventh- century power struggle proved to be remarkable.

Although Dorval's feelings usually led her *into* the roles she was preparing, her incarnation of Lady Macbeth, she realized, required a different approach – infinitely more cerebral. Her acting would have to be cumulative: ranging from instances of rapt joy upon learning of her husband's military plans, to bravado as the slaughter of his enemies began, to murmured asides, and thunderous maniacal verbal clamorings once dementia had taken root. So too did her hand gestures have to be worked on. They had to span a gamut of poses: from subdued, subtle, clenched, at times, quixotic finger and hand-pointing movements, to extended fingers, separated from one another, as they slowly advanced forward. Flailing arms, expressing a desire for revenge, revealed her utter joy at the thought of Macbeth's future enthronement. Dorval's subtle facial expressions, eye movements, and body language, when scoffing at her husband's fears and scruples, were so unnerving to him, that he failed to kill the king of Scotland which would have seated him on the throne. Instead, the brash ironies she spoke to Macbeth achieved a boomerang effect on her, unleashing her murderous passion for blood-letting. After completing the frenzied act of murder, and glorying in an orgy of gore, the terror and guilt she experienced resulted in an excoriating self-awareness, driving her insane in the process.

Lady Macbeth's famous sleep-walking scene was lived on stage in a medley of ponderous staccato pacings. At certain moments Dorval would throw her body backward, and at other times move about in silence and terror. Some of her words were uttered with clarity, others in muffled agony, accompanied by macabre hand-wringing in her vain attempt to wash away the blood she had caused to flow.

> Out damned spot! Out, I say...What, will these hands ne'er be clean?...Here's the smell of the blood still. All the perfumes of Arabia will not sweeten this little hand... (Shakespeare, *Macbeth*, 5.1)

Under Dorval's aegis, a world of Evil and ever darkening shadows had come to life in nineteenth-century Parisian theater. No melodrama could compare with the kinetic energy suffused in, and emanating from, the bard's words.

Vigny had not only been intoxicated by Dorval's shifting surges of emotion, but marveled at her capacity to change from encouraging wife to imperious commander, from feelings of rapacity to those of dread. Each stage of Lady Macbeth's development seemed to catalyze Dorval's tortured verbal ejaculations. The razor-sharpness of her diction created an increasingly reactive effect on her audience, and memorably on Vigny. When Soulié took Vigny back stage and introduced him to Dorval, his reactions were immediate. To say that he had been swept off his feet by the power vested in Dorval's being and personality would be to minimize the heights of his jubilation. Later, he wrote to Soulié to express "his marveling gratitude for the happiness he had brought him that night" (Ambrière, 191).

So overwhelmed had he been by this "great" actress' portrayal of Lady Macbeth as a powerhouse of evil, that the visual image recorded by the mind of this blue-eyed, curly and golden-haired aristocrat remained with him. The violence of the shock encounter served, happily, to arouse his own creative *élan*. The following days Vigny began imagining Dorval in a diametrically opposite role, that of Portia, in his translation of Shakespeare's *The Merchant of Venice*. After its completion in January, 1830, he sent a note to Baron Taylor, the royal commissioner of the Comédie-Française, informing him of his intent to submit his *Merchant of Venice* to the Ambigu theater where Dorval was performing temporarily. His choice of this theater was surprising, given the fact that Vigny's successful translation of *Othello* which had been playing at the prestigious Comédie Française, was currently coming to an end (Ambrière, 191).

Vigny was born in 1797 into an aristocratic family in Loches, in the Indre-et-Loire region of France. One may wonder whether this particularly macabre city, with its ramparts and dungeon dating back to the eleventh century, had in some way affected the personality of the frail infant who, at eighteen months, moved to Paris with his parents. Solitary and sensitive, Vigny was unhappy during his school years. He found the student body vulgar and offensive. While bearing his pain in silence, his fantasy world was active. That he dreamed of a glorious military career was not surprising, given the accounts his father had related to him as army captain in the Seven Years' War. By 1814 the young Vigny had enlisted in the "Compagnies rouges de la maison du roi." As an officer in the infantry, however, the brilliant future about which he had fantasized was all but that. His life was reduced to endless days of tedium performing routine exercises in the barracks. What saved him from unbearable boredom was his need and talent for writing. He spent his leaves in Paris, mostly at Nodier's gatherings at the Arsenal, where music, dancing, and conversation were *de rigueur*. It was there that he met, cultivated, and was inspired by Hugo, Lamartine, Musset, Dumas, and other Romantic poets and dramatists. With the passing of days, he realized he could count on them as friends, at least for the present. At times they worked together helping each other overcome difficult passages in a text, or congratulating one another for having found *le mot juste.* On the eve of the opening of Alexander Dumas' play *Christine,* Vigny and Hugo had spent four hours improving their friend's verses. Such was their devotion.

Work, friendship, and dreams of future greatness opened the in-dwelling Vigny to a world of excitement, creativity – and passion. Not surprisingly had he fallen in love with the beautiful and charming Delphine Gay whose Salon attracted many artists. A fine poet in her own right, she became Vigny's muse. He proposed marriage to her.

Much to his sorrow, Vigny's mother, whose word was law to him, vetoed the idea. Delphine's lineage was not sufficiently aristocratic to suit her. As a consolation prize, the anglophile Vigny married the beautiful English girl, Lydia Bunbury, in 1825. Rather than a prize, however, she became a burden to him, though he never complained of her sloth, nor of her unwillingness to learn French. Even more importantly, she displayed no interest in her husband's writings or intellectual life. Nor did she offer him much in the way of sexual pleasure. In time, she became increasingly dependent on her husband and after three years of wedlock, she turned into a hopeless invalid. A principled man, Vigny spent the next forty years nursing his wife. He also looked after his mother, until she died of a stroke, after which, he mourned her deeply.

Philosophically speaking, Vigny was a stoic – a self-sacrificer. One may wonder whether he had perhaps unconsciously enjoyed playing the martyr. Such comportment, however, in no way precluded having a sex life of his own. He frequently had recourse to prostitutes.

It was the written word, nonetheless, that was, and would remain, Vigny's bridge to the world. Following the publication of his *Poèmes antiques et modernes* (1826) and his historical novel *Cinq Mars,* he turned his attention to the theater. A fervent admirer of Shakespeare, he translated his *Romeo and Juliet* into French verse in 1827, and his *Othello* was successfully performed at the Comédie-Française in 1829. His translation of *The Merchant of Venice* in verse was completed in 1830, a few months prior to the outbreak of the July Revolution. Although he had Dorval in mind for the role of Portia, what he had not anticipated was the government's law forbidding secondary theaters from performing dramas in verse. Because Dorval was not performing at the Porte Saint-Martin during the summer months, but at the Ambigu, considered a secondary theater, Vigny's translation of *The Merchant of Venice* had been placed on hold. He was crest-fallen. Understandably so, since Dorval had become the passion and torment of his life. For the present, however, his eagle eye having pierced the niceties of first meetings and first impressions, he realized, as had Dorval, that she was frittering away her time on insignificant works such as *Pablo* and a revival of one of her great hits, *Thirty Years of a Gambler's Life*, both featuring the adulated Frederick Lemaître. At this time in her career, such works did little to further enhance her stature as an actress (Ambrière,193). Although Dorval was aware of the dearth of fine plays at the time, she also understood that genius was rare, while mediocrity was the rule.

Matters were not to change. On June 15, she, whose memory was so extraordinary and whose acting gifts were unique, was still performing at the Ambigu, winning rave reviews in run-of-the-mill plays, like Nepomucène Lemercier's *Les Serfs polonais*. Still, her rendition of the drama's Othello-like female lead won critical acclaim, particularly, for its kinetically engineered scene of jealousy in the second act. Like a maimed animal, Dorval's wailings accelerated amid a series of shrieking climaxes, only to tone down to barely audible sounds at predictably crucial moments. One of the reviews praising her acting talents appeared in the *Globe* on June 17. Although unsigned, it was later discovered that Vigny, who had thoughts only for her, had authored it. "Her concentrated and profound pain, her violent and contained gestures," he wrote, "incited enthusiastic and merited applause" (Ambrière, 193). Even more importantly, when he discovered, probably via his friend Soulié, that the moods, gestures, asides, and emotional vicissitudes dominating Dorval's performance had been inspired by his poem "Dolorida," written in 1823 during a stay in the Pyrenees, his joy was boundless. Moments later, a smile crossed his lips, as he recalled its lines:

> Est-ce la Volupté, qui, pour ses doux mystères,
> Furtive, a rallumé ces temps solitaires?...
> La gaze et le cristal sont leur pâle prison. (Vigny, 63, OC, Pléiade, 1950)

Deeply introverted and controlled, Vigny's passionate desire for Dorval remained thus far unrequited. Was it she who had been taken aback by his poise and reticent demeanor? Had she interpreted these character traits as lack of interest on his part? Or was it the repressed stoic in him that forbade him to leap unthinkingly into an affair? The thought that she, who was forever learning new lines and performing in so many different plays, had taken the trouble to read his poems, moved him deeply.

The fact that Vigny considered the twenty-nine year-old Dorval to be France's leading tragic actress inspired him to compose *La Maréchale d'Ancre,* in which she would star. He worked like a man possessed – non-stop from the beginning of August, 1830 to October of that same year (Bassan, 48. Correspondance, 231). He smiled with satisfaction following his final run-through of his manuscript. This historical drama, he mused, was worthy of Dorval's talents. It brought him even more pleasure when he looked upon his play as an act of altruism: the monies Dorval would earn would help her deal with her mounting debts.

Vigny's *Maréchale d'Ancre*, with its *Sturm und Drang* motif, mirrored the tempests, passions, tumult and impetuosity of many Romantic works. It was melodramatic to the core, the plot being drawn from seventeenth-century history and certain "fateful" coincidences occurring during King Louis XIIIth's minority. Its focus revolved around a passionate love story featuring the young and beautiful Galigaï, and certain members of the well-known Medici, Concini, and Borgia families. A history buff, Vigny spared audiences none of the details of his protagonists' grandeur, vice, rivalries, depravities, duplicities and murderous instincts. His philosophical focus, the abolition of the death penalty, was incorporated into his drama's purview, together with two other important concerns of his: the notion of "Destiny," each individual's inexorable march toward death over which no one would seem to have any control, and "Honor," over which some, notably the Stoic, has some authority.

After setting down the last line of his drama on October 9, Vigny brought the manuscript to Dorval's home. It was customary at the time to read one's drama aloud to those involved. She felt warmly disposed toward Vigny since she had known since the play's inception that the starring role would be hers. Vigny's visit simply confirmed his belief, which he had shared with her, that she was "the first female tragedian of our times" (377, OC. II). Deeply flattered by his remark, and desperately searching for a great play in which to perform, Dorval sat down and listened attentively to his reading of the entire manuscript. For Vigny, such a session was a dream fulfilled. Strangely enough, though seemingly pleased by his play, she remained mute at its conclusion. No matter, plans were distilled and hopes surged.

On another positive note, the Porte Saint-Martin had reopened its doors under the directorship of the enterprising François Louis Crosner, who immediately invited Dorval to return. Since she attracted large crowds, her presence spelled financial health for the institution. She accepted, despite her still unfulfilled, perhaps even impossible dream of becoming a member of the Comédie-Française, which still was a hot-bed of rivalries, jealousies and connivings.

During this emotionally and financially strained period, Dorval, although immensely taken with Vigny, could no longer wait on the sidelines for his or any other playwright's masterpiece. With her usual modesty and realistic approach to life, she was prepared to accept whatever theater piece would draw a crowd, whether shocking to some circles or not! Let us note in this regard that the regressive pro-Church and ultra-royalist regime of Charles X, which had been swept away following the July Revolution, had given rise to a wave of anticlericalism. Although Dorval was deeply Catholic, when it came to feeding her family, she not only accepted to perform in clergy-bashing works, but did so willingly. Why not feature a play designed to please audiences, she thought? Ergo, she opened on August 19, 1830, in *Cloistered Victims* (*Les Victimes cloîtrées*) by François Boutet de Monvel, a revival of a drama which had drawn crowds in 1792 during the great French Revolution. That it was replete with lecherous Dominican priests eyeing young convent girls made it all the more savory and provocative for nineteenth-century audiences.

Dorval's stage appearances, despite the quality of some of the plays in which she performed, were greeted with applause. *Cloistered Victims* was no exception. Indeed, The Porte Saint-Martin flourished financially thanks to this kind of drama. In contrast, the Ambigu's less provocative fare obliged it to close its doors at the end of August. L'Opéra-Comique was failing as well.

The love and attention bestowed on Dorval by Vigny during the next months was moving. To say that he was obsessed with her is no exaggeration. He attended her performances virtually nightly, his devotion serving to increase her confidence in herself, both as an actress and as a woman. Strangely enough, despite the fact that she had been performing since childhood, she still felt insecure, both in her art and in the social world in general. She thrived on adulation, particularly Vigny's. In their still spiritual or platonic relationship, feelings of well-being, pride, and utter joy were evoked in her by his unmitigated attentions – his gifts of poems, such as the following:

> Vous que l'Illusion couronne, inspire, enivre
> De bonheur ou de désespoir,

Reine des passions! qui deux fois savez vivre
   Pour vous le jour, pour tous le soir,
Pensive solitaire ou tragique merveille,
   Coeur simple, esprit capricieux,
Riant chaque matin des larmes que, la veille,
   Vous fîtes tomber de nos yeux,
Des chants inspirateurs respirez l'ambroisie
   Loin du vulgaire âpre et fatal.
Vivez dans l'art divin et dans la Poésie
   Comme un Phénix sous un cristal. (A, 201)

Dorval loved the thought of being loved, courted, and adulated, not merely as an artist, but for herself. Vigny was so different from other men in her life, she mused. Handsome, to be sure, he was also charming and ingratiating when he chose to be. His inborn reticence, studied intellectuality, which Dorval realized she would never fathom, attracted her, nonetheless. While they lived on two different planets, she was dazzled by the fine manners of this suave and elegant aristocrat. He adored her for what he had never known: freedom of manner, the viscerality of sexual banter and fulfillment.

     While Parisians had lived through their July Revolution and theatrical institutions had been awarded greater liberties, inherent jealousies and collusive practices at the heart of these institutions existed as before. Will human nature ever change, some wondered? Since plays were difficult to place in theaters of one's choice – a truism, particularly at the Comédie-Française – authors frequently had recourse to well-known performers who might intercede on their behalf.
     When, to the shock of all concerned, it was announced that the lead in *La Maréchale d'Ancre* was to be given to the celebrated tragedian, the forty-four year-old Mlle George of the Comédie-Française, gossip-mongers were quick to add: not only was she considered a splendid actress, but she had had the additional *honor* of having been Napoleon's mistress, and that of Lucien and Jérôme Bonaparte – and outside of the family, Talleyrand, Murat, and Dumas (Whitridge, 103). Clearly, networking between the author of the play in question, or its director, had been speedily at work in 1831. So be it. What remains a mystery is why Dorval had not fought to keep a role in a play written expressly for her, and for which she had been

waiting many a year. Vigny's work would have lent her career the dignity and prestige she so cherished. One may also wonder why Vigny had so readily acquiesced to handing the role over to Mlle George? Was power alone at work?

La Maréchale d'Ancre opened at the Odéon on June 21, 1831. Much to the author's and, possibly, the audience's shock and chagrin, after the curtains descended, at the conclusion of the second act, the manager came on stage to announce Mlle George's indisposition. Or, had she been terrified at the thought of the endless tirades and speeches awaiting her in the third, fourth, and fifth acts? Time seems to heal all, at least in Mlle George's case. By June 25, she garnered her courage and performed the entire play. While whistling and hooting were sounded at its conclusion, the play and her acting earned a *succès d'estime*.

In Victor Hugo's letter to his poet friend, Antoine Fontanay, he described La Maréchale d'Ancre, as "distinguished and valuable, rather than powerful, a novel, rather than a play" (Ambrière, 221). Jules Janin, one of the most important critics of the day, voiced his approval of the work loud and clear: "One more dramatic poet: he was badly needed" (OC, II, 377). Some critics, however, stated outright that La Maréchale d'Ancre had been conceived by a "learned and cold mind" *(Débats*, 27 June). Outside of the lead, "the characters seem pale and vague" (*Le National* 28) (OC. 377, II, 1948). *Le Constitutionnel* underscored a certain "pretentiousness" on the dramatist's part. Whether favorable or not, La Maréchale d'Ancre was not a financial success and closed after thirty performances (Bassan, 51).

Was Vigny guilt-ridden for having so readily accepted Mlle George as lead and for not having fought for Dorval as star? Whatever the answers, he sent her the manuscript of *La Maréchale d'Ancre,* together with a newly published copy of his play, a note, and a sonnet for her birthday on August 15, 1831.

> I have only this means of returning this drama which was written for you, Madam.
> You wanted to perform in it, but you are Queen in your Theater by virtue of your talent... (Bassan, 50) (Ambriére, 222)

He then presented her with his poem:

D'autres yeux ont versé vos pleurs. Une autre bouche
Dit des mots que j'avais sur vos lèvres rangés. (Ambrière, 222)

Only at the end of 1832 did Dorval star in the revival of *La Maréchale D'Ancre*, but not at the Comédie-Française, as she had hoped, rather at the Porte Saint-Martin. Vigny's friend, Antonie Deschamps, wrote him, praising her interpretation: "I do not know how Mlle George understood the role, but I find Dorval excellent, her acting is natural and filled with true pathos. The conclusion is perfect" (Bassan, 54).

As a working woman, Dorval had no time to daydream. She did, nonetheless, fantasize during her acting stints, transplanting and renewing herself in her ever-novel and frequently spellbinding roles. That of the "admirable Marie Beaumarchais," in Léon Halévy's *Beaumarchais in Madrid,* was a case in point. Based on Goethe's five-act tragedy *Clavigo,* it was of typical *Sturm und Drang* vintage. Whether hackneyed or not, the tale of a Spanish knight who, for ambition's sake, reneges on his promise to marry his fiancée, the beautiful Marie, realizing the depth of his passion for her only after her death, remains powerfully dramatic.

It was as if the role of Marie in *Beaumarchais in Madrid* had been designed for Dorval; with ease and abandon she glided into each romantic episode – even into death. No one knew better than Dorval the secret of wrenching tears from her audience. In this work, perhaps, more so than in many previous ones, her spasmodic sobs were heard throughout the house. Dorval was far too great an actress to neglect the truism that "variety is the spice of life." She peppered her words and the expressions incised on her face with nuanced feelings, instinctively altering the tempo of her delivery, the cadences of her voice engendering in so doing almost painful excitement. Though her delivery sounded harsh and scratchy at times, the scale of her verbal modulations, when heightened or diminished, conveyed both the pathos of the moment and stirred the viewer's auricular needs as well. She, who had suffered such emotional turmoil, particularly during her early years, knew better than any actress of her day how to convey pain, and draw upon those special, sometimes harrowing inner forces to evoke both the terror of abandonment and those admirable moments of joyous play when in her lover's arms.

There was nothing fictitious about Dorval's *acting*. It was *real*. It had been lived.

The anguish she projected as Marie, and in previous dramas of unrequited passion as well, drew astounding reviews. Theater aficionados praised the "infinitely nuanced art of this remarkable actress... Everything was conveyed with truth...Tears flowed from every-one's eyes" (*The Jounal des comédiens,* 3 March, 1831). *The Figaro*, perhaps piqued for some unknown reason, focused on Dorval's daring *déshabillé.* So too did *Le Journal des Débats.* In the latter, we read, "I know nothing more vaporous than her costume, barely attached with a pin, ready to fall to the ground at any time, allowing one to peer at one and then at the other very white shoulder. Rarely does one see such coquettish and decent nudity as this" (Ambrière, 201). Were critics mocking her? Or were they perhaps titillated by it all? Dorval was above such commentaries. But they did make her smile with satisfaction.

Three weeks later, Dorval was featured in another anti-clerical drama which drew even greater crowds: *The Incendiary (L'Incendiaire)* by Benjamin Antier and Alexis de Comberousse. May it be noted here that the multiple burnings of churches in Paris and elsewhere in France had been another aftermath of the July Revolution. Most of these macabre destructive acts had not been perpetrated by lay people, but were surprisingly instigated by the clergy itself, with the intent of inflaming French citizens against the government. A case in point was the arson at Saint-Jean l'Auxerrois and its archbishopric in February, 1831.

In *The Incendiary,* a fanatic royalist Archbishop, brilliantly played by Bocage, convinces a young, mystically oriented peasant girl that heaven had awarded her the signal honor of setting aflame the factory of a rich Republican industrialist. The act was accomplished and the young girl was duly arrested and imprisoned. She asks for a confessor.

> Mme Dorval was admirable in the confession scene. Kneeling at the feet of the priest, or rather squatting on her heels like a repenting Madeleine, she stared vaguely about, lamenting in the manner of a mad woman who suddenly becomes conscious of her act. During the fifteen minutes this scene lasted, the audience sat breathless in their seats – anguished, to the point of no longer breathing. Hallucination and mysticism triumphed [on this night] in theatre. (Léon Séché, *Alfred de Vigny et son temps*, 55)

In time, the agonized penitent throws herself into the river to expiate her crime.

Dorval's ability to encapsulate emotions attracted audiences of all persuasions, classes and religious denominations to *The Incendiary*.

Vigny was there every night, so deeply was he "haunted" and "fascinated," perhaps even possessed, by Dorval's "mystical spirit" and acting (Séché, 55). It was as if electric currents permeated the atmosphere.

In a good mood – that is, a mood for love - Dorval took the tall, thin, and appealing Bocage to bed with her.

One evening, Vigny was accompanied by a heavily veiled woman whom he took backstage after the performance. When this mystery creature began congratulating Dorval and praising her enormous talent, Dorval grew curious. Who was she, she wondered. No sooner had the stranger lifted her veil, though her eyes were still red from the tears she had shed during the performance, Dorval recognized her as La Malibran, the world-famous opera star. So moved was Dorval by the lavish praise this renowned artist accorded her, that she took her by the arm and walked her to her dressing table, pointed to a small painting on it and said, "This picture alone has accompanied me to all of my dressing rooms in France. It is a portrait of you: La Malibran, singing the *Romance of the Weeping Willow*. I consider it the Madonna of art." And with that the two women hugged each other (Séché, 56).

Was she living out a dream or a fairy tale, Dorval asked herself later that night. She sensed that no man had ever loved her as deeply nor as passionately as Vigny. If this was so, how was it they had not yet become lovers? He was reserved, to be sure. Some of his friends had even referred to him as cold. Perhaps he was. Nonetheless, he had been her admirer since 1829. What held him back she wondered? There was certainly some kind of electric current vibrating between them! In the back of her mind, she recalled having heard about Goethe's novel, *Elective Affinities*. It told the story of a couple drawn together by mysterious means. Goethe, she had been told, believed that everything in the differentiated world is merely an emanation of the *All*: universal sympathies act and react on everything, whether these be visible or not, organic or not, conscious or not. The isolated pulsation, thought, or sensation simply does not exist. Each in its own way, Dorval concluded, reverberates, acts, and reacts like chemical substances, upon feeling, nerve, or particle.

Could such "Elective Affinities" be at the root of her relationship with Vigny, Dorval questioned. Their demeanors and education were poles apart. She was expansive, spontaneous, earthy, alive, open, freely displaying tears of joy or of sorrow. He, on the other hand, was repressed, rigid, cerebral, introverted, an aristocrat who harbored certain inalienable and unalterable principles. His rigidity in part must have resulted from the years he spent under the tutelage of strict school masters and army discipline. Yet, her bywords and Vigny's were, nonetheless, strangely similar – "love, invent, admire" (Séché, 58).

Unlike Vigny, Dorval had always had a casual approach to sex. Like food, sex for her was a necessity, a part of life. She had had lovers since her early teens, not to mention her three illegitimate children. Neither feelings of dread nor guilt inhabited her. She enjoyed love making and, unlike Vigny with his repressed behavioral patterns, she had no scruples about indulging in sexual play with whom she chose and at the time she determined. The thought of being faithful to one man was, in her mind, an absurdity! The double standard was non-existent for Dorval. Vigny, on the other hand, shared no such opinions. As a male, he had all the rights. While he did not flaunt the names of his sleeping mates, he saw them when he desired. A woman, such as Dorval, however, must –and in this regard, he was adamant – have only one lover, at least only one at a time.

Vigny grew increasingly mesmerized by Dorval, as he observed her night after night playing Louise in *The Incendiary*. Her slightest gesture was meaningful to him. When they were alone in her dressing room, later on that evening, she laughed when he told her she was beautiful. She described herself as a woman of the people, who was not *"belle, mais pire"* (Whitridge, 111). He admired her every word, gesture, feeling. Indeed, it could be said that he venerated her.

Dorval was drawn to him as well. Never had she been treated with such courtesy, admiration, and, awe. When he knelt before her

106

and she gazed at his beautiful "face framed in curly golden hair, his clear blue eyes expressing such love for her, she was overcome with feelings she had never experienced before. Something new and deeply tender had entered her life" (Séché, 57).

Sainte-Beuve described the poet at the onset of his burgeoning love as "living in a perpetual seraphic hallucination." His ideal of woman had until now been difficult, if not impossible to realize. He lived his loves in his poetic imagination." His dream woman was the thirteenth-century Francesca da Rimini "ascending to heaven, holding her beloved Paolo in her arms." Vigny had always considered "ecstasy of the soul superior to physical ecstasy" (Séché, 58). Like Tristan, he would soon imbibe his magic potion of love. Though carnal, his union with Dorval was mystical as well. Who better than the seventeenth-century Jansenist philosopher, Blaise Pascal, could describe such a union of body and soul.

> The longer the path to love, the more a delicate spirit senses pleasure.
> The first effect of love is to inspire great respect; one has veneration for what one loves.
> Respect and love must be so well proportioned, that they sustain each other without respect ever crushing love. (Séché quoting Pascal, *Sur les passions de l'amour,*59)

It happened unexpectedly, in 1833. Dorval had been enervated that day. For some reason she "looked directly into the white of Vigny's eyes and said to him in her *gamine* way, 'When, Monsieur, will the count's parents come and ask for my hand'?" (Séché 64). Vigny was so surprised by her question, that he answered her challenge in a matter of moments. Not love, it was sexual "ravishment," with its religious ritual, its altar, its orations, its prayers, its liturgy, its sanctification, and its beatification (Séché, 64). Caresses! Ecstasy! Fulfillment!

How could Dorval have expected such rapture from one who had never before courted her openly: no gifts, no walks together, no dinners. Vigny had sometimes visited her in her apartment on boulevard Saint-Martin, but only to talk (Séché, 60). She smiled when recalling those tender moments when he called her "duchess," or "my angel." She cherished his respect for her. Vigny's love had become a "purifying agent" for her (Séché, 61).

That they had conjoined so suddenly was for her all-encapsulating, a meeting of the minds, bodies, and spirit in joyous lust and mystical fulfillment. For Vigny, it had been a traumatic and unparalleled visceral experience.

Dorval always kept up-to-date with trends in the theater. The works of dramatists such as Casimir de la Vigne, the author of *Marino Faliero,* in whose play she had starred, piqued her curiosity for possible future productions. When time permitted Dorval still visited Nodier's salon. She had always admired his pen, his subtle humor, his soft and harmonious voice and way with words, not to speak of his immense knowledge of literature, myth, and mystical matters.

The tempestuous Dumas also continued to frequent Nodier's *cénacle.* Dorval, among many other women, still fascinated him. Marie knew Nodier to be intrigued by Dumas and his plays. There was something that attracted Dorval to Dumas. He was not, of course, in Vigny's class. Nonetheless, he was endearing. Was it his warmth, his bold approach to the female that drew so many women to his orbit? Some considered him priapic: reminiscent of Priapus, the Greek and Roman generative God. Or was Dorval intrigued by the high tension suspense factor in his plays, by their daring themes? Or was it simply kismet? Whatever the answer, Dumas was the antithesis of Vigny – an extrovert, a chatterer, bombastic, flamboyant, a womanizer, confident in himself and his purpose in life. Marie continued to work when she could. No one was making headway in the theater for the simple reason that the theaters had been closed. As for Dumas, he was busy helping the revolutionaries in real life. Dorval had heard nothing from the great lover since he had given the role supposedly "perfect" for Marie, in his play *Antony*, to her arch rival Mlle Mars.

Dorval knew *Antony* to be partly autobiographical, and acknowledged it for what it was – high drama, and utterly different from what had been produced on Parisian stages. Recognition scenes were touching, to be sure, but neither honesty nor virtue, nor goodness were lauded. The controversial nature of the play fascinated her. She related fully to its blatant emphasis on society's double, if not triple, standard. Hadn't she herself been victimized by this hypocritical behavior pattern? Unlike the play's protagonist, Dorval had lived by her own rules, her own credo, not by society's artificial conventions. How readily did she identify with the wretched, the plight of the orphan, the forlorn, and the deserted? Illegitimate herself, she understood the suffering and pain of the outcast. She was too perceptive to overlook the originality of Dumas' play. She would forgive him for his machinations with Mlle Mars after all; he had to fend for himself, as she, for herself, with one great exception: she did not resort to deception. She had learned to take people in her stride, or so she thought. Besides, she knew Dumas to be quixotic! All instinct! Nonetheless, there was something of the lost soul about him that was endearing.

She even had a pet name for him: "mon bon chien." Did they live a passionate liaison in her apartment, and/or in her dressing room, when her husband, Merle, was away? Were there secret trysts? No matter, love making was simply a fling for both of these sexually focused beings. She was playing! Amusing herself! As was he. One should not expect too much from him, she kept telling herself, nor from herself, at least not on the sexual level, she admitted.

Important to Dorval was whether Dumas' *Antony* would help her become the great artist she aspired to be. Surely she was prescient in this matter. Although she had not read the play, its theme, nonetheless, spoke to her. On another level, she knew that she and this opportunistic, womanizer and panderer to the rich and famous were kindred spirits.

When Dumas finally appeared at her door after a sixth-month absence, Dorval had her maid ask the visitor's name several times. "Are you going to refuse me admittance?" he bellowed. Whereupon she accused him of having abandoned her. With his usual bravura, he replied:

> "What do you want from me, my darling? Since I saw you last I have made baby, I fought in a revolution, during which I was nearly twice shot." Dorval did not react.
> "So this is how you kiss returning ghosts?" he clamored.
> "I cannot kiss you any other way, mon bon chien! I am like Marion Delorme, love has remade me a virgin...My word of honor...I have become a good girl! I swear it."
> "Ah! my dear, I was referring to a revolution in which I fought. This is a second one. Who the devil is responsible for this?"
> "Alfred de Vigny."

"Do you love him?"
"Don't talk about it. I'm crazy for him! He treats me like a duchess. He calls me his angel" "My sincere compliments," Dumas answered, a bit taken aback (F. Moser, 41).

While chatting, the tall muscular Dumas tried to extract a less than fraternal kiss from Dorval. He failed to do so. With that, she announced that she was going to star in Victor Hugo's new play, *Marion Delorme,* which, she added gleefully, Mlle Mars had coveted.

This time Dumas told her in no uncertain terms that he had come to offer her the lead in his play *Antony* and that he wanted to read it to her, adding that if "Vigny treats you like a duchess, I shall treat you like a queen!"

Dorval agreed to listen to him read his play. Would he like some kirsch? "No, water", he answered. With that, she went to her bedroom to ask the maid to bring her a table. Dumas followed, grabbed her, tried to extract a kiss from her, but failed. She pushed him away and in no uncertain terms threatened to have him thrown out. No sooner had the maid brought the water, than the door bell rang. Dorval put her finger to her lips indicating silence.

"Go and hide in the living room," she murmured to her *bon chien*, you must not be seen in my bedroom, she whispered. Dumas guessed the name of the visitor and decided to leave. Dorval asked him to return that evening. No one would disturb them. Her husband, Merle, was away on business, the children were in the country. He would have ample time to read his play to her. Dumas had time to slip out the back way. In his *Memoirs,* Dumas adds, humorously, "though Vigny calls Dorval his angel, he awaits less ethereal joys from her" (Moser, 43).

Dorval responded to Vigny with unbridled sensuality. And he to her with profound and all-enduring passion. She adored him. When the time drew near for him to return home to tend to his ailing wife and mother, Dorval was chagrined even more so when she read the look of anguish on his face. She did not urge him to stay that night, anxious as she was, to listen to her *bon chien* read his *Antony*.

When Dumas returned as promised, she warned him not to tempt her with his kisses. Were he to do so, she confessed, she would not have the strength to resist him. She loved Vigny deeply and completely and did not want anything to distract her from him, at least at this time.

As planned, Dumas sat down and read his play. Dorval listened carefully, sometimes walking behind his chair reading the lines herself. At other moments, she simply wept at the pathos depicted. "How do you know so much about women?" she blurted out. "You know them by heart." (Moser, 45). She did, however, comment on the weakness of the fifth act.

"How tastes differ," Dumas remarked. "Mlle Mars thought it was too hard" (Moser, 45).

"I'm certain it was not like that before," she replied (Moser, 45).

Dumas admitted having rewritten the act at Mlle Mars' request. He would now rewrite it for Dorval, and return it to her the next day. Knowing Dumas as she did, she suggested that her bon chien stay the night. Since her husband was away on business he could occupy his room. Her maid would bring him tea. Dorval would look in on him every now and then. As planned, he completed the rewrite that night. It was just as she wanted.

Dumas suggested Lemaître for the lead. Dorval disagreed. She wanted Bocage, her partner at the Porte Saint-Martin. "But his voice is too nasal," Dumas countered. She insisted. He could not but agree.

The thin, lanky, melancholy, disheveled Pierre Bocage (1797) had become the ideal romantic actor. So deeply had he been influenced by the British performer Edmund Keene, that he developed a unique sardonic laugh of his own. His rise to fame, however, had been difficult. In 1823, because he felt his career would be stunted at the Odéon should he remain there, he left for the provinces to develop a technique of his own. By 1826 he was back at the Odéon, left it again to join the Gaîté, where he enjoyed much success. Having realized that his talents lay in Boulevard theater, his success story pursued its course (Carlson, 68). Dorval's choice of Bocage as *Antony's* leading man prevailed over Dumas'.

Antony, Dumas' passionate stage blending of love, rage, and adultery, opened on May 3, 1831 at the Porte Saint-Martin. As a social commentary on the role of the bastard, it underscored the idea that whatever the achievements of Dumas' hero, society would look upon him as a pariah. Who better than Dumas was equipped to probe this painful topic? Hadn't his father, General Dumas, been the illegitimate offspring of a French nobleman and a black woman from Santo Domingo? Unlike Antony, Dumas had the consolation of knowing that his parents had loved each other and him as well. He further added, that although he was a bastard, he was not an orphan. His father who had died very young, had always been deeply devoted to his mother. As for Dumas, he loved her always!

Once the curtains rise on *Antony*, audiences are made privy to Adèle d'Hervey's elegant drawing room. As Adèle, Dorval is dressed simply but stylishly, as befits the society women of the day. She is in deep conversation with her sister, Viscountess Clara. Adèle's husband, Colonel d'Hervey, is due to return soon after a year's stay in Algeria.

Dorval's sometimes throaty voice seemed at first unsuitable to the charming Adèle. Not so, however, after opening and reading a letter delivered to her by her maid. The audience is taken aback by Adèle's sudden and searing mood swing. Her voice, taking on lower and more troubled tonalities, becomes spasmodic when she reveals the contents of the letter to Clara. Someone she had loved and still loves, but has not seen in years, has returned. Tension rises. In due course, Clara leaves. Moments later, a terrible noise and clatter are heard outside. Adèle rushes to the window. Someone has just stopped the runaway horses hitched to her sister's carriage and was severely wounded in the process. The bleeding lacerations suffered during the young man's struggle have caused him to faint. He is being taken into Adèle's home for immediate care. Audiences witness him being lifted on to the stage. As happenstance will have it, Adèle recognizes him, both as the young man she had loved and as the one responsible for the heroic deed.

After regaining consciousness, he speaks frankly to his beloved Adèle, evoking his love for her and his suffering as an outcast. The strain is yet too great and he again faints, only to regain consciousness moments later. It is at this time that he confesses his anguish at having been unable to marry her – the love of his life – because he had neither name, nor family, nor fortune.

Antony reveals himself to his beloved Adèle as a complex, somber, and somewhat Hamlet-like being filled with gloom, doom, and self-pity. He can no longer stand his pariah-like existence. His origins, wrapped as they are in mystery, have come to haunt him. As a bastard, he had been marginalized by society, and had been unable to make his way in the world. He despises humankind and rages against the role of the outcast and the victim, forced upon him by the general public. His unhealed pain, having turned into inner rage and violence over the years, now dominates his being.

Disdain for a world that has cast him aside prevails. His litany of hatred against society is cumulative. Revenge will be his due. If need be, he will use violence to quell the murderous inner rage that haunts and obsesses him. It is impossible to empathize with the sorrow endured by someone who has never had a birth certificate, he cries out. Unlike other young men, the misanthropic Antony has now decided his future. He will have his beloved, no matter what the social repercussions such an act incurs. No longer will he allow the chance factor to decide his destiny, he cries out, thereby giving Dumas the means to bring forward his anti-society arguments. No one can predict one's plight in the world. Each one casts his lot unknowingly. It was fate that dictated they meet again, he tells Adèle.

A good bourgeoise, Adèle, who responded years ago to Antony's love, yielded yet to her family's wishes and married Baron d'Hervey. At this juncture in her life, she leads a comfortable life. Soon her husband, who has been garrisoned in Strasbourg, will be returning home from army service in Algeria. Indeed, he is due any day. The couple has a delightful young daughter.

Adèle, the perfect wife and mother, is adamant about adhering to society's mores despite her passion for Antony and the emotional toll such repression has caused her throughout the years. Her greatest fear would be to commit adultery. In so doing, her beloved child would be taken from her and life would no longer be worth living.

The drama takes crushing hold as both Antony and Adèle become increasingly enmeshed in their passionate world of extremes. Adèle takes matters into her own hand and flees to Strasbourg to join her husband. The insidiously clever Antony, however, sets a trap. No sooner does Adèle arrive at the Ittenheim inn where she is to spend the night, than he, who had rented the room next to hers, steps on to the balcony, walks toward her room, breaks a window pane and enters. Antony then takes her in his arms, places a handkerchief on her mouth, and drags her toward him. There is no resisting him now, she realizes. They return to Paris. Colonel d'Hervey comes home and resumes his righteous existence. Despite her terror at the thought of discovery, and the certainty that her child will be taken from her, Adèle continues to see Antony. Rumors abound. Adèle's husband receives an anonymous letter disclosing his wife's liaison. Antony has been apprised, rushes to Adèle's home, and asks her to run away with him to another country. Never would she leave her daughter. Footsteps are heard. It's her husband. She begs her lover to kill her. Death, rather than a life of shame bestowed on her by society!

Colonel d'Hervey's thunderous voice resounds loud and clear. "Open! Open it!" he orders. If she refuses, he will break the door down.

As if paralyzed, Antony stands transfixed. Adèle begs him to stab her. She longs to die. "I am lost," she cries out. Seconds later, Antony's dagger does its work.

At this very instant, the door is broken open and Colonel d'Hervey rushes in. Shocked by the sight of his dead wife and Antony standing over her, he listens in stunned disbelief to Antony's lines, which made theatrical history that night and forever after:

"She resisted me," he said. "And so I killed her!" Adèle's honor had been saved, in this extraordinary *coup de théâtre*, after which Antony throws down his dagger at Colonel d'Hervey's feet.

Mistakes frequently occur on opening night in theater. Because the stage manager had failed to place an armchair near Dorval, rather than falling into it, she tripped over the arm of the chair, injecting in so doing an incredible sense of reality into her death scene.

The curtains came down to deafening applause. The audience was aghast. Traumatized. Madness had set in! Many sobbed. Others screamed. Every emotion possible had been injected into Dumas' play: grief, murder, love, sexuality, passion, rape, rage, hate, conformism. Even the latest psychological findings on these matters by French doctors and physiologists – Bichat and Broussais, and the German phrenologist, Gall, had been used by Dumas to make his point.

Théophile Gautier, poet, novelist, and critic had never truly underestimated Dorval's genius. But on this night he experienced the truth of her feelings, as revealed by her facial expressions and gestures, particularly when she raised her arms, threw her hat on a chair, and trembled with anguish, as never before. While descanting on her pain and despair, her voice reached moments of sublimity. He reviled those critics who focused only on her small, slightly hunched body, large forehead, tiny-veined hands, and coarse speech. She was not beautiful in the classical sense. Little did they understand that this frail-looking creature was a powder keg on stage. The potency of her emotions and feelings were contagious, explosive, like streams of currents which ignited and radiated throughout the house. Everyone in the audience had been caught up in her electric field of splendid desolation. Such was the miracle of Dorval's power of transfiguration.

The *Figaro* wrote that "Dorval cried as people do cry, with genuine tears; she shrieked as people do shriek, cursed as women do curse, tearing her hair, casting her flowers aside, rumpling up her dress to the knees without any consideration for conservative standards of the Conservatoire" (Carlson, 85).

A disquieting glance, a hand brought to the forehead, Dorval's very reticence created sentience. Her simplicity of gesture, realism in distress, the sincerity of her metered responses, even her stature broadened during her stage ordeal. "The audience was in a state of delirium; they applauded, sobbed, cried, screamed. Even the play's shaky passion had 'inflamed all hearts'" (Moser, 50: Gautier, "La Reprise d'Antony, 167).

When Dumas rose to leave the theater, those seeking a memento of the evening, simply tore off parts of his green jacket until not a square centimeter of it was left (Gautier, 171).

As Antony, the tall, thin, and blue-eyed Bocage, though not an Adonis in the classical sense of the word, dressed as he was in "a black frock coat, buttoned over a white waistcoat", fulfilled the masculine ideal of the day. Within him existed that "fatal and Byron-like beauty" (Maurois, 245). Bocage was heard to have said: "When I perform with her, I am moved, transported; this woman electrified me" (*Marie Dorval, Documents inédits,* 8).

Critics longed to discover Dorval's secret. How could this woman, whose physical state seemed so disappointing to some, extract from that small, slightly hunched body such blood-curdling sounds of sorrow? What magic did this woman, whose enunciation was so coarse, possess that enabled her to impact so forcefully on high society? She was a mystery! "Essentially modern, she owed nothing to tradition, she followed the fate of innovators... She was woman, while others would have been content with being an actress" (*Marie Dorval, Documents inédits,* 8)

One of the several unpredictable moments associated with *Antony* occurred during a performance when Bocage exited after some water pipes had begun leaking on stage. Unfortunately this incident occurred prior to having spoken the last crucial lines of the play. The disappointed spectators refused to leave their seats. Aware of the situation, she [Dorval] rose from the dead, faced the audience, and cried out, "I resisted him and he killed me". The satisfied audience renewed their thunderous applause, rose from their seats, and left (Marcel Pollitzer, *Trois Reines de Théâtre,* 55).

Now that Dorval had won another success, she was invited by the Baron Taylor to join the Comédie-Française troupe. This tidbit, reported by *Le Journal des comédiens* on May 12, 1831, might mean a dream fulfilled for Dorval.

> Mme Dorval, who has just enjoyed such a great success in *Antony* was very nearly lost to the Porte Saint-Martin... One of its strongest supporters has been hired by the Comédie-Française. M. Crosnier, who had been notified on time, offered this remarkable actress a highly advantageous three-year contract which she signed. (Ambrière, 219)

Vigny, unsurprisingly, was mesmerized by Dorval's performance. His unblinking eyes followed her every move, tremor, gesture, and heartbeat. She had been born to express the moods of frenzied, disconsolate hearts, but also their tender and well-meaning innuendoes. The ever discreet Vigny refrained, understandably, however, from revealing the depth of his personal feelings for the actress in his critique of *Antony* which appeared in the prestigious *Revue des Deux Mondes.* Vigny considered Dorval "a miracle worker. She speaks her flat and totally insignificant words in such pathetic, passionate, warm tones, that one feels one has understood it all and one weeps and groans thanks to her pantomime." The confessional scene in *Antony* was a marvelous example of her manner. (Ambrière, 203)

Vigny, and frequently Nodier, among others, were in the habit of repairing to Dorval's dressing room after a performance. Her visage had been incised in Vigny's mind. He saw her as dazzling, breathtaking, prodigious. Her performance had become the talk of the Salons. In his article, "A Letter on the Theater Concerning Antony" (June 1831), he readdressed, as others had before him, the greatest of all questions, perhaps prophetically in his case, since it revolved around the meaning of "devotion in love." He conjured up the tragic fate of Dumas's heroine in *Antony* to make his point. No one laughs when seeing this drama. There is little weeping, but a great deal of suffering. One experiences the nervous agitation of the characters whose hands and feet grow tense" (Baldensperger, 267).

As Mme d'Hervey, Dorval was melancholy, tender, and kind. One senses from the outset that if the man she loves ever reappears, she would be lost. So touching were her tears and so powerful her emotions that Vigny compared her "depth of reverie" and her emotions to the great English actors of Covent Garden and Drury Lane.

When emotional pain struck her protagonist, Dorval knew how to "develop these tormenting thrusts, these powerful moments of terror and anguish, characteristic of melancholy and tender souls;" she was capable of injecting feeling into each gesture, sigh, facial, and bodily expression (Baldensperger, 275). She knew how to cry in the most touching of ways – tears filled with emotions and human tragedy flowing.

Vigny commented on the very special nature of Dorval's voice as Mme d'Hervey. He suggested that speaking well on stage did not consist only in pronouncing one's words clearly and distinctly, but in "choosing among the natural and true movements of one's heart, those which are beautiful, in keeping with art, for were they beautiful only in keeping with nature it would most probably not be sufficient" (Baldensperger, 276). Vigny's "Lettre sur le Théâtre à propos d'Antony" (June 3, 1831) was of decisive benefit to Dorval's reputation.

Although not wanting for sexual encounters, by comparison with Dorval Vigny was a novice in these matters. Moreover, he had never really loved this completely before. She had swept him off his feet. She had become his muse. He worshipped her despite the world that separated them. She had been brought up in poverty, in the coarse, lower classes with little or no formal education, speaking the language of the streets, accustomed to the rough-and-tumble ways of her class, to the amorality of the senses – like Dumas. When the body called, and attraction was there, it had to be assuaged. No petty restrictions were evident on her part. Dorval was in no sense immoral; she was amoral in this respect. Like the run-of-the mill man, she chose what suited her needs and offered herself the pleasures of the flesh when she so sought them. Yet when this man of ancient lineage knelt at her feet, his charming face framed in his blond and curly hair and delicately lit up by the tender azure of his eyes, she experienced feelings she had never felt before, as though a cup of cold well-water had been lifted to her burning lips (Léon Séché's monograph, 53-56 E, Gosse, 17).

Dorval was transfixed by Vigny's gaze. She was in love as she had never been before. George Sand, who had met her, described Dorval's encounter with Vigny: "Oh! Naive and passionate, and young and suave, and trembling and terrible" (Gosse, 18). Dorval dreamed, she floated, she rejoiced, and she smiled at the sight of him.

As for Vigny, he was a man possessed. Ecstasy dominated their lives. Questions arose. What role would Dorval play in the workaday world of this vulnerable genius? It was as if she had cut open his veins and let the blood of creation flow forth from him. Her voice, whose timber glided up and down the register, from raging to disconsolate anger to the most passionate love, knew well how to convey her adoration of him. While Vigny sat in admration before this monstrously magnificent artist, he alluded to her as a "Reine de passion, qui deux fois savez vivre" (Vigny, "A Madame Dorval") (Vigny, Pléiade I, 191). How better could he convey his love for her than by writing a dithyrambic review of her bedazzling performance:

Une heure sonne dans la nuit,
La journée enfin s'est éteinte,
L'ombre calme efface l'empreinte
De ses clartés et de son bruit;
Tout ce théâtre, où l'on adore,
N'est plus qu'une salle sonore
Où ta voix retentit encore
Comme un faible écho qui s'enfuit...
Et toi, tu rêves solitaire,

Toi l'âme de ce corps désert,
O toi, la voix de ce concert

Qui ce soir enchantait la terre,
Tu viens de remonter aux cieux
Ainsi qu'un oiseau gracieux
Se tait, et dans son nid soyeux
Cherche la paix et le mystère. (Baldensperger, 299)

These thrilling times for Dorval saw the star ushering in one success after another. On August 11, 1831, she opened in Victor Hugo's blood and thunder drama, *Marion Delorme*. Hugo would work closely with Dorval on the staging of his latest play. Although Hugo had completed *Marion Delorme* by 1829, and had offered it to the Comédie-Française a year prior to the July Revolution, the censors predictably vetoed its production. Following the July Revolution the play had been cleared by the governing forces at the Comédie-Française. Like Dumas, Hugo believed Mlle Mars should play the lead. When he learned that she was on bad terms with the establishment, and unwilling to involve himself in an imbroglio, he requested his play be returned to him. It was then that he offered his action-packed drama to Dorval, who accepted it.

Marion Delorme rang in on a seventeenth century courtesan who had left the capital for Blois with her beloved, Didier. Coincidentally, it is Didier, we learn, who, though unaware of the perils involved, had saved Saverny, Marion's former lover. Brawls, drinking, and dueling scenes, the last in opposition to Richelieu's interdict against fencing, heighten the momentum and brio of Hugo's complicated drama. Caught in the act, Didier and Saverny are imprisoned, then escape. When Didier discovers that Marion is a courtesan and not the virgin he had thought her to be, he repudiates her. In a tear-stained Act V, he forgives her upon learning that she has risked her life to gain clemency for her beloved, after which Didier and Saverny are put to death.

Shortly after Hugo and Dorval began working together, Vigny grew jealous of their close relationship. Had Dorval and Hugo become lovers, Vigny wondered. Hugo was known to be a lady's man, worse, a great lover as well. Dorval seemed to have some kind of hold over Hugo. That he had so readily accepted the changes she had suggested in his script was unlike him. Heretofore, he had always been the one to give orders! Not this time. He had confidence in Dorval's approach to, and experience in, the theater. Without flinching, he agreed to her recommendations: that the original title,

Un duel sous Richelieu, be changed to *Marion Delorme*, thus singling out her role in the title; that the curtain descend during the courtesan's absolution scene; that alterations that better suited her voice and demeanour be made in the text. During a rehearsal, she took Hugo by the arm, according to Adèle Hugo: "Monsieur Hugo, she said with the graciousness of her smile, your Didier is a bad person: I do everything for him, and he goes and dies without ever saying a nice word to me. Tell him he's wrong not to pardon me" (Ambrière, 226). In this instance, he may have acquiesced to Dorval's advice because the highly regarded Prosper Mérimée, author of *Carmen* and other tales, had given him similar counsel. (Ambrière, 226). The figure of this hero became memorable, whatever the reason.

> His visage lit by eyes glowing with somber fire, a muffled voice which, in scenes of passion, vibrated brilliantly, his words, now calculatedly slow, then violently staccato, a nervous and febrile spirit, an exalted and yet concentrated poetic sense, all gave an ardent and melancholy fire to his performance which had a real and unique attractiveness for spectators. (Carlson, 69)

Bocage was among the notables on opening night as were Ernest de Saxe Cobourg, Théophile Gautier, Célestin Nanteuil, Jéhan Duseigneur, Pétrus Borel, Mme Dosne, Thiers' mother in law, the dandy Joseph Bouchardy, Delacroix, Ingres, Gustave Planche, Balzac, Mlle Mars, Mme de Girardin, Dumas, Soulié, Vigny, to mention but a few.

Dorval loved people. So much so that her much-coveted Sunday get-togethers were the talk of the town although she only served punch and appetizing goodies to her young and handsome admirers at these simple gatherings. Perhaps, she could have mused, the guests might be her future lovers. Such a one was the young, handsome, emaciated, and still unknown poet, Antoine Fontaney. Much to Vigny's sorrow, it seemed to him that she had already developed an eagle eye for this theater fanatic. He heard her say to Fontaney, most tellingly, that before going on stage, she always chose sone face – one person – in the audience to whom she would play. He was understandably flattered and moved. What he might not have known, however, was that she had told her *secret* to many other men as well.

Fontaney was in the company of Lemaître, Piccini, and others, when Dorval extended her invitation to him to attend her much-coveted Sunday get-togethers. It was on these occasions that men such as Hugo and Dumas could vent their spleen and share their hopes. Hugo confided his high expectations for the success of his drama on one of these occasions, reiterating what he had written in his Preface to *Marion Delorme*: he *modestly* suggested that those who no longer believed in the existence of genius at this time might do well to heed the following words:

> At the outset of the nineteenth century, we had the Empire and the Emperor. Why wouldn't there now be a poet who would be to Shakespeare what Napoleon had been to Charlemagne. (Victor Hugo's *OC*, 959)

Hugo claimed that he would play this role himself.

That the first few scenes of Hugo's *Marion Delorme* were coldly received, was blamed in part on the claque who had not only clapped too much, but had done so at the wrong moments. What excuse could they give moments later, after Dorval uttered what were to become her famous lines: "Your love has turned me into a virgin!" The audience burst into roars of laughter. Fortunately, the outburst ceased almost immediately thanks to Hugo's friends, who not only insulted the offenders, but requested respect. The play dragged along, peppered as it was with ovations, along with whistles and jeers (Moser, 71).

The following day Dorval was relieved to read Charles Maurice's critique of her performance in the *Courrier des Spectacles*. That he lavished praise on her remarkable talents drew smiles of satisfaction from an artist who had grown accustomed to laudatory reviews. Other reviewers, however, were less generous in their comments on the rest of the cast. *Le Bon Théo*, as Gautier's friends had come to call him, praised the laughter, tears, and terror elicited by the play's fulminating lines, the performance, and Hugo's innovative approach to history! Days later, it was reported that Dorval had fainted several times from exhaustion in her attempts to quell hoots and jeers from unruly audiences. On the whole, *Marion Delorme* was not well received. It had to be conceded, Dumas was the winner this theatrical season!

While the triumvirate – Hugo, Dumas, Vigny – had been close friends in their youth, working and struggling together to brave the world, to make their mark as poets, novelists, and dramatists, the closeness and generosity that had once existed between them had all but vanished by 1831. No longer novices, their personalities jarred. Jealousy and rancor took hold of each one of them in specific ways. Nothing overt, to be sure. They were simply growing up. Each was going his own way. During the rehearsals of *Marion Delorme* Hugo had clearly lost patience with Vigny's latest bout of uncalled for jealousy over his entente with Dorval. Hugo's riposte, as noted in his diary, was anything but generous:

> A. de Vigny has two reasons not to like me. *Primo*, *Marion Delorme* made more money than *La Maréchale d'Ancre,* and *Hernani,* more money than *Othello. Secundo*, that I sometimes gave my arm to Mme Dorval. Envious and jealous. (Ambrière, 227)

CHAPTER 6

"MAKE ME A BABY SHE CRIED OUT IN A STATE OF DELIRIUM"
(Vigny, *Journal d'un poète,* Feb. March, 1832, 943. II).

Vigny loved to remain in Dorval's dressing room while she applied her make-up. These intimate moments allowed him to feel close to her. To listen to her chatter invited him to penetrate a whole unguarded secret realm. There was no acting on her part, simply an outpouring of revelations, an unburdening of unpremeditated thoughts and feelings. Her prattling revealed a paradoxically naive girlish charm. More frequently than not, they conveyed a dissatisfaction with the life she was living and the stage personality she was incarnating at the time. The modalities of her voice – ranging from sighs, cries, screams, groans, joy, rapture, anger, laughter, melancholy, and caressingly voluptuous tones – conveyed the richness of her inner emotional climate. At times she ululated her sorrows and frustrations, particularly when suffering through exaggerated bouts of seemingly unrequited love, or casting aside a tiresome lover. Her ability to intersperse her lamentations with well-placed sighs and pangs of passion during a fly-by-night secret affair, added moments of high drama to the occasion (*Journal d'un poète,* II, 966).

To accept Dorval's histrionic manner did not come easily to Vigny at this time. Nonetheless, he neither judged her nor attempted to change her nature, at least for the present. Instead, he turned to her background of poverty to explain their differences. They were opposites. He was a dreamer, she lived in the circumscribed domain of the workaday world, forced to deal since her earliest childhood with reality, be it in the theatrical productions in which she participated or in her relationships with people. Forever controlled on the outside, he followed what he considered to be his ethical injunctions. A flamboyant extrovert, she usually spoke her mind. Vigny had his limitations, most overtly in his relationships with women, and most unconditionally when it came to one to whom he was so deeply drawn.

On March 18, 1832, Vigny attended Dorval's latest theatrical adventure, *Ten Years in the Life of a Woman (Dix Ans dans la vie d'une femme),* by the well known dramatist Eugène Scribe. Heretofore, Scribe had been a favorite among the bourgeoisie. They admired his probity on social issues, and his light banter and accessible language. He subsequently seemed to have changed his priorities, emphasis being placed increasingly on earthy subjects, anticipating the writings of Zola and other end-of-the-century Naturalists who sought to depict life as objectively as possible, including well-placed crudities.

Vigny was repulsed, even offended, by what he looked upon as a raw drama, featuring a young girl from an honorable bourgeois family who marries, is seduced by a smooth-talking young man, then fritters her life away on mindless sexual encounters leading her ever more deeply into a morass of vice, crime, and degradation. Gone were the passionate love motif, the yearning, the tears, the cries of anguish, and the dreams of future happiness so dear to the Romantics.

Others as well, including many critics, rejected both the theme and writing style of *Ten Years in the Life of a Woman.* Vigny's friend, the young poet and critic, Antoine Fontaney, seated next to him at the theater, was likewise offended. He, who had heretofore published highly favorable reviews of Dorval and her work, would refrain from doing so this time. The play's coarseness, stylistic ugliness, and unmilled dialogue in no way gained entry into either Fontaney's or Vigny's sensitive and poetic worlds.

For fear of offending Dorval by speaking ill of the play, these two diplomats refrained from commenting on it when accompanying her home after the performance. Nor were critics, on the whole, kindly disposed to *Ten Years in the Life of a Woman.* How could it have been otherwise? Romanticism – love, heartbreak, ethics, and a search for beauty – was in the air, not the coarseness and vulgarities of the theater of the future. Nonetheless, the blatancy of the negative criticisms, based on anti-decency outcries, rather than discouraging audiences from buying tickets, encouraged them to do so. For the following two months nearly all of Paris had lined up in front of the Porte Saint-Martin to buy tickets. The goal of money-making, which

Dorval needed so much more desperately than esthetics, had been achieved – at least for the moment!

Only a month later, in April, 1832, the sweet charm of theatrical novelty suddenly shifted into a negative mode. The furor created by *Ten Years in the Life of a Woman* gave way to a climate of dread. The deadly scourge of cholera had descended on Paris. Vigny, his mother, and his wife came down with the disease in early May. So sick had Vigny become that each time he tried to rise from bed, he fainted. He thought he was dying. With this in mind, he burned his unfinished plays, fearing that money-driven publishers would seek to print them as they were. After six weeks, however, his strength returned. His joy was such that he wrote what subsequently became his *famous* letter to Dorval, entitled, "to be read in bed." So pornographic was it considered to be, that it never saw print, and was allegedly burned after Dorval's demise. It began…

> He is alone; he is thinking of the tragedian. All of his thoughts are drawn toward her, and it is this turmoil that he depicts in the fiery painting that whips up his imagination to paroxistic heights... He flies toward the one he adores, and gives himself to her full and burning. (Vigny, Corresp., 315)

On May 23, 1832, Dorval herself became deathly ill with cholera. Her fever skyrocketed. She was placed on the critical list. Vigny was in anguish. Weeks passed before her health returned. Still weak, but like the trouper she had always been, Dorval was prepared to return to the stage. She was, however, unprepared to be told by the unscrupulous Charles Harel, the Director of the Porte Saint-Martin, that she would be allowed to perform only on Sundays, and occasionally, on one or another day of the week in some revival. Knowing Sunday to be the least popular day of the week sent shock waves throughout her body. It was obvious to all involved that Mlle George, Harel's mistress, had been instrumental in instigating this latest plot against her. Dorval's severe bout with cholera and the time she had spent away from the theatre had favored such behind-the-scene manipulations. During the interim, Mlle George had become the new favorite on the *Boulevard du Crime* and was enjoying unprecedented success in Dumas' latest melodrama, *The Tower of Nesle*. Parisians flocked to this blood and thunder work, filled as it was with eerie dungeons, killings, incest, brutal and harrowing stratagems.

Mlle George had had both the time and the power to hatch her insidious machinations, which, if successful, would prevent Dorval from earning a living wage. Aware of her perilous situation and, worse, of the fickleness of audiences who have the capacity to forget even the best performers if they remain invisible for a certain amount of time, Marie was not one to mourn over her fate. Rather than lamenting or weeping over a precarious future, the optimist in her set to work. After all, she reasoned, she, who had been the product of want and hardship, had had the courage to build a life for herself virtually single-handedly. Her reserves of strength helped her not only to face facts, but to act on them. A will of iron had also served her well, and would again be called upon to work its wonders: this time, treading a different path, garnering the esteem of her wayward audiences. To accomplish her goal she would need to be seen in public: at theaters, dinners, meetings, and to participate in a variety of causes and significant events. She was certain Vigny would help her in this regard.

Not so readily! Strangely enough, the one who had stood in adoration of Dorval, who had spoken words of desperate love to her, who had kept a small bachelor's apartment at 18 rue Montaigne (today rue Jean Mermoz) for himself and for her, was too involved in his own writing at the time to help. Furthermore, he let it be known that his gifts did not lie in organizing functions and mingling with people. He was not a facilitator, nor even involved in theater. He was, on the other hand, deeply concerned with his writings. His first volume, *Stello,* had just been published and he was now at work on the second. Did Vigny, nonetheless, behave true to form? Certainly so, if one is to believe Fontaney's words concerning his character. He was "envious and jealous... saccharine, mannered, complimentary and bitter..." (Aug. 20, 1831, *Journal Intime,* 4).

To whom could Dorval turn for help? Of all of her acquaintances, only one man really had the heart for it: the good-natured, generous, kind, blustering womanizer, Dumas. She knew him to be available to her – and, of course, to many other women as well! Dorval had remained on good terms with him, and, one might add, *somewhat more*! A born extrovert with the capacity to size up people and situations in minutes, Dumas answered Dorval's plea and offered to help her in whatever way he could. Moreover, he claimed, and justly so, to be an expert at earning money, which he unfortunately spent as swiftly as he acquired it. He told Dorval that money could be easily made by writing a book. Despite her fear of opening herself up to ridicule, she accepted the suggestion. Dumas wrote the volume, which he entitled *Marianne*. It was published under Dorval's daughter's name – Gabrielle Allan-Dorval – and appeared in print the following year. Predictably, it earned the authors more than a few *sous*.

Dumas revealed his kindness and in-born *largesse* to Dorval in other ways. He organized special benefits for her, a custom that had been set in place in France years before, and was destined to help artists during hard times (Ambrière, 247). To this end, Dorval performed in *Antony* at the Ambigu, *Tartuffe,* at the Vaudeville, and *The Two Convicts (Les Deux Forçats)* at the Odéon, to mention but a few of her appearances. Dumas arranged theatrical evenings in which Mlle Mars, happily no longer Dorval's rival, agreed to participate. Newspapers, such as the *Courrier des Théâtres* and *Le Corsaire,* printed highly favorable reviews and articles on her theater work.

Hugo's comportment toward Dorval, or lack thereof, for having failed to invite her to the opening of his new play, *Lucrecia Borgia,* on February 2, 1833, hurt her deeply. Had his omission, she wondered, been intended to minimize her importance as an actress? After all, he did choose to star Mlle George and not her. Was it the dread of alienating Mlle George that had precipitated such discourtesy on his part? Whatever the motivations, one might be led to think that after performing at the Porte Saint-Martin for fifteen years, the management of the theater would have seen fit to invite Dorval to this particular opening. To point up the matter, Dorval wrote the following delightful note to Hugo requesting a seat for the event:

> My dear Monsieur Hugo,
> Will I suffer the disappointment of not being invited to your opening performance? Would it be possible for you to give me a small loge for the première? And despite your many commitments, would you be able to send me a very brief note? If I am granted the pleasure of being given a loge, I intend to bring Mme Sand and Miss Smithson. (Ambrière, 250)

Rather than taking the chance of displeasing his star, Mlle George, who despised Dorval, Hugo never even bothered to reply. Should he have acquiesced to Dorval's suggestion, he would have certainly feared a slowing of his precipitous rise to fame. All was not lost, however, since one of Dorval's friends, Delphine Custine, invited her to sit in her loge. Although neither jealous nor envious by nature, Dorval must have smiled, at least inwardly, upon reading the deprecating reviews allotted to Mlle George. Particularly venomous was the one appearing in *Le Voleur*:

> Mlle George does not know how to convey the nuances of a role. Her diction is halting and forced. Her continuous declamations are fatiguing. We would have wanted to see Dorval play Lucrecia, her reputation being synonymous with drama. According to us, she would have been more authentic and, happily, more energetic, than Mlle George. (Ambrière, 250)

With the passing of days, theatergoers, well informed as to Mlle George's insidious machinations, began siding with Dorval against her rival's offensive dictates. Some felt sorry for Dorval. Others considered the interdicts imposed on her unjust and unwarranted. Dorval's reputation was beginning to soar once again. Her comeback was virtually a certainty at this time. Even her love life seemed to be relatively smooth – at least for the moment. She and Vigny were seeing each other in their small hideaway on rue Montaigne. As the days passed, nonetheless, the passionately possessive Vigny complained that their meetings were not sufficiently frequent. She tried to make him understand that he would have to accept this situation. As her popularity increased, her days and evenings grew busier. She began breaking rendezvous with Vigny and accepting invitations from those who were in a position to help her broaden her circle and thereby her career. Unlike Vigny's restrictive life – he had to spend so much time caring for his mother and his wife – Dorval's was gregarious and open. She was instinctively drawn to new faces and good times, rather than to the frequently ponderous and irascible Vigny. Perhaps she could take so much of him and no more!

To be seen, had become her by-word! She attended theatrical performances, musical events, dinner parties, and other festivities. At a performance of Rossini's opera, *Moses,* she became friendly with the wealthy Marquis Astolphe de Custine, a pederast, and, at the time, the butt of scathing antagonism. His drama, *Beatricia Cenci*, which had been rejected by various theaters for its focus on incest, its blood-thirstiness, though, covertly, because of Custine's homosexuality. After much persuasion on Custine's part, Harel finally agreed to have it performed, providing the author fund the production. Custine agreed. In return, he requested that Dorval and Lemaître be given the leads (Carlson, *The French Stage,* 89).

That Harel asked for Mlle George's approval prior to validating the contract was to be expected. Convinced that Dorval, whose forte was prose drama, would be unable to handle the poetic tragedy required by the role, she felt that the play would close after two days. Since her reasoning failed to threaten her ego, Mlle George acquiesced to the production. When the reviews in *L'Artiste, La Revue de Paris,* and the *Gazette des Théâtres* proved to be more than enthusiastic, Mlle George demanded that the play close after the third performance. True to form, Harel, agreed. The public was outraged. Newspapers denounced the persecutors of Dorval and Lemaître. The exquisite sets had cost Custine a small fortune and the financial loss suffered by the actors and the theater were equally significant. Lemaître was so infuriated with Harel that he "came to blows" with him and promised never to return (Carlson, 90).

Meanwhile, Vigny was growing increasingly annoyed with Dorval's apparently lackadaisical ways. He was jealous of her escorts, even of Custine. As was his wont, he found momentary solace in his profound belief in stoicism and in his *creed of honor* (Whitridge, 117). Little did he understand that Dorval was *incapable of fidelity to one man*. Like Dumas in this respect, and many other men and women as well, she was a philanderer at heart, seeking out those capable of answering her sexual needs and, if possible, filling the ever-gaping void in her heart. At times, and thankfully for her, some of her lovers helped her allay her serious financial concerns, her persecution by Mlle George, her fears for the future, and for her health. She was, nonetheless, not a dreamer. Her feet had been too well planted in the precarious real world. Neither health nor happiness was tangible or secure. Life for Dorval, had always been and would remain a floating mass of uncertainties.

Never before, she noted, had she suffered such protracted pangs of anxiety. No longer the young charmer with a life ahead, the thirty-five-year-old Dorval would have to begin focusing on the difficult years to come. Heretofore, she had been taken by the merry swirl of new plays, receptions, and audiences who loved her. Perhaps the after effects of her serious bout with cholera had weakened her both physically and psychologically. She seemed incapable at this point, even more so than in the past, of addressing what now appeared to be her insurmountable financial problems. Rather than face them, she chose, but fortunately only in part, to escape them.

Randomness, an integral part of the human experience, insinuated itself, for better or for worse, into Dorval's life. Back in 1831, during an intermission of *Marion Delorme*, Hugo had introduced her to the young and handsome poet, drama critic, and future diplomat, Antoine Fontaney. It was common knowledge among theater people that he had loved and had wanted to marry Marie Nodier. Her parents, however, did not consider him a suitable candidate for their daughter (Moser, 81). After coping with his disappointment, Fontaney began socializing again. He was taken by Dorval's vivacity, wit, and in time, with what seemed to be her visceral interest in him.

In his *Diary*, he could not help but convey his reactions to the many courtesies she had extended to him. Nonetheless, he admitted to the "curious nature of her looks":

> Her large, bulging forehead, her small nose, her thin pinched lips which forever seemed puckered, her dusky skin, the vivacity of that animated face, that witty mind... (Fontaney, *Journal Intime,* Monday 22, August, 1831, 7)

Dorval invited Fontaney to visit her in her dressing room where he had occasion to meet some of her friends, namely, the dramatist Frédéric Soulié. In a matter of days, the charmingly delightful Fontaney was welcomed at Dorval's dinner parties at her home on rue Mesley. All was very proper. Her placid husband, Merle, usually presided. Nothing seemed to bother him. Not to worry, Dorval was meeting the bills, at least for the most part.

The more Fontaney saw of Dorval, the more he was taken by her outgoing personality and what he judged to be her strength of character. It was no simple matter, he reasoned, to perform nightly to frequently rowdy audiences. Nor must one minimize the concentration needed to memorize line upon line in the many plays in which she performed. In his eyes "Mme Dorval was very beautiful! ...full of wit and charm" (*Journal Intime*, Sept.1, 1831, p.23). One might even call her a heroine in her own way.

Instantly aware of their outward intimacy, the petulant Vigny grew "jealous" and "envious" of the interloper, erroneously believing him to be Dorval's latest flame, Fontaney noted in his *Journal Intime* (August 20, 1832, p. 4).

Merle was antipodal to Vigny. He was the essence of discretion. He was so anxious to please his wife that when Vigny – or any other lover – came to the apartment to visit with her, he did his best to see to their privacy and tranquility. Fontaney attests to Merle's incredible – virtually unique – attitude toward his wife's lovers and their love-making. On one occasion, when Fontaney arrived at Dorval's apartment, simply as a friend, he was told that she was occupied at the moment – which meant, that she had a lover in her room – and was summarily shown the door (Moser, 85).

At a propitious time, Fontaney was introduced to Dorval's daughters: Caroline, who sang well; Louise, the oldest, who was determined to become an actress, though her mother believed she lacked the talent to realize her goals; and Gabrielle, who was a beauty. It was the latter who accelerated Fontaney's heart beat. At the same time, he was immediately aware of the fact that Dorval's daughters had been brought up in keeping with strict moral and religious credo, which meant they were taboo to him, at least for the present (Fontaney, *Journal Intime,* 20 August, 1831).

Fontaney differed from other visitors who came to Dorval's home. He was not in love with her. It was the seventeen-year-old Gabrielle, whom he later referred to as his "beautiful and tender bee," who captured his fancy at first sight (Fontaney, *Journal Intime,* Sept. 9, 1831, p.31). So caught up was Dorval in her own seductive powers, that she failed to notice that Fontaney's world did not revolve around her, but around his "beautiful" Gabrielle. In time, Dorval must have sensed that she was no longer the center of attention: the archetypal "mother" had been displaced by the archetypal "young virgin." The age-old love/jealousy relationship existing between generations began festering. The thought of having a married daughter was emotionally unacceptable to Dorval. Not that she did not love her daughters. She did, and very deeply so, but in her own way. Since she had rarely been home during her daughters' early years, she had entrusted their upbringing to governesses and maids. As sole money-earner she could not have done otherwise. When old enough, her daughters were enrolled in convent boarding schools. The prospect of having a married daughter at this juncture was traumatic for her. It meant that her youth had been spent and that middle age had come upon her. Unable to accept these facts of life, tension mounted in the household. Life was said to be at its best when *Mother* was occupied elsewhere.

On January 17, 1832, Dorval was called upon to star at the Odéon in *Jeanne Vau-bernier,* a slight three-act comedy by Rougemont and Laffitte. Because the action took place during the reign of Louis XV, the costumes and décors were redolent with beauty and elegance. The mood was one of misplaced joy, arrogance, and conceit. As the curtains rose, the splendidly beautiful Madame Dubarry, one of Louis XVth's favorites, is busy playing a game with two of her admirers. As if she were casting oranges into the air and then catching them, her lightly bantering voice is heard ordering two well-known and powerful men about: "Jump Choiseul!," she says with the impudence of the *parvenue* to none other than to the Minister of Foreign Affairs, whom she disdains for heeding her folly. Moments later, she again cries out, "Jump Praslin," this time directing her command to the Minister of the Navy, belittling him as well for obeying what she knows to be a foolish request. The joy of her contagious laughter, and the selfishness of the spoiled child about her, permeate the atmosphere (Ambrière, 242).

As the play meanders from act to act, provocative pleasures diminish in intensity. Horror strikes in act IV, with the unleashing of the French Revolution. A mood of sorrow, of suffering, and of blood-letting floods the atmosphere. Gone is the privileged, pleasure-seeking and abusive aristocracy. Du Barry will be guillotined under the Terror. Louis XVI will be executed under the Convention in 1793. How much gore could audiences stand? Very little, judging from the cat-calls, jeers, and whistles greeting *Jeanne Vaubernier*. The fact was that audiences were no longer entertained by scenes of carnage.

Horror had been replaced by mitigated pleasures, hope in the future, and in a world of moderation.

Rather than derided and negativized, Dorval's role in *Jeanne Vaubernier* had been reworked to feature a joyous, humorous, coquettish, and clever adventuress, whose bouncy personality elicited cheers from the audience. Gone were Dorval's melodramatic weeping scenes, her pathos and tragic demeanor. Audiences must have welcomed the change since they greeted her revamped cheery personality with continuous applause.

Vigny's review of *Jeanne Vaubernier* helped matters along as well. Rather than pointing up the mediocre aspects of the play, he praised Dorval's new and broader acting techniques.

> Mme Dorval's originality is of the most unpredictable type; without batting an eyelid her serious blitheness elicits laughter; the brusqueness of her repartees, the tone of her bold gestures, the frankness of her good naturedness, her happy-go-lucky gait take on the nonchalance of a spirited *grisette,* ready for whatever you want, providing it amuses her... go and hear her and you will see how the cleverness of this consummate actress enables her to make something out of nothing. The best actress in the best comedy has never done anything better. (Ambrière, 242)

Most importantly, the play earned its success and Dorval adulation from grateful spectators.

Less heartening events, however, were to impose themselves on Dorval's daily existence. Fontaney's continued and reciprocated passion for his "beautiful" Gabrielle was creating an increasingly painful, even harrowing, atmosphere in the Dorval home.

When Fontaney visited Dorval's home unexpectedly on September 29, 1832, "Gabrielle was there," he noted delightedly in his *Journal intime*. So powerfully smitten had he been by her beauty that he was determined to visit her more frequently (Fontaney, 151). At times, he arrived with gifts. On October 17, he brought his some English books, his goal being to increase her fluency in the language. "I look at her with all my soul," he admitted to himself (Fontaney, 153). When accompanying Dorval to a friend's house that same day, however, the mother attempted to attract his attention away from her daughter. She sought to elicit pity by confiding to him that Vigny was "tyrannizing" her, that she was "bored" with him, and that he was jealous of Fontaney (Fontaney, 153). On October 19, the love-stricken Fontaney again returned to Dorval's home. He dined there.

"Gabrielle is so admirable!" he noted in his *Diary*: "I glide my hands over hers as we pass each other. And how we shudder!" (Fontaney, 154). On October 24, Fontaney meets Dorval and her daughters at the opera. In the darkness enclosing them, "I leaned toward Gabrielle. I kissed her hair. I pressed her beautiful shoulders with my hands and she seemed to respond to my touch. I looked at her with all my soul" (Fontaney, 154). Fontaney wondered whether she understood how he felt about her. "This young girl is so very beautiful and gracious!" (Fontaney, 154). He could not help but sing her graces. By November 7, the situation was becoming grotesque Fontaney noted in his Diary:

> I leave home at 1 o'clock to go to Mme Dorval's – My situation is again becoming dramatic – She gives me the impression of wanting to love me! "Do you have a mistress?" she asks. "Does seeing me mean something to you?"
> It's incredible! (Fontaney, 159)

On Wednesday, November 21, 1832, Fontaney returned to Dorval's home. Gabrielle was alone.

> Without telling her formally that I love her, I insinuate it in a thousand ways. I get down on my knees and press her hand to mine. – she tells me that I am just playing a game. When I leave, I kiss her hand and do not wait for Mme Dorval. I do not want to ruin the pleasure I had of having seen her alone. (Fontaney, 160)

Fontaney returned on December 3. He complained that after only one minute with his beloved, her sister, Louise, came into the living room to chaperone them. Worse, no sooner does the *mother* return, than he becomes the brunt of her anger. Why did he stay so long, she questions (Fontaney, 160) . Dutifully, he accompanies Dorval to the Porte Saint-Martin Theater where she is still performing in *Jeanne Vaubernier.* Prior to leaving the Dorval home, however, he steals a second alone with Gabrielle. He kisses her hand fervently.

Days pass. As critic for the *Revue des Deux Mondes,* Fontaney was forever going to the theater and meeting playwrights. Despite his busy life style, nothing deterred him from courting his beloved Gabrielle. He again noted with great disappointment, that Gabrielle's sister, certainly in keeping with the *mother's* orders, was usually present during his visits. When, on one occasion, he found himself alone with his beloved he worked up the *temerity* to outline his plan for her to accompany him to London. It was madness, he realized. But he could not help himself. "My God, she is so beautiful," he kept repeating! (Fontaney, 162, Nov. 28).When he arrived at Dorval's home on Dec. 8, and discovered the *mother* was out, he luxuriated in the blessed moments which allowed him to be alone with his beloved. In Gabrielle's demure way, she confessed to being deeply annoyed with both her mother and her sister.

Whenever Dorval was home, matters took a turn for the worse. Still believing herself to be the favored one, she made certain that Gabrielle would not intrude at the wrong moments. Not a difficult task, she simply locked her in a small room in the apartment. Fontaney refrained from all comment on the subject.

Impatient to the extreme, Fontaney decided to try another tactic: to visit Gabrielle after making certain the *mother* was out; to no avail. She would return minutes later. Did she have a sixth sense, he wondered. Fontanay yet pursued his secret courtship of Gabrielle. The two made plans to slip away to London. François Buloz, the director of the prestigious *Revue des Deux Mondes* had asked Fontaney to be his London correspondent and report on English theater, so popular in Paris at the time.

Rage seized Dorval when she finally realized that Fontaney was in love with her daughter and not with her. Incensed beyond endurance, she went directly to his home, where he lived with his mother. No sooner had the frenzied Dorval entered his apartment, than shock and consternation overcame Fontaney. He asked his mother to stay in the living room. He and Dorval went into his bedroom. Evidently stunned by Dorval's brazen ways, Fontaney remained strangely mute on the personal issues involved. As recorded in his diary:

> This visit staggered me. It will, all the same, remain a secret between us. Yet it may be better that it happened as it did. (Fontaney, January. 19, 1833, 172)

Still obsessing over Gabrielle, Fontaney returned to Dorval's home on Monday January 21 (Fontaney, 173). While prepared to sacrifice everything and anything for his beloved, he obviously remained silent on the matter, particularly since both Dorval and her latest lover, George Sand, were present. "I don't like Mme Sand, he wrote; she is a pretty boy; she is a mediocre woman. Just as her novels have only a first volume, she has only a head. But my Gabrielle is a woman" (Fontaney, 174).

During his Friday visit to Gabrielle, on January 25, she whispered to him that she had left a letter for him in the pocket of her grey coat. On Sunday Jan. 27, she and Fontaney met secretly on the Boulevard Saint-Martin, took a fiacre, and spent two hours together. The following day he visited Gabrielle at home. "She is in bed with a sore throat. Her health had always been fragile," he wrote (Fontaney, 177). The lovers, nonetheless, made love in her bedroom. The maid very nearly walked in on them. Fontaney begged her to remain silent on the subject. The next few days were lived in the terror and the fear of discovery.

Meanwhile, the unstoppable Dorval had dreamed up a more efficacious scheme of catching her prey and of putting an end, at least temporarily, to her daughter's romance. Fontaney was offered the post of secretary to the Spanish Embassy in Madrid. If he accepted the work, she promised him Gabrielle on his return. She hoped inwardly that he would stay away a long time. Neither he nor Gabrielle could alter the *mother's* dicta. Should Gabrielle not adhere to her rulings, she made it quite clear that she would have her incarcerated in a convent! A very plausible threat since such happenings were common at the time. However, Gabrielle had already served her convent time. Enough was enough, she felt!

By January 1833, Vigny's jealousy over Fontaney, or any man or woman approaching Dorval, had reached new heights. Despite his agonizing fantasies, which happened to be realities, Dorval remained his muse:

> Oh my muse! my Muse! I am separated from you. Separated by living beings who have bodies and make noises. You, you have no body; you are a soul, a beautiful soul, a goddess... (Vigny, 21 Feb, 1833, *Le Journal d'un Poète*, II, 979)

Paroxysistic jealousy took hold of Vigny and all hell broke loose. Not over a man this time, but over a woman. It had been kismet for Sand and Dorval. The two marveled at each other, understood each other, and from this day on, loved each other, powerfully and completely (Ambrière, 258). Sand's midnight visits to Dorval, and worse, that she spent the entire night by her side were unbearable to Vigny. This "monstrous woman deceives her lover for whom she left her husband" (Vigny, *Journal inédit*, 21 Feb, 1833). Despite his frenzied remonstrances, Sand and Dorval would continue their felicitous and sexually intense affair, soon to take on the luster of sincere friendship as well (Baldensperger, 333). Nonetheless, high drama was to inhabit their relationship. After the fiasco of Vigny's *Unscathed, but For Fear,* Dorval basked in sorrow and irritability. During one of her torturous mood swings, she raged jealously over Vigny's courtesies to Sand. When, for example, Dorval returned home with her husband and her three daughters after a performance of *Unscathed, but For Fear,* Vigny courteously saw Sand home. That same night Dorval's fulminating rage against Vigny marked her letter to him:

> I want to inflict any kind of wound on you; find any type of bullet that will pierce your heart, and return to you the torment of this night. (*Histoire de ma vie, Chapt.* IV. Baldensperger, 334)

Vigny, who had accompanied his house guest home for courtesy's sake, was surprised by Dorval's uncalled-for outburst. It served no purpose. By April 22, 1833, as an aftermath to the incident, Vigny noted, regretfully: "When one finds oneself in love with a woman, prior to committing oneself to her, one should ask who her friends are. Determine what her life is like. All future happiness rests on this point (O.C.*Journal*, II, 985).

Vigny's relationship with Dorval was a taxing experience. Moments of forgiveness were followed by love fests; scenes of intense jealousy by recrimination; anger by moving reconciliations, pardons and exquisite periods of intimate love-making. So intense, so audacious had their sexual encounters become that they left Vigny giddy, exhausted, living and breathing his days with inexplicable voluptuousness. Addiction to such moments of supernal pleasure were frequently followed by periods of intense depression and anger, during which he lived and relived each of their encounters in total abandon. Clearly, he was enslaved by Dorval's love-making power and her success as an actress. His masochistic jealousy, at the thought that she had been, and was still, possessed by Sand, as well as by other men, knew no bounds. It could be said, that they were, at times, pleasurably abrasive! Vigny compared his passion to that of a martyr, to that of Christ! He was living out his torture, his punishment, his felicity!

As for Dorval, no matter what her anguish or joy, life went on as did her acting career. On May 18, 1833, she opened in *Edward's Children* (*Les Enfants d'Edouard*) by Casimir Delavigne. On May 21, 1833, she performed in Custine's *Beatricia Cenci* at the Porte Saint-Martin. On May 30, she enthralled her audience at the Opera, in a benefit performance of *Unscathed, but for Fear* (*Quitte pour la peur)*, which Vigny had written and labeled a "proverb" or "bagatelle".

While Vigny alluded to *Unscathed, but for Fear* as a simple work, this brief play, unlike his other writings, was delightful, charming, and scintillating. Its repartces were clever, pithy, and filled with verve, conviviality, and gentle banter. Few could have divined the torture Vigny was suffering when composing this work and attending its rehearsals and performance. His pain was a private affair. It remained so. The banter, litheness, charm, and delight implicit in this work masked his hurt, transcended his morbid world of feeling. The stoic in him had willed it that way. On those occasions when Dorval had been good to him, and their love-making intense, his sense of well-being surged, and his *bonhomie* was miraculously restored. The tongue-in-cheek dialogue, terse humor, and rapid back-and-forth quips in *Unscathed, but for Fear* were unlike anything Vigny had written. So different was this non-ponderous, non-morose, and non-distressed *oeuvre,* that no one would have judged him to have been its author.

Ironically, *Unscathed, but for Fear* might be identified as an early feminist work for pointing up a husband's complete control over his wife's actions in eighteenth and nineteenth century France. While painters from the previous century, such as Watteau and Boucher, garnished the walls of the homes of the rich and famous with their mood-making sensuous country or boudoir settings, fine manners and elegant comportment, Vigny's bagatelle centered on what preoccupied him most intensely at this juncture – the searing question of adultery! Rather than dwelling on the subject in his playlet, *Unscathed, but for Fear*, he chose to emphasize the injustices suffered by women: the man being awarded all the liberties, and the woman, none! This same subject was broached in a flighty and delicious entry in his journal:

> The adulterous wife of 1778 had to fear neither the dagger of the middle ages nor the avenging saber of the outraged National Guard of 1832. It was one of those times of religious and moral confusion where men no longer had any other guide to comportment but their individual feelings of honor or of goodness. Externals, and what was considered suitable, were alone respected then. (May 1, 1833, 988)

In *Unscathed, but for Fear,* Vigny incorporated a story related to him by Princess Béthume, which pointed out a husband's beautiful character trait.

> Mr. X knew very well that his wife had a lover – but events were lived with such stunning decency that he remained silent on the subject. One evening he enters her room – which he had not done in five years.
> She is surprised. He tells her: "Remain in bed. I'll spend the night reading in this armchair. I know you are pregnant. I came here to save your reputation."
> She ceased talking and wept. (Vigny, II. 966)

Unscathed, but for Fear takes place during the reign of Louis XVI. A young duchess is impatiently awaiting the visit of her elderly physician, Dr. Tronchin. No sooner does he arrive than she begins chattering away about her lover, the Chevalier de Malte. No one thinks ill of her, she tells him. She and her lover are invited everywhere together. Should she become pregnant, however, she knows society would shun her.

Dr.Tronchin, looks at her knowingly. The anxious duchess asks him to indicate the nature of her malady in writing. He notes that she "will be a mother in eight months." She is abashed at the thought that the good doctor intends to relay the news to the duke, her husband. Not the least bit angered by the news, the duke informs the doctor that he had married his wife when she was virtually stepping out of convent school, and that he had never felt anything for her. Furthermore, he is in love with a marquise. His exquisite refinement, however, encourages him to visit his wife immediately. He does so at midnight, just as she is about to retire. She is paralyzed by fear at the sight of him. He will certainly kill her, she believes. To stave off such a happening, she takes the offensive and blames him for not having visited her in five years. Not to worry, he replies, as we have seen.

For appearances' sake, he will spend the night seated on a chair in her bedroom. She is both relieved and delighted by his willingness to help her face what would have otherwise been the tortured months of her illegitimate pregnancy.

Well-mannered in every way, this most courteous of courteous centuries accepted any kind of elegant behavior to allay scandal. Keeping up appearances was *de rigueur*. Vigny's surprisingly pro-feminist stand decried the sorrowful lot of married women. Since men were stronger than women, they had "made the laws," which were of necessity "very unjust" toward women, and increasingly so, since they were reinforced under the Napoleonic code and thereafter: if a husband discovers his wife has betrayed him, even if he does not love her, he "must seek revenge." Vigny's humor goes even further. He blames the "coward" Adam, for foisting on Eve all responsibility for his disobedience. Eve, he adds, "will avenge herself" (O.C., II. 681). Vigny must certainly have had Merle, Dorval's complacent husband, in mind when focusing on the theme of flagrant *delicto*.

Jules Janin considered Dorval's portrayal of the pregnant wife fascinating, "truly inspired."

> She speaks about everything in charmingly exaggerated tones. She gets excited about small things, screams, groans, laughs, sighs, and gets angry, all in one minute. She claims she is ill, in pain, cured, feeling well, weak, strong, happy, melancholy, angry, and she is none of these; she is as impatient as a young race horse awaiting the go sign. She stomps in her way, she looks in the mirror, puts on her rouge, then removes it, tries out various expressions, perfects them, vocalizes by speaking her words in high tones and exercises her soul by going through all pitches and their feeling tones. She gets dizzy on theatrical art. She gets drunk on it. (Dupuy, *Les Amitiés littéraires d'Alfred de Vigny, 65 / Débats, 28 January*, 1833)

Sainte-Beuve conveyed his pleased reaction to this *Unscathed, but for Fear* in a letter to its author (June 1, 1833). He was fully aware of its innovative sallies, the finesse of its wit and praised *Unscathed, but For Fear* for its committed stance.

> Your duchess is very charming, ingenuous, coquettish, loving, embarrassing, and a daring philosopher for her ingenuity... Please compliment the duchess on my behalf, so beautiful under her powder and so naturally at ease in this gracious role. (Baldensperger, 340)

The majority of critics, however, failed to understand the profound nature of Vigny's satire: irony, black humor, and compassion for neglected and abused women. (Baldensperger, 340).

Much to Vigny's sorrow, Dorval left Paris on a protracted tour. He had asked her to write to him frequently. She responded flippantly by telling him that her daughter Louise would be in touch with him. He accused her of torturing him. On June 5, 1833, her mood seemed to have suddenly changed. Her letter from Bourg revealed distress. "I have had no letter from you for three days." Following this outburst, their correspondence pursued its tortuous course" (Baldensperger, 341). The desperately busy Dorval wrote few letters. Vigny detailed his sorrow to her at this omission. In his July 4th letter, he underscored the fact that he did not want her daughter, Louise, to write to him instead of her.

> I need your handwriting, the trace of your name on the paper, every single day of my life, your handwriting and only yours, and let no one else come between us. How cruel of you to accuse me, me of all people, of not helping you enough in your career! You know my life, what more could I do. But you will soon see, if you will only trust me, how much I can still do for you. (Baldensperger, 347 / Whitridge, 119)

At this juncture, Vigny's home life was becoming increasingly untenable. His mother had had a stroke, after which she was given to uncontrollable tempers. She despised the very sight of the self-effacing Lydia. Vigny buried his sorrow, his loneliness, and his inability to communicate his love to his mother, or to explain the pain of his existence to Dorval. His financial plight also gnawed at him. But this Dorval knew only too well, having tussled with poverty, homelessness, and inadequate food supplies since birth. While Dorval had lived it, Vigny talked it. As a woman of action, she did not have the capacity nor the time to luxuriate in thought, certainly not in Vigny's particular meditative brand of sorrow – that of the cerebral aristocrat who suffered in silence, who bore his pain like the stoic he was. But did he? Nor did Dorval understand his daily struggle with finances. He supported his family mainly on the sale of his books, at best a difficult task, since medical expenses were high and constant, and funds were never adequate. Nor could Dorval understand why, unlike her other men friends, he never invited her out for dinner. Why couldn't this handsome aristocrat, this well-mannered being, wine and dine her? What she perhaps resented most, was his inability to have her accepted at the Comédie-Française. In the latter case, she simply failed to realize the difficulties involved, namely, the role prejudice played among the members of the august Comédie-Française against Boulevard actresses. Although Vigny had tried his best to have Dorval perform at this prestigious institution – in his translation of *Othello,* and in his play, *La Maréchale d'Ancre* – Mlle Mars and Mlle George were forever being awarded the leads.

His pain was somewhat assuaged upon recalling the times they had spent together, and he had been able to

> review her entire soul, and, after our four hours of kisses and love-making, it opened again as it had before... I ask your thanks a thousand times, my angel, my dear beautiful one, I have found you anew. Your tender repentance erases everything, my child; I entrust you to the charge of your love, *to your happiness and to your kindness!* Never forget this. (July 3, 1833, Baldensperger, 346)

Dorval's departure left Vigny worn, torn, distressed and discouraged. His natural introverted temperament invited him to dig deeply into the world of his feelings.

> For the first time in my life, I feel a secret shame within me. The words that I forced myself to pronounce yesterday outraged me more than I can say. While avenging myself, I cut and wounded myself with the sharp edge of my weapon. That this occurred was horrible for me, and for me alone it is painful.
> Until tonight. (Baldensperger, 347)

On July 4, Vigny writes her in pain and sorrow.

> How cruel it was to accuse me, me! Of not having served you sufficiently in the theater! You know my life. Could I? You'll see henceforth... I beg you, my beautiful Marie, rather than frighten and threaten me as before, do nothing else but reassure me of the future, so that I may think of writing for you. (Baldensperger, 347)

He begs her to write him frequently. The following morning Vigny awakes in tears. For many months now, he had used all of his influence to have Dorval accepted at the Comédie-Française, and he would continue to do so until her dream would be fulfilled.

Whether on tour or in Paris, Dorval's correspondence with Vigny continued, eliciting tears, joy, love, and pain on both sides. On Aug. 23 and 24, 1833, she wrote of her anguish over Vigny's silence. "How happy your two letters made me this morning" (Baldensperger, 354). She realized he was deeply preocupied by his mother's continuously deteriorating health. On August 26, 1833, Dorval writes Vigny a compassionate letter from Rouen. "My angel, you are still so very unhappy? My God how very sorry I am for you. And how can I speak of the theater, knowing how worried you are? Nor am I rich with your letters here...You do not tell me to return. Don't you want me anymore?" (Baldensperger, 354). In her letter of August 27, Dorval detailed the happy news about her performance in *Edward's Children (Les Enfants d'Edouard)* by Casimir Delavigne. Audiences are "in adoration of me...Except they do not want me to make them laugh...They want to remain in a drama modality. For them, I am an imaginary being, an ideal. They want me to remain forever passionate" (Baldensperger, 356).

On August 29, 1833, Vigny reassures Dorval of his love and of his admiration of her as an artist. Nonetheless, she is a tragedian and will remain a tragedian, even if she played one hundred comedies as perfectly as she had *Jeanne Vaubernier* and *The Young Angry Girl(La Jeune femme en colère*) (Baldensperger, 355*).* Vigny worried about the type of plays in which Dorval performed. The first resembled vaudeville, and the second a parade during which "one suffers through the ordeal of seeing you drawing laughter from your audiences by kicking and punching people" (Baldensperger, 355).

While Vigny considered her a brilliant artist, he never failed to give her advice. No matter what theater piece she performed, he maintained that she was a born tragedian and he gave her his reasons for thinking so.

> The gravity of your voice, of your features, of your walk, the natural sadness which inhabits you, everything about you made you a tragedian... If I were you, I would never play another comic role. Do you realize how enthroned you are in the hearts of men, who imagine finding in you an ever dreaming, melancholy, tender, and suffering being. (Baldensperger, 355)

Her two enemies, Vigny maintained, were brashness and anger (cf. Baldensperger, 355 Aug, 29, 1833).

Vigny is distressed over the extension of Dorval's tour in Rouen to September 5, even more so when he learns that Merle intends to visit her. In her letter of August 31, 1833, she tries to placate her lover's jealousy. She thought he was so concerned with his mother's health that he would not mind hearing of Merle's visit to Rouen. Vigny's mounting jealousy brings smiles to Dorval. She responds on September 3, reassuring him. "You know that my husband does not know how to enjoy anything" (Baldensperger, 357). From Rouen, Dorval admits that when reading Vigny's letters her "heart is filled with love, my eyes are filled with tears of joy" (Baldensperger, 358).

Although busy with revivals and new works, Dorval was still adamant about fulfilling a goal she had set for herself years back: to perform at the Comédie-Française. To lure her back from Rouen Vigny wrote to her early in 1834, that he had great news. He was able to realize her dream: he had succeeded in getting her an engagement at the Comédie-Française In return, he wrote, "promise me you are going to be nice to me when you come back" (Whitridge, 121).

Miracle of miracles, thanks to Vigny's intercession, Dorval thus opened at the Comédie-Française on April 21, 1834 in *A Liaison* by Edmond Mazères and Adophe Empis. At best, the play could be labeled mediocre. It was so poor, that Mlle Mars refused to appear in it. On tour in Bordeaux prior to the play's opening, Dorval conceded in her letter of February 4th to Vigny, that *A Liaison* was second-rate, if even that. Nonetheless, she thanked him for his intercession on her behalf, since it meant her debut at the much-coveted theater. But even after working her role as thoroughly as possible, or, as she frequently used to say, "inside and out," she admitted that she had found no redeeming feature in the work. Either she would be "punished" for having accepted to perform in it or Mlle Mars would suffer for not having accepted the role offered her.

Dorval's much anticipated debut at the Comédie-Française was to be a night of nights. Thanks in part to the press releases, many of which Vigny undertook to have written, *A Liaison* created a stir on opening night. The elite of the elite were present: government officials, high society, writers, artists, musicians, and more. It was on this night as well, that, despite the second-rate nature of the play, Dorval was crowned

"Reine du Drame" and made *sociétaire* by the four thousand people invited to the ceremony (Ambrière, 296).

Despite the honor bestowed upon her, Dorval fully understood the mediocrity of the work in which she had performed and the role she had brought to life. More disappointments were in store for her. On April 28, 1834, she was scheduled to perform in a revival of Dumas' enormously successful *Antony*. It had won accolades in 1831, when first produced at the Porte Saint-Martin. It was expected to entertain them once again. On the morning *Antony* was scheduled to open, the powerful government minister, Adolphe Thiers, who had contributed so stunningly to the establishment of the July monarchy, vetoed the production of the play for his own political reasons (Ambrière, 299). Not surprising was Dorval's fury at the interdict, not to speak of Dumas'. Not only did she refuse to perform in a brief revival of *A Liaison* offered her as compensation for her disappointment, but the spunky actress sent a letter to the Parisian newspapers informing them that she had signed a contract to perform in *Antony*, and that, despite the many performances this play had enjoyed, it had now been censored (Ambrière, 299). To save face following the catalytic effect of Dorval's letter, the immensely clever politician that Thiers was summoned Dorval to his office ten days later. He spoke in glowing terms of her talent and asked her to continue performing at the Comédie-Française, which she had failed to do for the past ten days. Thiers compensated her with 600 francs. Dorval returned to work at the Comédie-Française for financial reasons only, for she was featured in relatively uninteresting revivals: undistinguished works, such as *The Mother and the Daughter (La Mère et la Fille)* by Mazères and Empis, *La Fausse Agnès,* and *Misanthropy and Repentence,* to mention but a few *(*Ambrière, 300).

Clearly Dorval's career was foundering. The October 3 issue of *Le Foyer* assessed her situation perfectly.

> What has happened to Mme Dorval since she became a *pensionnaire* or a *sociétaire* at the Théâtre-Français? Didn't Mme Dorval glow even more brilliantly when she attracted all of Paris to the Boulevard? In another two years, this actress will be completely annihilated and forever lost. (Ambrière, 300)

Dorval needed a hit to surface again. Would the possessive, devoted, and passionate Vigny be capable of creating the rich theatrical brew needed to effect unforgettable moments in French theater? Could the subjective passion he was living be projected on stage? Could he transform age-old feelings into sparkling dialogue? Could banal feelings evoke riveting sensations in the hearts of each member of the audience? Only this kind of theatrical miracle could save Dorval's career.

Lest we forget, the first time Vigny had attended a Dorval performance, she portrayed the half-crazed Lady Macbeth. It was then that he declared her a tragic actress. That he now considered her France's top tragic actress demanded more depth of characterization on his part. Vigny knew that Dorval, in whose heart almost all human types were contained, was capable of drawing on her feelings to portray humankind's most subtle inclinations. Her ability to encapsulate feelings – be they love, hatred, jealousy, hypocrisy, intrigue, to mention but a few, and their variables in endless intensities – was equally admirable.

The waiting game was to pursue its course. During the summer of 1834, Dorval went on another lengthy tour of the provinces, spending most of her time in Bordeaux and Nancy. Once again separation caused Vigny much grief.

On November 6, 1834 Dorval opened in *Lord Byron* by Ancelot. She did not think highly of the play which featured one of England's most complex poets – the defiant, melancholy, brooding, idealistic Byron, hero and great lover, who took part in the war of Greek independence and died fever-stricken at Missolonghi in 1824. Ancelot's play was replete with scenes of conjugal fury and passion toward his wife and his mistress, in Venice, then in Greece. Dorval complained. She did not fit the role of Byron's mistress. Nor did Dorval's stage partner, Ligier, find Ancelot's Byron suitable to his personality. Both actors ever so courteously requested a meeting with the dramatist, Ancelot, and the managers of the Comédie-Francaise. Dorval's and Ligier's opinions on the subject were not even considered. The play was performed as planned. Although Dorval and Ligier would have wanted to take advantage of the opportunity of portraying a great poet, they felt it unseemly and in bad taste to reveal some of Byron's sexual escapades on stage while his wife was still alive. *Lord Byron* was, predictably, a disaster. Not because of its lascivious innuendoes, but because it was poorly constructed and superficial. The critics of the *Corsaire*, and the *Figaro* called it empty, devoid of interest. Nor did they allude to it as a play. Rather, it was simply "a conversation in three acts." Dorval's acting, by contrast was, yet, lauded. She proved "that one could make something out of nothing" noted The *Courrier des théâtres*. The *Charivari* called Dorval's acting "admirable and inspirational" (Ambrière, 313).

CHAPTER 7

The fact that Vigny was utterly focused on writing stage pieces for Dorval opened him up to new elements within the mysterious powers of theatrical art. Most alluring to him, and most suitable to Dorval's talents, would be the composition of fully fledged tragedy, interspersed with a variety of on-stage love motifs. While his forthcoming play, *Chatterton,* featured wan and moribund types, perfectly suited to the Romantic formula of the times, its innovative and austere ideas and poetics did not follow a conventional recipe. Violence did not intrude into the plot-line. Indeed, it was virtually non-existent. The play's simplicity was classical; its goal, intensely realistic.

As both dreamer and idealist, Vigny created protagonists that corresponded to the melancholy tenor sweeping France at the time, and to Vigny's own rather morbid personality traits. His ability to interiorize pain espoused a climate of sorrow. The genial idea of interweaving certain *causes célèbres* into the action of his play, served to center the happenings related to social justice and righteousness for all citizens of the land, particularly for creative individuals who tried in vain to earn recognition from an indifferent public. As a feminist *avant la lettre*, Vigny also pointed out the inequities foisted on women in general and on married women in particular. The stoic and aristocrat that Vigny was gave birth to a new hero figure: that of the young poet, Thomas Chatterton, prepared to suffer privation for his art, even to sacrifice his life, to bring the above mentioned causes to public attention.

Vigny's novel *Stello,* written in 1831, centered on the inhumane lot of three failed poets: Gilbert who died of starvation, Chatterton, who was starving and committed suicide, and Chénier, who was killed during France's Revolutionary Reign of Terror. Vigny's play, however, focused exclusively on the "gravity and intensity" of Chatterton's suffering (E. Gosse, *French Profiles*, 4).

Shakespeare's literary presence in Vigny's play may be said to have been striking. Understandably so, since he had been intensely moved, even traumatized, by attending Edmund Keane's performance of

Othello in 1828. Never had such energy, violent emotions, and brio been injected into a role by any French actor. William Macready's realistic touch in *Macbeth* had made a lasting impression on Vigny as well. Nor had he remained unaffected by the powerful unleashing of Charles Kemble's stage personality. Vigny's visits to London added to his enthusiasm and admiration of the bard's work, for it was then that he met and attended Sarah Kemble Siddons' performances. Her rich and warm voice awed him. While translating *Othello, The Merchant of Venice,* and *Romeo and Juliet* into French, Vigny lived and breathed Shakespeare's sensibility. His visceral reactions gained him entry into deeper and grimmer folds of his own and humankind's psyche.

By 1834, Vigny was in such possession of *Chatterton's* emotional and mental world that one understands why he spent only seventeen days and nights of intense work to compose his play. Entrenchment in a world of fantasy, unfortunately, leads some artists to discount the powers that be in the real world. In Vigny's case, the difficulties involved in dealing with the production process affected him deeply. A few days after his play had been presented to the reading committee of the Comédie-Française in August 1834, it was unanimously rejected. Even more invidious, but not surprising, were the reasons for the committee's negative verdict: Vigny's choice of Dorval for the lead.

Boulevard theater, with which Dorval had been associated for many years, was now looked down upon by the elitist Comédie-Française. Hatreds and jealousies among theater folk in general, although vicious, were particularly lethal among the actors in France's most august theatrical institution. Mlle Mars and her cohorts had mounted their cabal against Dorval years prior to *Chatterton's* submission. In fact, Mlle Mars was so astute in her manipulations of committees and *sociétaires* at the Comédie-Française that she nearly succeeded in bringing Vigny's entire enterprise to a halt. Fortunately, the administrator of the Comédie-Française, Jouslin de Lasalle, put a temporary end to her nefarious maneuvers, stipulating that Vigny's play would most, finally, open at the end of January, 1835. Such a positive outcome was due in large measure to the intervention of King Louis-Philippe and his Queen Marie-Amélie, whose reign had begun following the July Revolution in 1830. Nonetheless, the royal couple found themselves facing a delicate problem revolving around their sincere desire to see *Chatterton* performed and their equally sincere wish not to alienate the Comédie-Française, France's *first* theater company. Once the hurdle was cleared, Vigny noted in his *Journal:*

> Chatterton is to be performed. I am standing as I write this note. I find myself calm, convinced that if this drama does not succeed, it will only retard the inevitable success of spiritually-oriented plays.
>
> It is impossible to believe, that six years hence, if one must wait that long, what I wanted to do will not be felt.
>
> Unity, simplicity of action, the continuous development of the same idea. Poetry, philosophy (Vigny, *Journal d'un poète*).

Prior to the opening of *Chatterton* however, *Dorval* was again facing severe economic problems. With a husband and three daughters to support, and never certain of what plays would open and or close, she was forever obliged to go on tour to make up the funds lost during slack periods. A case in point was her three-week tour – from August 10 to September 1 – prior to finalizing arrangements for the opening of *Chatterton*.

What many failed to realize at the time were the expenses involved each time an actress or actor goes on tour – be it in Rheims, Lille, Rouen, Arras, Metz, Nancy, Brussels, or elsewhere. Dorval, for example, required a stage coach, sometimes two, depending on the number of cast members and maids she took with her, the length of the tour, the type of sets, costumes, decors, and sleeping space needed to insure a relatively smooth trip.

Whether performing in the evening and traveling by day, or vice versa, tours were exhausting, to say the least. While Dorval had been accustomed to physical hardships since the day she was born, age and increasing responsibilities seemed to add to the arduousness of each displacement. Lest we forget, making appointments with theater directors, planning future performances, looking over the size and type of theaters involved, intuiting the nature of the varied audiences in order to determine the plays best suited to production - all took up a great deal of Dorval's time. Nor must we discount the hours she spent writing letters to her husband, to her children, to friends, not to speak of those virtually daily missives to Vigny, who complained bitterly of his loneliness, of his jealousy of the men in her entourage and of the many unknowns she would meet *en route.*

While deeply perceptive, the touring Dorval at times misjudged the likes and dislikes of her audiences. She knew instinctively that certain plays, namely, *TheIncendiary, The Tower of Nesle,* and *Antony* would receive deafening bravos, and written criticisms would be replete with such adjectives as "sublime," "remarkable," and "great." When the consensus downgraded her choices of tragedy, drama, comedy, and melodrama, labeling them passé, attendance was sparse, and Dorval's entire venture proved to be a financial loss (Ambrière, 308). So inured was she to her problems that she sometimes failed to see the larger picture denoted: changing tastes required a change of program. What suited one generation, might bore another. The citizens of Metz and Nancy, she learned from bitter experience, were tired of *old-fashioned* romantic theater, with its outrageous extremes, obliging spectators to dwell on the rights and wrongs of each staged relationship, each action, and each facial expression. Entertainment was their goal and not the difficulties involved in probing philosophical, historical, or psychological issues. Some viewers demanded seductive, lyrical, and choreographed operatic works, gauged to beguile and delight them.

Meanwhile, other matters were troublesome to Dorval. Gustave Planche, the literary critic for the important *Revue des Deux Mondes,* began courting Dorval's friend and lover, George Sand. To calumniate Dorval, whom Planche despised, would, he believed, help him win Sand's favors. After concentrated thought on the subject, he decided that his goal would be best achieved by informing Sand of Dorval's "disgusting" Sapphism. His obvious manipulations not only aroused George's merriment, since she had been enjoying a lesbian relationship with Dorval for some time, but to the surprise of all involved, she left for Italy in December, 1833, on a tryst with Alfred de Musset.

Having lost all possibility of seducing Sand, Planche, unbeknown to his good friend Vigny, zigzagged in Dorval's direction, claiming he had grown passionately attracted to her. He brought his case before his latest flame in writing. His ineptitude and flippancy – vowing deep love to Sand and a few days later, to Dorval – aroused the actress' ill-will toward him. In response to his lack of delicacy with regard to Sand and to her, Dorval scoffed at him by passing around the "feverish" love letters he had written her. Cut to the quick, Planche apologized, and asked for their immediate return (Ambrière, 311). Not granted, Dorval informed him, in a charming, but nonetheless sardonic note. She would keep his letters to her as a souvenir of both her "*amitié*" and her "esteem for him" (Ambrière, 312).

When dealing with sick psyches such as Planche's, unpleasant repercussions are usually in the offing. Predictably rancor seethed in Planche. To allay any retributive suspicion on Dorval's part, Planche wrote two extremely laudatory articles on her acting talents for *La Revue des Deux Mondes*. He made up his mind to bide his time and wait for the propitious moment to vent his ire. His "good friend" Vigny, who had purposely abstained from becoming involved in Planche's venal manipulations was, nonetheless, destined to receive the brunt of his mephitic lucubrations. In Planche's sick mind, Vigny, above all others, was the culprit and thus merited punishment. Hadn't he loved and been loved by Dorval? Planche finally vented his ire, jealousy and rage on Vigny alone.

Ill-will, grudges, and dissension have always been rampant in theater: be it in the choice of E.A.F. Geoffroy as Chatterton, Joanny as the Quaker, or Dorval as Kitty Bell in Vigny's drama. Particularly insidious were the insults aimed at Dorval during the rehearsals by members of the Comédie-Française. Elitist to the core, they deprecated this queen of Boulevard theater with gusto and venom. Since they were competitors, they feared her power and popularity. Less understandable was that highly placed government ministers, such as Adolphe Thiers, resorted to these base and uncalled for tactics as well.

One evening, when Thiers happened to run into Vigny in the foyer of the opera, he congratulated the playwright on *Chatterton's* acceptance by the Comédie-Française and for having chosen Mlle Mars to play the lead, though he knew this not to be the case. Vigny corrected him politely by naming Dorval as the star. That King Louis-Philippe, on his way to a ball, also stopped Vigny to congratulate him on his choice of Mlle Mars as lead for his drama, left the dramatist, accustomed to the vicissitudes of fortune, completely unruffled, at least on the surface.

Unlike Vigny, the extroverted and highly volatile Dorval suffered from the cast's hurtful behavior during the entire rehearsal period. Surrounded daily by the snooty and verbally malignant members of the Comédie-Française who reveled in mocking her, be it by ridiculing her accent, her stance, her mannerisms, or by simply avoiding her, knowingly stepping aside as she approached them, or remaining aloof, distant, and cold toward her – Dorval, nonetheless, stood strong. She maintained her calm, at least outwardly, on important issues, most notably her firm intent not to rehearse her last scene in *Chatterton* prior to opening night. To maintain secrecy over what she considered to be her innovative method of falling down a flight of stairs, was crucial to preserving the play's shock factor, thereby clinching what she believed would both make for *Chatterton's* howling success and memorialize the play's finale as well.

Dorval had read rightly into the minds of the cast. As enemies of Boulevard acting techniques, and of her, as its representative, they had planned to do their utmost to subvert the surprise factor she had in store for them. Even more dangerous for her, though she down-played such a possibility, was the physical risk she ran – that of a broken back – should she make one false move down the flight of stairs.

Vigny worked closely with Dorval during this arduous rehearsal period, adjusting scenes to suit her needs, talents, and taste. Her infallible theatrical sense not only helped him to hone certain important aspects of the play's dialogue, but to center it, flesh it out, and articulate matters in accordance with his own tempestuous but controlled inner feelings.

As a play, *Chatterton* gave Vigny the opportunity to vent his spleen against society, and most significantly, against "the Man of Action," the business man, the money-maker, the merchant, the materialist; and to convey his sympathy for the "Man of Art," the poet, the creative individual. The "gravity" of human suffering is at the core of Vigny's play, wrote the English poet, Edmund Gosse (Gosse, *French Profiles,* 4). Its subject, so aptly delivered in the drama, focuses on the "usual and inevitable martyrdom of the Poet, against whom all the rest of the successful world nourishes an involuntary resentment, because he will take no part in the game of action" (Gosse, 4)

Like Vigny, who lived his writings inwardly and who was unable to relate to society's increasing brashness and vulgarity, his protagonist, Chatterton, withdrew into his own isolated world of creativity, with his admonition to society, "Protect us, but touch us not" (Gosse, 20), for only then may the poet retain his ethical understanding of the world and of his own powerfully individual nature.

Other factors in *Chatterton* were equally novel. Unlike romantic drama, such as Hugo's *Hernani,* or classical drama, like Corneille's *Horace,* filled with action, at times violent, at other moments tender, and even *osé,* Vigny's discreet and painful love motif left viewers on the edge of their seats throughout the performance although it had virtually no action. In keeping with French classical drama and to better tighten the play's emotional intensity, Vigny maintained the unities of action, place, and tone. Love was subdued and painful. Rather than assuage the protagonist's anguish, the poet in Vigny's play was invited to suffer his mute passion and martyrdom to the last day of his life. *Chatterton* was premeditated tragedy at its height. First of its kind, it was the drama of "pure thought." In this respect only, it may be considered a type of precursor to Samuel Beckett's stage work.

Vigny's stage piece revolves around the idealistic poet-pariah Chatterton. As the symbol of the creative and imaginative being, he is destined to be crushed by society's materialism and insensitivity. Although Chatterton readily admits to suffering from some type of mental illness, he sees no reason for himself, as a poet, to be forced out of existence. Isn't there a place for poetry in society? He simply asks for leisure, lodgings, and some bread, to be able to compose his writings. He questions the reason behind the need to destroy the world of the dreamer. Rights are accorded to every member of the state, save, seemingly, to the poet. Why should those yearning for reverie be deprived of state support?

Vigny's drama was based on the life of the English poet-martyr, Thomas Chatterton (1752-70), who had been misunderstood, neglected, and rejected by the society of his day. On the brink of starvation and too proud to ask for help, he resorted to poisoning himself. While Vigny's grim play focused on contemporary times, its scope addressed virtually all eras. Rarely had the true artist been appreciated prior to having made a name for himself, if he was ever fortunate enough to do so.

During his bouts of inspirational fervor, Vigny's protagonist, the eighteen year-old Chatterton, spends his days and nights struggling to extract his words, feelings, and "pure" and "rare" passions from within. Although he was one of those who indulged in what he loved most, *his art,* he, nonetheless, lived an excoriating *caveat* as well. He remained apart from mainstream existence. His poetry was misunderstood, and rejected by those interested only in material gain. Even more importantly, he was in debt. For Vigny, the poet was the perfect example of the perpetual martyr.

Audiences learn that, as a boy, Chatterton had been a spendthrift. During his student years at Oxford, he spent his days happily hunting wild boar with his society friends. In his late teens, however, he had had a change of heart and mended his ways. He gave up games and follies, devoting himself exclusively to his one passion, poetry.

As presented on stage, audiences learn that Chatterton, a lodger in the inn of John and Kitty Bell, is literally starving in his cold and fog-encircled garret. The presence of the kindly Quaker, who figures importantly in the play, is reminiscent in function of the ancient Greek chorus: although aware of the happenings, he is unable to avert the coming tragedy. On another level, the Quaker may be compared to the old-time father confessor, who hears out and advises both Chatterton and Kitty Bell, the beautiful, meek, sensitive, reserved, and loving mother of two young children. It is she who reads the Bible, cares for the house, and observes Chatterton, who observes her as well. The mystical relationship the two live out is conveyed in "unarticulated thoughts," revealing the "infinite passion and the pain of finite hearts that yearn" for each other (Gosse, 21,23).

Kitty Bell's husband John, a rich London merchant, is tyrannical, rude, abusive, demanding, avaricious, and cruel to his gentle and subservient wife. His tempers traumatize her and cause her to weep and to tremble. Like a "vulture who crushes its brood," John Bell, as head of the household, is a terrifyingly rapacious force in the home, an ideal foil for those espousing the cause or feminism. Kitty Bell is an object for her husband, a vehicle by means of which his seed may be reproduced, thus allowing him to continue his bloodline. Although inferior, and essentially weaker than her husband, Kitty Bell is capable of tending to his home, to his needs, and to his children who, like their mother, cringe before this mightily unpleasant presence.

Because of Chatterton's devotion to his art, the misunderstood poet lives a pariah-like existence. To add to his agony, he has just been accused of not having authored the "Rowley Poems," which he had been composing since the age of twelve. Adding insult to injury, he has been told that should he wish to earn a living, the Lord Mayor of London is prepared to offer him a job as first flunkey. Chatterton is cut to the quick by what he considers to be a degrading offer which increases his sorrow and limits his alternatives. As a man of "reverie," of solitude, and of intellectual liberty, Chatterton keeps reinforcing his strong commitment to the "martyr" principle that vibrates so actively in his brooding soul. In his agony of sorrow and his fear of being sent to debtors' prison, this aristocrat of the word reaches a stage of such despair that he tears up his manuscript, and, unbeknownst to Kitty Bell, imbibes a slow-working poison, allowing him sufficient time before his death to articulate his love for her, and she, hers for him.

"A dead man is now talking to you," Chatterton tells her. Struck with terror, Kitty sinks down to her knees and prays. He kisses her forehead, then walks up the stairs to his attic room – using the spiral staircase Dorval had kept carefully hidden from members of her cast during the rehearsal period. Moments later, the trembling Kitty Bell hears the thud of a body slump to the floor.

More dead than alive, she walks toward the staircase, clutches the banister and mounts the stairs leading to his room. She stops at the top step, takes hold of the door knob opening into his room, turns it, pushes the door ajar, sees the near-dead Chatterton lying on the floor, and emits a blood-wrenching cry. The Quaker rushes in and takes Chatterton in his arms. Seconds later, the young poet heaves his last breath. While Kitty Bell's scorching scream of terror still resonates throughout the theater, she slumps over in a faint, spasmodically throwing herself backward, falls down the flight of winding stairs, and dies. This sequence, known as Dorval's memorable *dégringolade* scene, made theater history that night. Few realized, save the actress, the serious physical consequences her heroic stage act might have had on her spinal column, had not her fall been meticulously planned, and rehearsed in secret during those long

> Once the intensity of the mood had been spent, Dorval returned to the natural poetic techniques required by her role. When dreaming of her love in some mystical clime, she would caress her words with gentleness, only to descend into the human sphere seconds later, to tend to the more menial tasks of mother and wife. She ran the gamut of emotions, from tenderness to pain, to sequences of melancholia, suffering, and anguish. Her depth of feeling, the variety of poses, smiles, frowns, eye movements, conveying fear and pain, had transformed her into the most accomplished French actress of her day. (Barbier, 71)

No one, but Dorval, Théophile Gautier declared, could have brought such fullness – and depth of being into the role of Kitty Bell. Dorval was a woman transfigured!

One may imagine how the young would-be performers, poets, and painters, seated in the *parterre* – many of whom were poor, undernourished, wan, unpublished, and seeking to make a name for themselves – identified with Chatterton's martyrdom. For them, and for other generations of creative youth, Vigny's stage words rang out clear and true. Hadn't they, like Vigny's desolate hero, experienced rejection of their works by the establishment? It is the latter, Vigny maintained, which determines the destiny of the starving poet.

Vigny's friends surrounded him with praise and adulation in his moment of triumph. The composer, Hector Berlioz, the dramatist, Eugène Labiche, the author Maxime du Camp, poets, such as Alfred de Musset, Auguste Barbier, and Antonie Deschamps greeted him with screams and tears of joy: for he had just depicted the sorrow of those unsung heroes of the written word.

Vigny was idolized. He was living his fantasy. Elation, joy, pride, happiness, and the realization of a dream: that of thought, philosophy, poetics, and love wrapped in one.

Edmund Gosse may have best encapsulated *Chatterton's* thrust and mood, when writing:

> The mystical passion of Chatterton and Kitty Bell is sutble, silent, expressed in thoughts; here were brought before the footlights "infinite passion and the pain of finite hearts that yearn" without a sigh. It is a marvelous tribute to genius that such a play could succeed, yet it was precisely in the huge psychological soliloquy in the third act – where the danger seemed greatest – that success was most eminent. (Gosse, 22)

The redoubtable and frequently acerbic critic Jules Janin, praised Dorval's creativity, deftness, finesse, and force. She was herself an inspiration on stage:

> It was, nonetheless, the eloquent and touching Dorval, who lent her grace and her charm to these paradoxes. She was their soul and their life; she was their finesse and their strength. She was the truly inspired creator, reminiscent of the most charming phantoms that you entertained in your dreams of yesteryear. (Jules Janin, *Littérature dramatique,* 208)

The memory of Vigny's sensational opening night would remain embedded in the hearts and minds of many throughout their lives. A case in point was Maxime du Camp's depiction of Chatterton's opening night, forty-six years after the fact.

> Were I to live ten thousand eternities, I would never forget Marie Dorval and Geoffroy playing Kitty Bell and Chatterton...Marie Dorval could be incoherent, irregular, average, mediocre, or sublime in keeping with the suitability of the role. She spoke from the throat, like Parisians; she had vulgar intonations; but the breadth of her play, of her intelligence, when portraying delicate situations and overflowing passions, transformed her into the greatest dramatic actress I have ever known, including Mlle Mars and Rachel. I obstinately focused my eyes on her: she fascinated me. ...She wiped real tears from her eyes. She suffered all the pains she expressed. I can still see her with her black lace gloves, her velvet hat, her taffeta apron. She manipulated her children like a mother and not like an actress; with rapid movements, sometimes repeating them with her hand, as she did when pushing up a lateral lock of hair that forever fell down on her face. Despite her lusty voice, her tones were at times sweeter than a caress. The expression of contained passion when looking at or listening to Chatterton, of which she was perhaps unaware, stirred her heart, perhaps crushing it. Repressed anguish to the point of admiration...

> I don't remember the exact moment in the last scene, when Kitty Bell collapses and dies, and someone in the audience cried out, "Enough!" The entire audience rose from their seats. Screams of terror, of commiseration and enthusiasm echoed throughout the theater. When the author's name – M. le comte Alfred de Vigny – was proclaimed, the audience remained standing for nearly ten minutes: the men were applauding, the women were waving their handkerchiefs. Never since have I seen such an ovation… (Pierre Flottes, 124).

An important article on *Chatterton*, written by Vigny's alleged friend, Planche, appeared on February 15 in the *Revue des*

Deux Mondes. Who could have suspected such duplicity on Planche's part. His courting of Vigny and of Dorval, his pretence at friendship toward them both had been put aside when writing his ferociously deprecating article on *Chatterton*. With the exception of Dorval, he averred the acting and the play to be below par, due to the playwright's "ineptitude." He accused Vigny of having tampered with the facts revolving around Chatterton's very existence, simply to heighten the thrust of the drama. Planche claimed that Chatterton was "arrogant" and not the unrecognized genius Vigny had claimed him to be (Ambrière, 321). So masterfully planned was Planche's diatribe on the unsuspecting Vigny, that it was clear that his review had been written for the most part prior to the play's opening. Planche's retribution smacked more of venom emanating from a disenchanted lover than of the cool, lucid judgment of a reviewer. By ridiculing Vigny, Planche's monstrously sick psyche must have thought he would win Dorval's favors, and she would detach herself from Vigny. How miscalculated had been his plan!

Vigny's reactions to Planche's deceptive manipulations toward him were accusatory. He believed, to some degree, that Dorval had been in cahoots with Planche, hoping to play one side against the other, in her attempt to win back Vigny's love (Ambrière, 323). It was not to be. Vigny was no longer in a mood to allow himself to be manipulated. He was adamant. He would change his ways, no matter the wear and tear on his psyche. He had grown as a writer. His fame had become a certainty.

In many respects, *Chatterton* was an autobiographical work. Vigny's passion for Dorval transformed her into a beautifully kind sensitive young girl whose misfortune had been to have been brutalized by her husband. Despite her perpetual state of trauma, she found room in her heart and being to live out a mystical love experience in all of its radiant beauty and tragic overtones. Her virtues of character, having been projected by the living Dorval on stage, transformed the ideal into the real. As an actress, she had learned the art of dissimulation. Vigny, the author, believed in the reality of his theater piece. Chatterton, the poet, represented Vigny's sorrow, his sense of isolation. He despaired at the cleavage existing between society's lack of understanding and the finesse and sensitivity of the artist. Although he lived increasingly in his ivory tower, Vigny realized that the poet – the creative individual who lives before his time – would remain a pariah throughout his life. Was Vigny ready to accept such a fate?

Tragedy struck only days later! From the heights of jubilation to the depths of despair, as Goethe had written with such prescience. Strangely enough, however, it was no longer despair that overwhelmed Vigny. It was numbness. Or was it a condition of beatific "calm"? The warmth, understanding, and powerful response of his audience had not only imbued him with a deepened sense of confidence in his talents, but had caused his passion for poetry to be reborn that night. A closeness with his art, with his inner world, had come to the forefront. Everything seemed to be falling into place on that night of February 12, 1835. It was at this moment that he finally realized that Dorval "had been the instrument of his genius" (Flottes, 126). On this night, however, Vigny started to break with Dorval inwardly. He believed himself able to fly on his own; to live on his own. The following morning he wrote to his mother, "I won my small battle. Kiss me, dear mother" (Flottes, 126).

Unable to understand Vigny's sudden coldness and seeming indifference to her on the days which followed, Dorval confronted him. He responded only on April 3, 1835.

> You make me very sad. I can no longer live this way… For the past four years every hour of every day and night has been spent trying to make you happy, and during this time, you seem to have been busying yourself trying to think up new ways of mortifying me, of dreaming up new afflictions you have in store for me. The contrast has become too painful at present…Don't lead your offenses further than my love and my kindness allow. (Letter quoted in Flottes, 126-7)

Unwilling to deprive herself of Vigny's loving relationship, Dorval tried other tactics to win him back. She accused him of courting Sand, of making believe Sand was her rival. Vigny was adamant in his coldness. He felt only pity for her now, or so he maintained. He wrote Dorval derisively, "Poor Marie! Jealous of Sand?" Unable to contain his anger any longer, he told her she was "mad" (Flottes, 127). While her increasingly frenetic and hysterical letters to Vigny attempted ever more blatantly to win back her "angel," they seemed to have had little to no effect on him at this time. Or was he dissimulating his hurt? Still, she pursued her course. Soon there would be a reversal.

By September, 1835, Dorval was on tour again with *Chatterton*, among other dramas. While she performed in Douai and Brussels, Vigny brooded in Paris, unwilling or unable to accept the thought of Dorval's flagrant *man-izing* on tour or whenever the spirit moved her. He needed her. He wanted her with him. His loneliness was unbearable. She must return. One wonders whether Vigny had been capable of really severing emotional ties with Dorval? Or was it his *thinking principle* that had convinced him he had done so? No matter, conflict raged within him!

A year later, in 1836, Dorval was in Lyon. Vigny not only conveyed his loneliness to her in his missives, but to her close friend, the writer, Mme Marceline Desbordes-Valmore: poet, short story writer, actress at the Opéra Comique and at the Odéon, among other theaters. Sensitive to the sorrows of others, having lived so many of her own, she "gently" reprimanded Dorval for having paid so little attention to Vigny. How could it have been otherwise, Dorval questioned. Her need of funds compelled her to continue touring, hoping that Douai, Brussels, Lyon, and other cities would be more receptive to her plays. She could not change her ways. Indeed, no one knew better than she that she was a spendthrift, lavish to a fault. No, she admitted, she had no sense of money, spending it as rapidly as she earned it. Only after everything had been spent, she opined, did she realize the gravity of her financial situation. She vowed to be more frugal next time. She could not alter her ways.

Fully aware of her concerns, Vigny had to deal with his own torments. His sense of utter loneliness when Dorval was on tour could in no way be assuaged by his asthmatic wife and his paraplegic mother, each in her own way sinking ever more swiftly into their miasmic worlds.

New problems aroused Vigny's ire and jealousy. His rival Hugo, jealous of *Chatterton*'s success, made another play for Dorval. This time, he asked her to star, along with Mlle Mars, in his new drama, Angelo, *The Tyrant of Padua*.

To stave off his increasingly morbid frame of mind, Vigny took to taking long walks around Paris. These seemed to have a steadying effect on him. It gave him time to contemplate and probe what he considered to be his moments of sorrow and isolation. It also awarded him the leisure to plan his future writings. To steer his thoughts elsewhere, Vigny began reading the works of the eleventh-century monk and philosopher, Abélard, known for his passionate affair with the young nun, Héloise. It had, coincidentally, appeared in print 1836. He lost himself in the vicissitudes of Abélard and Héloise's sorrows in this passionate medieval tale. He even spent an entire day roaming about the Sainte Geneviève mountain, where Abélard had trodden. He allowed his thoughts to wander back to medieval times: to Paris, with its small, dark, narrow, winding streets, and to the sufferings of the monk Abélard, and his self-castration, a common punishment for sex crimes at the time.

At home again, Vigny's increasing concern over his mother's failing health preoccupied him. Not only had the doctor predicted her end to be imminent, but the seventy-six year-old had suffered a stroke which had left her paralyzed on the right side and intellectually impaired. Thanks to her son's protracted solicitude and love of this demanding and difficult person, she recovered somewhat. During this period, Vigny enjoyed a sense of mitigated well-being at the thought that he had brought her back to virtual normalcy. Her previous onsets of dementia following her many strokes, her uncontrollable temper and the enormous patience required of him to quiet her down, allowed him to live at peace with his martyr's conscience. Nor did he ever stop caring for his asthmatic, invalid wife, who had during these passing years grown so obese that she even found moving around the house difficult. Because of his mother's hatred for his wife, mother and son lived separately: Vigny, with his wife, on rue des Ecuries d'Artois, and his mother, on rue du Faubourg Saint-Honoré. Obedient to his conscience and sincerely devoted – or perhaps emotionally *enslaved* to his mother - he made it a habit of visiting her at least twice daily, sometimes more frequently, thus adding to his already burdensome life style. Nor was having to tend to the family's finances, frequently short-funded, a simple task. The upkeep of the beautiful family estate in the Maine-Giraud, left to him by an aunt, had to be taken into consideration as well.

During these painfully difficult years, Dorval was to disclose to him another facet of her character. Whether in Paris or on tour, always solicitous of her beloved's welfare, and anxious to help him in whatever way possible, she habitually sent him notes during the course of the day. There were times when attempting to apprise herself of Vigny's mother's state of health, she accomplished her mission in the most charming of ways, by hiring a *fiacre* and having the driver stop at rue du Faubourg Saint-Honoré to linger in front of Vigny's mother's rooms. After observing the happenings on the fourth floor apartment, which gave onto the street, she claimed to be able to sense the mood of those within. On some days she even saw Vigny's mother seated comfortably in front of the window taking the sun. On other occasions, Vigny might be seated near his mother, simply talking to her in utter calmness. When concerned about her health, he had taken to pacing the floor. If the scene augured well, Dorval returned home happy as a lark. If she judged her beloved to be anguished and pale, she knew trouble to be in store. On these occasions she sent him notes admonishing him to have courage, strength of character, otherwise

> You will kill yourself and others with you. You owe it to yourself, to your wife, to your friend – to your poor Marie, who lives through you - and finally to yourself, to your glory. You owe your beautiful and great works to sustain humankind. (Ambrière, 272)

Dorval gave body and soul to Vigny. On March 30, she wrote to him from Rheims, where she was on tour, promising to respect his anguish. She wanted to be his friend. Nonetheless, his scenes of jealousy and of recrimination, which, she reasoned, served only to add to his burdens, were increasingly frequent. If he only knew how much she longed to be simply his friend. How good she would be to him. Only then would he begin to see into her innately kind and happy being (Ambrière, 272). She knew he needed time for himself: to study, read, philosophize, and to write poetry. It was his way of turning pain into art. There were moments, however, when the unthinking Dorval would act on impulse and make demands on him: to find new roles for her, new plays, and playwrights, to help her develop her art, and, most importantly, to pay her continually growing debts.

Try as he did, Vigny could not help obsessing over his new rival, Dorval's latest young and handsome admirer, Jules Sandeau, one of George Sand's cast-offs. Not that he had not wanted to believe in Dorval's innocence: he did, but there were lingering doubts in his mind. Jealousy was in both their natures. They would have to make a choice: either accept each other as they were or break all contact. Neither was capable of such *reasonable* action. Vigny mused on the years he had spent loving her, naively believing that she would mend her ways.

Dorval was, nonetheless, touched by Vigny's kindnesses toward her in her times of need. Nor did she minimize his *macho* qualities as a lover. Never would she forget the sexually explicit letter he had sent to her after their four-hour love-making bash. She too knew the meaning of jealousy. The fact that he loved women as sexual playmates sickened her. His encounters, unlike hers, were kept in the dark. Hers were brief, for the most part, and open. She simply loved to be caressed – and the art of love-making was part of her daily fare. When seriously engaged in a love affair, as was the case in her relationship with Vigny, she suffered, pained, and howled inwardly in joy and in sorrow. Sensual to the extreme, she loved Vigny for himself, for his art of love-making. She simply wanted her man about! He, on the other hand, was hurt by her overt and frequent affairs. On April 3, 1835, he let his feelings be known.

> You make me very unhappy. I can no longer live this way. Last night put an end to so many of your calculatingly mean-spirited ways, when speaking to me, in front of your husband in the coldest and most ungrateful of ways… I have never been mistaken about the contents of your nasty, calculating, and egotistical feelings. To reveal your complete ingratitude does not satisfy you, you have to flaunt it in front of the man who most hates me; you have turned it into base flattery for him, undoubtedly so you may simply tell him later, "You see what I said to him..." Ah! I beg you. Don't go any further. Don't allow your insults to go further than my love and my kindness can go. I feel them always watching over you, but in truth and kindness. But in truth, I am beginning to not know how to use them, so powerfully do you repulse me, and how deeply tired I am of this continual struggle. (Ambrière, 327)

CHAPTER 8

December 1835 was a harrowing month for Vigny. It was at this juncture that he discovered Dorval's flagrantly unfaithful nature. Emotional devastation followed. For him, the earth seemed to have pulverized. He could not, nor would not, forgive her. His corrosive grief was all-consuming. In his mind's eye, his beloved had taken on the guise of a venomous, snake-like creature, whose invasive toxins had spread rapidly throughout his body and psyche. She had become a vagina *dentata*: a sinister Eve, a rapacious Delila, whom he would now immortalize in verse.

> Toujours voir serpenter la vipère dorée
> Qui se traîne en sa fange et s'y croit ignorée;
> Toujours ce compagnon dont le coeur n'est pas sûr,
> La femme, enfant malade et douze fois impur!
> Toujours mettre sa force à garder sa colère
> Dans son coeur offensé, comme en un sanctuaire,
> D'où le feu s'échappant irait tout dévorer;
> Interdire à ses yeux de voir ou de pleurer.
> C'est trop! Dieu s'il le veut, peut balayer ma cendre.
> J'ai donné mon secret, Dalila va le vendre.

Poetry served Vigny as both art form and as *catharsis*. It enabled him to convey his pain and rage – his powerlessness – against Dorval, now viewed as a crushingly seductive force. This palliative rid him only momentarily of his fixation. Possessive to the extreme, he sought from her the same kind of *total adoration* he had received from his mother. It was not to be. While aware of Dorval's infidelities toward previous *amorati,* he had expected her to alter her ways once he had declared his love for her. Vigny's despair at the thought of sharing her body with multiple men, particularly with Dumas and Hugo, was unparalleled. Clearly she had become incised in his flesh. Like the ancient Harpies, she was tearing him apart piece by piece. To endure his sorrow, Vigny sought ways to penalize himself, naively believing that punishment would purge him of this lesion-filled canker. Reminiscent of Christian penitents of old, he too resorted to self-flagellation. It was all for naught. The more he whipped himself and cursed his beloved in his poems, the more deeply bound he was to her. So mesmerized had he become by Dorval's aura that even his *heroic* intentions not to visit her at home, particularly with her husband Merle always there, evaporated into thin air. Vigny attended her dinners, her Sunday lunches, her social events, and rarely, if ever, did he fail to appear in her dressing room following a performance.

The poet's hurt, nonetheless, was lacerating. In time, it stained his entire outlook on the world. Vigny's self-protective path encouraged him to turn increasingly inward. Rather than socialize, he withdrew into an ivory tower. His belief in sublime isolation as a cure-all for pain, invited him to pursue philosophical readings, be it of the Bible, Shakespeare, or the stoic Zeno, to mention but a few. Since his youth, he had sought and had found comfort, understanding, solace, spiritual strength, even rapture in intellectual inquiry. Intensely sensitive to human suffering, particularly his own, the stoic in him called upon *thought* to reign supreme in his life. Only in this way, he felt, could he find a *modus vivendi*, which would enable him to transcend his sexual dependency, even, enslavement, to Dorval. While he frequented prostitutes at times and had passing affairs, *no one* had affected him as powerfully as Dorval. Nor had he ever reached such heights of sexual exaltation with another. The *passion* he had lived with her had been all-consuming – a jubilation – experienced in consort with nature, a felicitous and turbulent bewilderment. Unable and unwilling to share Dorval with anyone, Vigny's period of sexual rapture was coming to an end. Passionate self-indulgence was to be replaced by rage, by periods of penitence and isolation. Stoic morality, to which he now clung with such adamancy – that of performing one's duties in life – would allow him to live in accordance with his dicta, but not in harmony with his nature. While he struggled to adapt to society and overcome his great sorrow, the knowledge of Dorval's continuous infidelities opened up a deeper fold of his psyche: the stoic's belief that "Silence alone is great… all the rest is weakness."

While trying to dominate his clamorous emotional upheavals, his control over his emotional world had slackened at times, inviting his charismatic utterances to grow strident. He ululated his pain, both in his scenes with Dorval and in his letters to her. Most agonizing to him at this time was the thought that she was to act on April, 19, 1835, in the première of Victor Hugo's latest play, *Angelo, the Tyrant of Padua.* Wasn't it a well-known *secret* that Hugo and Dorval had had a sexual *entente* back in 1829, prior to, during, and following the rehearsals and opening of his verse drama, *Marion de Lorme* at the Comédie-Française? Could, or should he expect her to alter her behavior at this jucture? After all, was not Hugo the lady's man *par excellence*? He, above others, knew just how to win favors from the opposite sex. Vigny was seething at the opening of *Angelo, the Tyrant of Padua.* Not that he did not want Dorval to triumph as an actress. To the contrary, he had always wished her well. Indeed, he was thrilled when dramatists such as Casimir de la Vigne adulated her for her superb performance in his play, *Edward's Children.* Dorval's theatrical ventures, be they in Vigny's *Chatterton* or in Dumas' *Antony,* had been unique: each in its own way, a stepping stone toward a greater understanding of the performing arts. Much to Vigny's dismay, however, each time she appeared on stage she seemed to attract more and more men to her orbit. How could it have been otherwise, he reasoned. Dorval radiated personality, charm, and her very own brand of sensuality. Who could, or would even want to, resist her?

Most recently, the painter, Célestin Nanteuil had fallen in love with Dorval. It was easy bait in his case, for he had been called upon to work on the sets of Hugo's *Angelo, the Tyrant of Padua.* He sent her passionate love letters. For her, however, their affair was but a minor *passe-temps*! To work with Hugo was optimum! One of France's great lyric poets, whose *Odes and Ballads* (1828) had earned him esteem, and whose play, *Hernani,* had brought thousands of youths into the Romantic movement, had been and was again to be, a volcanic experience for Dorval. Hugo's novel, *The Hunchback of Notre Dame* (1831), resurrecting the essence of medieval life and times in France, had won adulation from critics and readers. Singled out was his capacity for tenderness, compassion, and sensitivity, directed most specifically to the deformed, the poor, and the disenfranchised. That same year of 1831, Dorval had starred with brio in his play, *Marion Delorme* at the Porte Saint-Martin. Their working friendship had been not only artistically sound, but had gone far beyond professional bounds. From the very outset, Dorval and Hugo had not only been genuinely attracted to each other, but had bonded. Each enjoyed the other's company. He was attractive, dynamic, charming, imaginative, and exciting to her. She was spirited, articulate, and a master at love-making. Their sensitivities again coalesced. The instinctive Dorval knew exactly what to expect from the instinctive Hugo. Unlike the rigid and ponderous Vigny, Hugo had charm, humor, and levity. He was a born lady's man in every sense of the word. He knew how to attract and to cradle them in his arms. He listened to them, was understanding of their needs, jocular when appropriate, loving and tender when called for, gentle and firm when need be. Dorval enjoyed his talk and admired his genius and charm. As the perfect lady's man, he knew what she liked to hear and did what she liked to have done. They captivated each other. That harmony reigned between them became quite apparent during the rehearsals of Hugo's *Angelo, the Tyrant of Padua*.

Despite Dorval's seemingly amenable and conciliatory behavior during the pre-performance run-throughs, problems cropped up from the very outset. Since Hugo's play called for two female leads, he had understandably chosen Dorval to play Tisbé, Angelo's flamboyant courtesan, and Mlle Mars to play Catarina, the tyrant's faithful wife. While Hugo's decisions in these matters almost always prevailed, a spirit of contrariness on the part of Mlle Mars broke out almost immediately. The well-connected and much adulated Mlle Mars, one of the Théâtre-Français' glories, and known to have been Napoleon's favorite actress, insisted on playing Tisbé. Under these circumstances, Hugo felt compelled to yield to her wishes in spite of his strong reservations. First and foremost, Mlle Mars was fifty-four years old and no longer the slim, sensual, and vibrant woman she had once been. Given her age, he asked himself whether it would not be a mockery for her to portray the lush concubine called for in his drama, when Dorval was ideal for the part. The wise *entrepreneur* that Hugo was, decided to opt for political correctness and complied with Mlle Mars' wishes on this issue. Furthermore, he despised theatrical sparring, which he considered unproductive and certainly deleterious to the project at hand. Aware of Hugo's predicament, Dorval acquiesced.

That Dorval had been relegated to playing the role of Angelo's chaste, *ergo* dull wife, while shocking to some, in no way perturbed the actress. She had such confidence in her histrionic abilities and such imaginative reserves hidden within her larder of endless characters, that she instinctively *knew* she could not only handle the part assigned to her, but would make her portrayal of Catarina the centerpiece of the drama.

A minor problem, however, still remained to be ironed out. Hugo's mistress, Juliette Drouet, although a beauty, was less than a mediocre actress. In fact, she had once been nearly booed off the stage. That she was financially dependent on her lover simplified matters for Hugo. Minutes after she asked to play one of the leads, Hugo informed her unflinchingly that casting had been completed.

Throughout the rehearsal period Hugo was impressed by and grateful for Dorval's malleability, her ingratiating ways, her intent to please him, and most importantly, for her in-depth understanding of the play. Her responses and imaginative suggestions with regard to certain difficult scenes in *Angelo* were equally impressive. That she seconded him on specific cuts and rewrites and complimented him on the appropriateness of others, made for an atmosphere of congeniality which reined a good deal of the time. Unlike Dorval, Mlle Mars was adamant concerning certain deletions, additions, and emphases which she urged on Hugo. On occasion, her surly outbursts clashed with his intents. She might have reasoned that she too had the right to express her thoughts on the manner in which specific scenes should be played. After all, was she not still a great star? It is averred that, to make matters even more unpleasant, during a rehearsal of one of Dorval's key scenes, Mlle Mars placed herself, "like a jealous wall," in front of Dorval, thus depriving future audiences of seeing her rival in her momentous scene of agony. Aware of her ploy, the outraged Hugo spoke out unequivocally. Known for her rapid repartee, Mlle Mars replied forthwith, that he was "more of a tyrant than his Paduan Tyrant" (Ambrière, 331).

Hugo's *Sturm und Drang* dramas, replete with dungeons, vaults, tombs, multiple plots, and heroic adventurers, were usually interwoven with political, social, and satiric innuendoes. His *Angelo* was no exception. It played up the ruthless and despotic actions of rulers, the piteous lot of the poor, the disenfranchised, and the suffering of maltreated women. His stage works were known for their radiant poetic lyricism and their charming dialogue, for instance those between the young lovers in *Angelo*. Memorable as well was the adroit and gripping suspense he knew how to engender in his viewers.

Angelo, the Tyrant of Padua dramatizes the misfortunes of "two grave and pained" actresses: Angelo's faithful, self-abnegating, and noble wife, Catarina, who, by dint of her proper marital status is accepted by society, and his equally trustworthy, virtuous, and gentle courtesan, Tisbé, who is rejected by the class-conscious community because she lives out of wedlock. While both women are in love with the handsome Rodolfo, neither one knows his preference. No sooner does Tisbé discover that Rodolfo has eyes only for Catarina, than she succumbs to devastating anger, followed by pain. Rather than inflict scenes of jealous rage upon her rival, however, this "noble" woman opts to help Catarina fulfill her yearnings. Only at this stage of emotional development, Hugo maintained, may real love rise to its purest heights.

Hugo's stereotypical tyrant Angelo, convinced that his wife, Catarina, has been unfaithful to him, orders her to reveal her lover's name. Should she fail to do so, she would be decapitated. Outwardly composed, but inwardly terrified, Dorval's Catarina stands strong as she denies the accusation, never shuddering, never fearful, nor faltering in her resolve to live out her decision, no matter what possibly horrific consequences await her. When alone or with Tisbé, Catarina yields to her fears – weeping, praying, and shuddering. The scale of Dorval's verbal tonal effects, ranging from *crescendos* to *diminuendos*, conveys her character's increasing or diminishing surges of inner resolve and mounting terror.

That Dorval had sung opera and operetta since childhood, and still did when a role demanded it, enabled her to once again call on her musical expertise to not only convey tonal beauty, but hyper-emotional character traits in the multiple mood sequences called for by her role. When, for example, she valiantly sought to maintain her composure when facing Angelos's dictates and threats, particularly his accusation of infidelity, Dorval's voice grew firmer, her words increasingly resilient, and her tones huskier. Rather than shouting or crying out her feelings, she spoke them movingly and candidly in her attempt to sway Angelo's suspicions. Her periods of reasoned restraint, alternating with moments of unleashed horror served to not only intensify her truth in this matter, but to reject any thought of conforming to her husband's accusations. The verbal onstage sparring sequences with Angelo, revolving around Catarina's infidelity, were so powerfully under Dorval's control, that even while enraged to the extreme, she never divulged her great passion for Rodolfo.

Only during Tisbé's secret visits with Catarina did she confide the disgust she felt for her venal persecutor. The realistic and compassionate Tisbé, who had been present at Catarina's disavowal of Angelo's imputations, feared for the latter's life. She knew from past experiences that no one daring to countermand the tyrant's orders had escaped unpunished. Tisbé mounts a secret plan to help Catarina. Moments later, Angelo hands Tisbé a silver vial destined for Catarina, who conspicuously casts it aside. In a pitiful mode this time, Dorval's now barely audible tones declare both her innocence and her fear of death. The adamant Angelo, having lost his patience, now wills to have Catarina stabbed to death. Such is Hugo's way of revealing to his audiences the magnitude of the Paduan tyrant's cruelty.

Dorval, known to have her own startling and inimitable way of creating theatrical climaxes, takes center stage and heroically rejects her husband's orders, after which she launches into an unprecedented and unforgettable *coup de théâtre*! She gets down on her hands and knees and drags herself half way across the stage, howling all the while as she begs for Angelo's mercy! The audience is aghast by her mood change! Not a sound is heard in the theater!

Dorval's stunt was unacceptable, however, to one member of the cast. During a rehearsal, Mlle Mars lashed out at her rival. In an attempt to derogate what she considered to be Dorval's cheap acting stunt geared to attract attention to herself, she told Hugo in all of her condescending arrogance, "As for myself, I don't perform tragedies on all fours" (Ambrière, 331).

Meanwhile, the play must go on and the altruistic Tisbé, unlike the self-centered Mlle Mars, learns of Rodolfo's love for Catarina and devises a way of saving her erstwhile rival. Time is running out but not sufficiently rapidly to prevent Hugo from inserting a passionate, albeit tawdry, scene between the lovers. Tisbé wisely warns Catarina to remain mute on the subject of her lover and in barely audible tones, tells her to drink the poisonous brew she will soon be handing her. The trusting Catarina whispers her gratitude to Tisbé in mellifluous tones.

Forewarned by Tisbé, who remains on stage throughout the scene, no sooner does Angelo hand Catarina a vial of poison, than

Dorval, a master in the art of hesitation, slowly takes the lid off the vial and looks at it suspiciously. Suspense having reached its height, she raises the vial slowly toward her mouth. Seconds pass. Dorval hesitates. Her expression, ranging from dread to uncertainty, gives way to one of determination. She drinks the brew unflinchingly and apparently dies moments later. Angelo orders his henchmen to carry Catarina's corpse down a secret passageway to be placed in one of the innermost vaults of his palace. Once the deed is done and the tyrant's departure assured, Tisbé returns to the vault, hands these same men a pouch of gold, orders them to countermand Angelo's directives, after which she arranges for a horse-drawn carriage to take Catarina away. Rodolfo, who serendipitously arrives at this moment, believing Catarina to be dead, accuses Tisbé of having planned her murder. In a sudden and unexpected but predetermined mood change, she ejaculates her words. "Yes, I hate this woman," she screams. "I hate her. Yes, you were told the truth, I avenged myself, I poisoned her. I killed her!" (Hugo, *O.C.*, 675). "What I did, I would do again," she rages. Unknown to Rodolfo, however, there was a reason for Tisbé's verbal outburst. Once she had learned that Rodolfo had eyes only for Catarina, life had no longer any meaning for her. She wanted to die. Her goal was to bring Rodolpho to such a crescendo of rage that he would kill her.

Tisbé implements her character's on-stage maneuverings by pointing to the dagger Rodolfo clutches. She incites him, she taunts him to stab her in the heart. "Stab me," Tisbé cries out (Hugo, 675) The heightened rhythmicality of this mobile scene reaches a climax as Rodolfo swoops down on his victim and impales her with venomous bravura. Tisbé falls to the ground. "What I did, I would do again!" he proudly announces" (Hugo, 675). Whereupon, Tisbé takes his hand and most lovingly thanks him for delivering her from an unbearable life.

Seconds later, Catarina's mellow voice flows into the atmosphere. Overjoyed at the sight of his beloved, Rodolfo runs towards her and embraces her. He asks who had saved her life. Before uttering a word, Tisbé's now frail, barely audible voice, emerges as if from the dead, to utter words that subsequently became famous: *"I did, for you!"* (677).

Unbeknownst to all assembled, Tisbé had been the architect of the plan that saved Catarina. She had deceived the tyrant by substituting a sleeping potion for the poison Angelo had intended for Catarina. The guilt-ridden Rodolfo kneels before the saintly Tisbé. Gathering her last bit of strength, she tells the lovers to "Flee immediately. In three hours you will be outside the state of Venice. Be happy." (Hugo, *O.C.,* 677). Dorval's Catarina stands transfixed.

The theater-goers' frenzied applause continued on. Many in the audience wailed, others grieved. Each in his or her way was transfixed by the power of the emerging feelings and horrified at the violence of the killings, the heroics and audaciousness involved in the bloody on-stage murders. Particularly impressive was the scope of Dorval's flawless acting: the multiple mood tones she ushered into her stage play, the fears she instilled in others at the prospect of her excoriating fate. Her infrequent strident tones, like involuntarily stabbings, and her passionate embraces, punctuated the atmosphere. The empathetic effects emanating from her dialogues ran the gamut of emotions – from searing, to loving, to supplicating, to despising, to passionate. The pacing of her words, timed to play up the mood of the moment, be it condescending, murderous, vulnerable or treacherous, reached peaks of frenzy. Dorval's chaste Catarina even blanched at critical times, particularly at the outset of the play, when she is still naive and ignorant of the manipulations of highly placed and sophisticated government officials. Only after the audience becomes aware of Tisbé's sacrifice do Catarina's roaring verbal crescendos reveal the magnitude of the courtesan's sacrifice.

Hugo's wife, Adèle, described how her husband was received by the nearly hysterical Dorval in her dressing room after the play.

> Mme Dorval had lost complete possession of herself, she was drunk, she had just removed her clothes, her *chemise* virtually *alone* remained, as she lunged toward the author's neck, had him sit down, and sat on his lap, caressing him all about, saying to him: "You are my author, I love you, my great author." She conveyed such grace in her abandon that this grace acted like a chastity belt. (Ambrière, 333)

While Hugo was beaming on this night, Vigny was seen prowling around the theater. Bitterness was incised on his features, for he must certainly have been told of the warm, understanding and tender relationship existing between Hugo and Dorval prior to, and during, the rehearsal period. That Dorval and Hugo had seen eye to eye was her way, she might have told Vigny, of helping a director resolve whatever disputes might arise with Mlle Mars or other members of the casts. Vigny sorrowed. He knew Hugo and Dorval to be partners who worked as one!

Strangely enough, Dorval's and Hugo's relationship had been made even more secure and secretive thanks to Célestin Nanteuil's adoration of Victor Hugo. Although it had been he, paradoxically, who had loved Dorval, once he realized that she did not return his passion but loved Hugo, at least for the moment, he served as epistolary intermediary between the poet and the actress. In one of Nanteuil's letters to Hugo, we read:

> My dear Mr. Hugo, I have just this instant left your Catarina who would very much like to speak with you about several matters and many others. On what day will you have a few moments to sacrifice to her? It is for this reason that I ask you to be good enough to answer me forthwith, if this is possible. (Ambrière, 334)

Other circumstances fueled Dorval's and Hugo's relationship. Most notable was their desire to work together at the Comédie-Française. As for love-making, it could be said that Hugo had met his match in Dorval. The two went well together, for a while at least, until critics averred that Hugo was a great poet and story-teller, but only a mediocre playwright. As for Mlle Mars and her despised rival, Dorval, neither actress was finally sorry when the curtains fell on *Angelo, the Tyrant of Padua,* for the last time on July 20, 1835.

The same could be said of Vigny. His confirmed jealousy of Hugo, particularly vis-à-vis Dorval's relationship with the master, aggravated his already jaundiced outlook on life. The crystallization in his mind's eye of Dorval's and Hugo's love-making seared him like a branding iron. She belonged to him, he affirmed. She was anchored to him. Like a *mother* he expected her to cling to him. Nothing else was acceptable to the intransigent, tight-lipped and restrained Vigny! As for Dorval, who had made her own way in life since childhood, she was like a bird in the wild, not only refusing the cage, but unaware of its very meaning!

But, although Dorval did at times romp and frolic, she was not spared her share of excoriating sorrow. The joys of an adolescent love experience between her daughter Gabrielle, and the young poet, Fontaney were to have dire repercussions. The charming but naive Gabrielle, who had nurtured fantasies of becoming a successful actress, had been warned by her mother that talent and beauty without training did not ensure stardom. She refused to take heed of her mother's wise admonition. Gabrielle and Fontaney left secretly for London. Predictably, she failed to find work. Nor did Fontaney succeed as poet or as journalist. Indeed, he grew bored writing articles about England and its arts. The couple experienced their rude awakening once their meager savings had run out.

London's damp and cold climate had not helped matters. Tragically, the pallid and frail Fontaney developed tuberculosis. As for Gabrielle, prone to sore throats, she became so run down during her stay in England, that she caught her lover's illness. Dorval wailed when told the news. Upon the couple's return to Paris in mid-July, 1836, the beautiful Gabrielle took to her bed.

Dorval's great lover, George Sand, did not refrain from accusing Fontaney of thoughtless behavior. He never should have eloped with the poor girl, she insisted harshly, unless he had the means to care for her. So angered had Fontaney become with what he considered to be Sand's hypocritical "moralizing," that he wrote a strong article in the *Revue des Deux Mondes* "railing about her pretentiousness" (May 1, 1836. Antoine Fontaney, *Journal Intime,* (Jasinski, xxvi).

Gabrielle died on April 15, 1837. Fontaney's increasing suffering, mainly the guilt he felt for not having married his beautiful Gabrielle, who according to him would thus have known "supreme joy," had become virtually unbearable. To allay his sense of culpability yet justify his stay in London, he told himself over and over again that he had tried his best to acquire the necessary papers to make her his wife, but had failed to pursue the matter to its conclusion. Sand took to exacerbating his sense of guilt by hammering away at him, accusing him outright of infecting Gabrielle with his malady, thus blaming him for her death. Fontaney, nonetheless, defended himself in his *Journal Intime,* against her accusations. Because Gabrielle had been "the victim of wretchedness and despair," he wrote, she had been "overcome" by illness in just a few weeks, (Fontaney, *Journal Intime,* xxviii). He further stressed her dangerous ill-health prior to their departure. "I sobbed in the arms of my angel; and the poor child tried to console me" – "She lacked nothing. She is not to be pitied. She knew how life used to be when she lived under her mother's roof – deprived of stockings, shoes, and other essentials" (Fontaney, *Journal Intime,* xxix).

Fontaney died two months later, on June 11. He was buried beside Gabrielle in the Montparnasse cemetery. "In vain may people search for their two names: their tombs, which poverty could not render durable, have today disappeared" (Ibid, xxxi).

While devastated, the incredible trouper that Dorval was went on with her life!

As the clock struck midnight on December 31, 1836, Vigny got down on his knees as he had once a year since childhood, kissed his mother, and wished her a happy New Year. Upon looking at this eighty-year-old woman with love in his heart, he had the auspicious feeling that she would live out another year and was thus comforted at the thought that he was and would remain his mother's adoring son.

A year later, Vigny experienced a lasting – but not his last – sorrow, with the passing of his beloved mother on December 19, 1837. Rather than being grateful for having had her so many years, he simply went to pieces. Compounding his great loss were Dorval's continuing infidelities which not only wounded him to his depths, but divested him of his pride, hope, and passion. He felt as if "the earth had given way under his feet." His world had crumbled before his very eyes. He prayed for hours in front of his mother's casket and rejected all thought of consolation. Pain, tears, and sobs invaded every segment of his being. "I no longer have her," he cried out (Flottes, *Alfred de Vigny,* 168). Nor did his sorrow cease after her burial. He visited his mother's grave regularly, dreamt of her on April 25, and wept. He frequently thought of the sage advice she had given him back in 1815, when she warned him against frequenting actresses:

I shall say nothing about this type of woman, who is as rightly disdained for her circumstances as for her mores; I am talking about actresses; I truly hope you will never see them except at the end of opera glasses, and that you will never speak to them." (Flottes, 170)

Because he had disregarded his mother's words of wisdom, he found himself hounded by guilt. He again wrote of flagellating himself, of perpetrating other physical cruelties on his body, as was the habit of so many saints to prove their faith. Certainly, Vigny, the stoic, was a masochist. What disturbed him most crucially was his inability to break with Dorval – whom, we have seen, he had identified at times with the harlot Delila, thereby admitting a humiliating truth that flesh *had won over spiritual values*. During his six-year on again-off again relationship with Dorval, he had never succeeded in inuring himself to the lie he was living. Never had he been willing to face the truth of his own hypocrisy. Since his mother's demise, he was hounded by such abrasive feelings of guilt that the very thought of his love-making scenes was destroying whatever peace of mind he might have enjoyed.

One single irremediable event in his life proved to be far more painful to him than all others: that he had let his mother spend the hours prior to her death alone. In his Journal, and to the world at large, he claimed that he had been out until midnight completing some late shopping for New Year's day, when in fact, he was enjoying sexual pleasures with Dorval in the little room he had rented for this purpose (Ambrière, 413).

While reviewing his mother's last moments of life, he noted in his diary:

> Happy and sweet at dinner time, she kisses me, and then prepares to retire. As for me, I am getting ready to go out to buy a few last minute presents for the New Year. I return at midnight. She hears me pass and calls to me. I go to her. She complains of being too hot, then too cold, of pain throughout her body. "*I don't know what I have,*" she says. (Vigny, *Journal*, 1089)

He places an eiderdown coverlet on her feet. Her pulse seems slow. He rings for her personal maid. His mother's groans grow increasingly significant. He calls her companion, then others in the household. Shortly thereafter, Vigny fetches the doctor. They return around two in the morning. Moments later, she was in her death throes!

"Mother! Dear mother!, a word to your Alfred, your son who loves you, who has always adored you"! (Vigny, *Le Journal d'un* *poète,*1089). She squeezes her son's hand. Her head drops on to her chest. Life had ceased (cf. Vigny, 1090).

Immediately after having been apprised of the news on December 20th, Dorval wrote to Vigny with the tenderness and solicitude characteristic of her during moments of empathetic pain. For she did love Vigny lastingly and profoundly, albeit in her own way. She was a woman with heart!

> Alfred, Alfred, my poor friend! No words can convey your sorrow. Know only, that I share it with you deeply... I beg you to try to let me know in what state you are, and whether I can count on your strength to preserve your dear health. You understand my concern... *and my remorse,* dear angel! (Ambrière, 413)

The key word, in Dorval's note was, *"remorse."*
Another missive from Dorval:

> Yes, dear Alfred, I prayed for you, for us. I well understand your pain, I who so loved your mother... You must follow your heart's inclinations, and give vent to your regrets... No, you must not return to that room. I realize that fully! I'll look for another one. (Ambrière, 415)

The drama of trauma, of inexorable guilt feelings, and the horror of his comportment was about to unfold! Unable to bear his own culpability *vis à vis* his mother, who had rejected actresses *in toto*, Vigny was now prepared to resort to the most painful of all chastisements, that of depriving himself of Dorval. His sense of utter bereavement encouraged him to follow his mother's dicta by summarily cutting Dorval out of his life. To cleanse himself of everything that was associated with her was his goal – their rented room in which they made love, in particular. Like Adam, who labeled Eve the evil temptress, instead of blaming the Fall on his own weakness, Vigny would do likewise: cleanse himself of Dorval, thereby assuaging himself from guilt. The mere thought of Dorval had seemingly become repulsive to him. She lacked his *sensitivity.* She had never understood the *meaning* of love. Vigny begs God to assure him that his mother sees and feels his pain, and that she rests content (Ambrière, 415).

Vigny even castigated Dorval for not being sensitive to his unmitigated sorrow and for not giving him the time to deal with his pain. He must be allowed the liberty to mourn for his mother as he saw fit, he told her, and most importantly to begin dealing with his guilt toward the virtually sanctified woman who had given him life.

The deeply affected Dorval, while unaware of Vigny's intellectualized philosophy of pain, restraint, and self-flagellation, kept writing letters of condolence to him. Her sorrow for his mother had struck her deeply. As a woman of feeling, she sought to share Vigny's pain with him. What she failed to understand was the powerful urgency of his anger toward himself, his guilt, his sense of doom, his masochism.

Jealousy marked her world as well. She was still in the habit of hiding opposite his home, to observing the goings-on in his house from the outside. She had learned that he was seeing other women, thereby perpetrating another cruelty against her. By January 3, she bewailed his silence. She asked for another meeting. She needed her "angel!" As fate would have it, when Vigny did finally call on her unannounced, she happened not to be home. They met, however, on January 11. Passion again took over, only this time the *heart* was no longer to be found! It was over.

Vigny's scourging of Dorval – for what he considered to ber her hard-heartedness, her use of people, her promiscuity – was not only evident in his *Journal,* but would play an even more prominent role in his poems.

Dorval, still mourning the death of her Gabrielle and increasingly preoccupied with her two other daughters whom she was supporting, neither understood Vigny's sudden coldness toward her, nor his projection of Evil on to her.

With each passing day, he looked upon her soul as increasingly base and material, the antithesis of spiritual. A believer in the double standard, he considered her continuous philanderings, her sexual adventures, her belief in sex for its own sake, her one night stands, unpardonable. Only one solution was left him: to sever relations with her and devote his hours and days to the hard work of writing.

Failing to understand Vigny's change of heart toward her, Dorval wrote him about her problems with her daughter Louise, who was now pregnant by the twenty-five year-old Félix Bibet, an engraver without a steady job. But her great and everlasting sorrow was the loss of her beloved daughter Gabrielle.

In many ways Dorval was naive. A case in point was the comportment of her allegedly close friend Pauline Duchambge, whom she introduced to Vigny to soothe and calm his anguish during her latest tour, which lasted from June 1836 to June 1837. This insidious gossip-monger, rather than placating Vigny, wrought havoc with their relationship. Little did Dorval realize that this false friend was not only maligning her but falsifying facts, deprecating Dorval in the subtlest of ways. Hadn't she been the one to stir Dorval's jealousy when she reported to her during her tour that two lovely American ladies, the Battlegang sisters – friends of Vigny's wife Lydia – who had come to France with their mother to study, were living temporarily in Vigny's home? One of them, the twenty year-old Julia, the same age as Dorval's daughter, Louise, was particularly beautiful. She was told that Vigny enjoyed looking at Miss Battlegang paint in the *atelier* he had rented for her on rue Saint-Louis in the Batignolles area of Paris (*Georges Sand et Marie Dorval, Histoire d'une correspondance,* 43). Although Pauline Duchambge attempted with all of her might – so she claimed – to break up the couple, she failed to do so.

Still on tour, and still jealous of Vigny's roving eyes, Dorval wrote him a relatively angry letter, "promising him" she would remain calm and not weep at the thought of his infidelities and abandonment of her (Ambrière, 418). What Dorval did not know at the time was that Julia Battlegang, at twenty-one years of age, had already given herself to the poet. Meticulous in every way, Vigny made note of the incident in his diary.

Duchambge attempted to destroy the reputation of other friends of Dorval, including that of Marceline Desbordes-Valmore, the delightful poet, author of short stories, singer at the Opéra-Comique, praised and helped by such giants as Hugo, Lamartine, and Sainte-Beuve. Vigny had met her and her husband as a youth, when still in the army. Although they hadn't seen each other for years, their friendship still held. Indeed, Vigny considered her the "greatest feminine mind of her day" (Ambrière,, 379). It had even been rumored that Vigny had fathered one of her children. So close had Dorval's friendship been with Valmore, that Dorval's daughter

Caroline used to play with Valmore's daughter Marceline at the latter's home. Seemingly they were all compatible.

Time seemed to assuage misfortune, for when Dorval and Vigny met on January 11, 1837, they were in each others arms in a matter of minutes. Once again sexual ardor prevailed. She called him her Hercules. Not that mutual recriminations, hurt, and pain were not articulated. He castigated her for having taken the young and handsome Jules Sandeau, among others, as a lover. Her denials were immediate. She did not even love him. Reconciliation prevailed, but not for long. Unconvinced of her innocence, Vigny ordered a coach and driver on June 17 to follow Dorval at 3 in the morning. When her coach stopped at rue du Bac where he knew Sandeau to live, his sense of betrayal had been confirmed. Hurt again dominated. This time, however, he was even more determined to sever relations with Dorval.

Dorval's reaction to Vigny's stand was heart-rending. It would be impossible for her to separate herself from him. She was part of his being, forever linked to him! He must absolve her, she cried. He must forgive her! Each time she hammered away at the word "forgive," her voice grew increasingly strident, guttural and grating. "Forgive," she bellowed again and again "Forgive." She begged him to return to her home the following night. He did so, but by this time had grown weary of the masquerade: the scenes of jealousy, repentance, anguish, were being played out too frequently for his taste. Every act of hers and – one might add, of his as well – had become predictable. A pattern had been set, which he was now determined to destroy. No other alternative seemed valid to him. Vigny had his poetry, most notably his creation of "Eva." Dorval had her acting.

Importantly, for the economic security it afforded her, Dorval signed a five-year contract on November 1, 1837 with the Gymnase Theater on Boulevard Bonne-Nouvelle. It included a clause allowing her the right to accept other engagements if she so desired, providing she notified them six months in advance.

The ups and downs of Dorval's world were to play in her favor once again, thanks to Hugo, whose voice now prevailed at the Comédie-Française. Dorval was awarded the lead, that of Doña Sol, in the revival of *Hernani* to open on January, 20, 1838. For her, it was a dream fulfilled! Her much talked about costume, copied from Goya's painting of the Duchess of Alba, was eye-catching (Ambrière, 419). Hugo beamed!

On March 8, 1838, she opened in another revival: Hugo's *Marion Delorme* at the Comédie-Française. Again rave reviews.

By this time, Hugo's mistress, Juliette Drouet, was wracked with jealousy. He was seeing far too much of Dorval, she told her lover. He reassured her as only the suave and diplomatic Hugo could, of his love for her. Whether she felt comforted by his words or not, she remained home while he pursued his theatrical needs in all senses of the word!

Dorval's schedule was frenetic at this juncture. But she liked it that way. Not only was she earning money to pay off her continuous debts, but she was in the limelight, which she had always enjoyed. Work was a boon for her psychologically.

By February 2 of the same year, Dorval's days were steeped in rehearsal of *The Crusader's Camp (Le Camp des Croisés)* by Adolphe Dumas, and on March 8,
a revival of *Marion Delorme* at the Comédie-Française. On July 3, 1838, she forged ahead in *The Sister in Law* (*La Belle-Soeur),* a relatively mediocre play *by* Duport and Laurencin, revolving around that all too familiar topic of jealousy. Nonetheless, Dorval found herself able to pay at least some of her forever mounting debts.

Vigny again renewed his demands on Dorval. If she wanted to continue seeing him, she must cease her relationship with Sandeau. Dorval was suddenly seized by terrible nervous trembling! Her unconscious must have pointed out the impossibility of such a move. How could she change her nature even if she had wanted to! While she loved Vigny deeply and tenderly, the sexual encounters she enjoyed with others such as Sandeau, though temporary and fleeting, were and had always been part of her life-style.

Although Vigny was to some extent too sensitive a man to believe that Dorval could mend her ways, he nonetheless hid his fears and not only accompanied her nightly to the Gymnase but attended some of her rehearsals and all of her openings (Ambrière, 439)

When luck turns sour, it does so mightily. Dorval's enemies, particularly those at the Comédie-Française who were so jealous of her popularity and talent, were waiting for the propitious moment to sling their arrows her way. What better means to reduce her to naught than to impose their influence on the reviewers. The *Gazette des Théâtres* would verbalize their spleen. They succeeded.

> Each day Mme Dorval's organic defects increase and her qualities diminish. Poetry in the mouth of this actress sounds like a raucous and alcoholic hiccup; passion with her mannered gesture offers no more than a revolting image. (Ambrière, 439)

All, however, was not lost. Sand and Dorval's real friends were to have their say as well. While some of the plays in which she performed, for example, *The Sister-in-Law,* were poor they conceded, her acting was, as usual, up to par.

To complicate matters, Sandeau returned to the scene on July 7. Dorval was still performing in *The Sister-in-Law*. As fate would have it, Vigny was present on the evening of Sandeau's reappearance! Vigny had warned Dorval not to see him. The question remains as to whether Sandeau arrived on the battle scene of his own volition, or whether Dorval had invited him to return. No matter. The deed was done.

Nor was Vigny's role in this affair sparklingly pure. On April 3, he was enjoying a fling with the beautiful young American, Julia Dupré, a student at the Beaux-Arts Academy. There was nothing emotionally profound in this relationship. Nonetheless, it was titillating to the senses.

Vigny's and Dorval's relationship had been, and was still, reminiscent of a balancing act. Whenever Sandeau was out of the picture, Vigny attended Dorval's performances, such as *Hernani, Marion Delorme, Le Camp des Croisés,* visiting her back stage, then accompanying her home. What enraged Vigny increasingly, was his conviction that whenever Dorval even spoke to another man, she would be making love to him shortly thereafter. The free-spirited, Dorval, on the other hand, could seemingly no longer bear Vigny's attempted domination. She went out of her way, whether out of spite or simply to tease him, to talk to other men. This was evidently her subtle means of rejecting all domination over her.

As for the well-organized Vigny, he had taken to noting each of what he considered to be her infractions. To write his thoughts had always soothed his sorrow. It helped him withdraw into himself, but more importantly, it triggered his writing instinct. It was at this juncture that he began preparing an edition of his complete works, which was, of course, to include *Cinq Mars, Servitude et Grandeur militaires.*

On August 17, 1838, Vigny, tired of Dorval's philandering, refused to see her again. The final break would occur several weeks later.

Although separated by distance, Dorval lived within his being, solidly, powerfully, painfully! Increasingly pessimistic, he brooded, spending his hours and days writing, thinking, reading, and praying. His mood changes veered from his interpretation of the mystic's *ataraxia* to bitterness and inner rage. There came a time, however, when his gentle, idyllic hopes found expression in the remarkable poems he wrote prior to and following his departure from Paris. In 1839, one of his best known poems, about which he had evidently been meditating for many a month – *Samson's Anger,* "La Colère de Samson" – emerged, bold and brash, when he and his wife were traveling to the home of the Earl of Kilmorey at Shavington Park in Shropshire, England (Castex, *Les Destinées,* 89) .

As the violence of the poem suggests, Vigny had never succeeded in shaking off his love-hate passion for Dorval. Throughout his life she remained the incarnation of the deceitful Delila, the viper! It had been she, Vigny was convinced, who had aroused Sampson's destructive powers, and he raged against women's deceit and man's helplessness, envisioning a volcano over a city, bringing irremediable agony without warning in the form of a ravaging cyclone, burning to ashes and burying everything in sight (Gosse, *Alfred de Vigny,* 27).

Vigny, the poet was a doomed man. No matter where he lived, no matter the hour of day, Dorval's image had forever been engraved in his mind, blood, and soul, forever there to haunt, taunt, tantalize and scourge him. He was lacerated even more deeply upon discovery of Dorval's new beau, the young and handsome Mélingue, who was fifteen years her junior, and whom she succeeded in bringing to the Porte Saint-Martin in 1838. Alone with his faithful invalid wife Lydia, occupied with his writings and philosophical forays into the world beyond, Vigny could appreciate the soothing loneliness and esthetic greenery of a small estate in Maine-Giraud which he had inherited, and to which he would retire for the last years of his life.

Without her beloved Vigny whom she adored in her very own way, Dorval would continue fighting for new and interesting roles, be it at the Comédie-Française, or at other theaters. It was an increasingly difficult task for a single and untitled woman without powerful male support. She had become, like Vigny, prone to bouts of melancholia. With reason, she declared. The critic Henri Monnier inquired as to the causes of her basically mournful temperament, which gave her such vast understanding of sorrow, pain, hurt, sadness, and other modes of feeling, which she was able to convey so authentically in the roles she portrayed. She answered him unequivocally by revealing her early years.

> I came into this world via the large roads, I was rocked in keeping with the bumpy jolts of *Ragotin* (the drunkard cart), I never knew the games or the joys of childhood... If I glimpsed the blue sky, trees, greenery, flowers, if I heard birds sing, it was only in my dreams.
>
> My poor mother would have asked no more than to love me. But did she have the time? Can one be a real mother in the atmosphere of struggles, misery, pride, violent or vulgar passions, which is the life of the nomad comedienne?
>
> I married the first man who wanted to take charge of my fate. Fate reversed the roles, I became protector of my protector. The suffering and the hard work involved in maternity, household worries, the difficulties of an actress living in the provinces, without fire and a place of her own, so to speak, struggling against the public's caprices, the financial failures of the directors, filled my youth. (Emma Sakellaridès, 46)

To others Dorval confessed the tears she had shed and was still shedding over Vigny's departure from her life. Whenever she contemplated Canova'a sculpture of the weeping Mary Magdalene, she wrote:

> I spend hours looking at this woman who weeps, wondering [...] is it repentence for having lived or regret at no longer being alive... Passion crowned with thorns where not one point is lacking. (54, Sakellaridès)

Nor would Vigny ever be consoled for having lost his Dorval, whom he immortalized in his poems, in his prayers, in his thoughts, in the countryside, and in his inner world forever! Jules Janin, the critic, wrote, it was the phosphorous which she thrust on Vigny, "the passion and the suffering beyond the words she pronounced" (Sakellaridès, 58). As Vigny wrote:

> D'autres yeux ont versé vos pleurs. Une autre bouche
> Dit des mots que j'avais sur vos lèvres rangés,
> Et qui vers l'avenir (cette perte vous touche)
> Iront de voix en voix moins purs et tout changés (Vigny, 192 O.C.I.)

For Vigny the gentleman, his love for Dorval prior to their sexual encounter and thereafter as well, had been volcanic, momentous – unparalleled. Although he gave himself completely to his beloved, he never neglected his duties as a nurse to his mother and wife. Ironically, he felt himself honorable and expected similar comportment with his intimates. Nor was he partial to the Bohemian life. Interestingly, although he felt discomfort when shaking hands with M. Merle, he never felt a lack of respect for him or the marriage contract. He did look askance, however, on what he considered to be Dorval's sexual play. He cringed when he saw his Dorval mixing with the lower echelons of society. Her familiarity with admirers hurt him. He was discomfited by her easy friendships, her ability to mix with any and all types while he observed, seated in the background. For him she was a goddess, a luminary, perfection incarnate. He refused to accept what he considered negative or dangerous qualities of behavior. He believed in ethics, certainly his own ethics; in the code of honor, but his code, twisting and turning these broad concepts to suit his emotional and spiritual and even physical needs.

In his *Journal* he wrote:

> Love that is physical and only physical pardons all infidelity... but you, spiritual love, passionate love, you can forgive nothing. (Whitridge, 118)

> Following one of their outbursts, Vigny could write: "I entrust you to the protection of your love, your honor, and your goodness." (Whitridge, 117)

CHAPTER 9

An important subtext for the final dissolution of Dorval and Vigny's turbulent love was Dorval's relationship with the author George Sand. Earthshaking, momentous, and pivotal was the meeting of the thirty-five-year-old Dorval and the twenty-nine year- old George Sand in Paris one afternoon sometime between the 14 and the 20th of January, 1833. Not only did their *rencontre* change their lives, *it gave them their lives.* So passionately were they drawn to one another, that Dorval invited her new friend to her home on January 21. That very evening, the two attended the Opéra Comique (Sand, *Correspondance,* 209).

Aurore Dupin Sand, born in Paris in 1804, was the daughter of an aristocratic officer who died young and of a lower class mother. Her childhood years were spent for the most part roaming about her paternal grandmother's rustic estate in Nohant, in the Indre district. Aurore fell in love with nature early in life, related to its beaming beauty and mesmerizing aromas. She was inspired by the chill of autumn. The starkness and solemnity of winter's darkness spoke to her young heart. As the bursting color tones of spring and summer inched their way through the fields and forested areas, Aurore lived the joys of warmth and awakening.

By 1817, her relatively strict grandmother, forever attempting to correct what she considered to be Aurore's unbridled streak, sent her to convent school in Paris. Two years later, the partially transformed Aurore had become an inveterate reader and began penning her own works. By 1822, she was married off to Baron Dudevant and bore him two children. Unwilling to live a stultifying life, and far from being faithful to her husband, the free-spirited rule-breaker left her mate in 1830, and moved permanently to Paris.

Strong, optimistic, self-confident, Sand found employment as an industrial painter, then tried journalism, and finally, in 1831, in collaboration with her lover, Jules Sandeau, wrote her first novel, *Rose et Blanche.* That same year, and strictly on her own this time, she completed her novel, *Indiana,* which was published under the name of George Sand. So began a virtually unparalleled literary career that would resonate the world over.

Independent and self-sufficient in every sense of the word, Sand went where she pleased, frequented those for whom she felt an affinity, enjoyed sexual gratification whenever the spirit moved her, and favored novelists and poets, dramatists whose works and points of view she admired and whose causes she upheld. A case in point was Dumas' *avant garde* play, *Antony,* which broached the *untouchable* subject of adultery, and starred none other than the flamboyant Dorval. The young, self-confident, and brash Aurore, together with some friends, not only attended theater, but made their feminist stand overtly, by seating themselves in the pit, an area forbidden to women at the time.

Sand frequently dressed in men's gear in the country, considering it far more comfortable than the complicated dresses worn by women at the time. She was to set her own trend in Paris – tight-fitting trousers, high boots with tassels and a top hat. Fearless in her rebellions, be they of a social or of a sexual nature, the criticism incurred by her unconventional behavior, flowed off her like water off a duck's back. That many looked at her askance in no way bothered her. Sand pursued her course in life as she saw fit. Her by-word was: "There is nothing stronger in me than the need to love." She acted on impulse and gratified her senses with her lovers whenever the urge came upon her. And it did frequently. Her writings followed a similar path – gusto, verve, passion, compassion, romance, interspersed with witticisms. Her readers were moved to tears, to smiles, to anguish, to pleasure, to love, to satisfaction, and to so much more, when perusing her works. Bourgeois conventions for Sand were neither battered nor dismantled. They were simply non-existent.

Both Sand and Dorval were so at ease with each other that whenever Dorval felt the impulse to visit with her friend, be it at her Quai Malaquais home overlooking glorious gardens, or elsewhere, she did so irreverently and impulsively. If Sand was not home, Dorval usually left a note expressing her feelings of disappointment. "How unhappy I am to lose a day of my life when you could have been there" (Curtis Cate, *George Sand,* 227). They saw each other whenever possible, and confided in each other fully. To add zest to their lives they either made love or swapped lovers, most notably the young, blue-eyed, and handsome poet, Jules Sandeau, whose entry into their worlds peppered both their lives.

That Dorval's home was open to Sand at any time of day or night drew frowns from Vigny, who looked upon her masculine attire as shocking and in bad taste. No matter, she thought, he would simply have to get accustomed to it. But, as we know, he did not. Not only did Sand and Dorval meet several times a week, but their epistolary relationship was equally bountiful. Sand wrote, "I do not live on the days when I don't see you, *dear soul,*" and suggested that, should Dorval not have found anyone better to escort her to the theater, she accept "me as your knight, and I shall call for you between 6 and 7 o'clock... I love you" (Lubin, Sand *Correspondance,* 249). Because Dorval had failed to visit Sand on Feb. 4, 1833, the latter sent her a note, "My very dear one, you are hopefully not ill. I am. Otherwise I would be with you tonight. If you are in the neighborhood, come and kiss me so I can heal" (Lubin, 251).

No sooner had they met than they were as one. Their personalities had melded. Each seemed galvanized by the other's personality and sexuality. The flow of dialogue was unstoppable. Dorval, accustomed to running the gamut of vocalizations had found a perfect audience and partner in the more poised and better educated Sand. Not a touch of guilt intruded into the lives of these two sexually emancipated women. Rejecting custom, tradition and any other repressive social measure aimed at containing feminine needs and yearnings, invited each of them to go her own way, to savor the same liberties men had known for centuries. Sapphic love brought them ecstasy!

Sand's assessment of Dorval and their relationship was incisive.

Only those who know how differently we were made can realize how utterly I was in thrall to her... God had given her the power to express what she felt... She was beautiful, and she was simple. She had never been taught anything, but there was nothing she did not know by instinct. I can find no words with which to describe how *cold* and incomplete my own nature is. I can express nothing. There must be a sort of paralysis in my brain which prevents what I feel from ever finding a form through which it can achieve communication...When she appeared upon the stage, with her drooping figure, her listless gait, her sad and penetrating glance...I can say only that it was as though *I were looking at an embodied spirit.* (André Maurois, *Lélia,* 137)

At the outset of their affair, Sand needed assurance of Dorval's love for her.

> Do you really think you can endure me? That is something you cannot know yet, nor I. I am such a bear, so stupid, so slow to put my thoughts into words, so awkward and so dumb just when my heart is fullest. Do not judge me by externals. Wait a little before deciding how much pity and affection you can give me. I feel that I love you with a heart rejuvenated and altogether renewed by you. If that is just a dream, like everything I have ever wanted in life, do not wake me from it too soon. It does me so much good. Good-bye, you great and lovely person. Whatever happens, I shall see you this evening. (Maurois, 138)

The smitten Sand attended Dorval's performances in rapt adoration of the great artist that she was. In her letter of February 4, 1833, Sand asked Dorval for seats to a commemorative performance of Beaumarchais' *The Marriage of Figaro* at the Comédie-Française in which Dorval was to play the Countess and Mademoiselle Mars Suzanne. Sand concluded her letter with these poignant words, "Farewell, my dear love... I wish someone loved me the way I love you." Needless to say, the tickets were forthcoming, along with a note conveying the actress's feelings. "My friend, I have two box stalls for you. Be there, I beg you. I shall need to feel there is someone out there who loves me" (Cate, *George Sand,* 226).

So impressed was Sand with Dorval's performance, that she sent her critique of it to the weekly newpaper, *L'Artiste,* referring to Mlle Mars' stiff and dry acting style, her inflexible speech and stance on stage, as opposed to Dorval's supple, feeling, and poignantly realistic manner. Sand's opinions were brashly attacked the following week in the *Courrier des Spectacles.* Certainly the article could not have been written by a woman, the author claimed. "We, for our part believe that it was the work of "a nasty man in petticoats" (Maurois, *Lélia,* 226). No matter, Sand was in love and was loved. "I know I am not worth one lock of your hair, and this is why I love you," Sand added (Cate, 226).

Although they met frequently at Dorval's or at Sand's home, on occasion Sand wrote sadly to her beloved Dorval:

> I can't see you today, darling – no such luck! But on Monday, either in the morning or the evening, at the theater or in your bedroom before you are up, I must come and give you a kiss. If I don't, I cannot guarantee that I may not do something mad! I am working like a galley-slave, and seeing

you is my only form of relaxation. Goodbye, you loveliest of women. (Cate, 226)

Dorval wrote less frequently to Sand, and understandably so, since rehearsals, performances, important social engagements, and her children took up so much of her days and nights. Nor was writing her forte.

Throughout March of 1833, and thereafter, the lovers did everything in their power to steal time to be together. Vigny's jealousy catapulted. Dorval had not set out to hurt him. In fact, she had done her best to spare Vigny, to placate him, to hide her lesbian relationship from him. To alter his focus was understandably an impossible task. His suffering distressed her deeply. She felt sorry for him, for she loved him in her own way.

Sand did not dissimulate her pain. She bemoaned the days she and Dorval were separated from one another. In moments of sadness, she wondered whether she was worthy of her lover's friendship, then panicked at the thought of losing her. Only when Dorval and she were together did she experience bliss. If only Dorval would let her accompany her on tour, Sand asked, they would not be separated. It could work out, she insisted. Could she be her dresser? To be with Dorval and to enjoy their love was her ideal. The more practical Dorval knew the hardships involved in touring: the long hours, the unpredictability of audiences, the endless stage coach rides. She did not accept her offer (Maurois, 152)

Dorval and Sand loved to talk during their hours of togetherness, to gossip, as men did, about their conquests, their mates, or their sorrows. Indeed, it could be said that palaver fulminated between the two women. Like men, they took pride in their prowess. The cynical, icy, and distant Prosper Mérimée, future author of the world-famous *Carmen,* who talked brilliantly on so many subjects including sex, offered himself to Sand one day. She accepted, taking his glib words concerning his sexual prowess to be reality. After trying him out for size, however, the poor Mérimée failed miserably to arouse her to a climax. She, on the other hand, felt so disengaged, even apathetic, in his clutches, that she failed to give him a "helping hand" during the procedure. Shocked and distressed by Mérimée's sexual failure, she related the incident to Dorval. Despite the latter's pledge of secrecy, the actress repeated the story to

Dumas, whose talent for *bons mots* encouraged him to *coin* the following phrase –"I had Mérimée last night, but it didn't amount to much." To Mérimée's chagrin, in no time did his sexual incompetency become the talk of Paris (Maurois, 154).

More than deeply attached, it could be asserted that Sand and Dorval adored each other. They were open and forthright, tender and loving. Their sexual compatibility was complete. No secrets between them, no grudges, and no feelings of remorse or guilt ever surfaced. If any problem arose between the two, it was immediately discussed and explained. One evening, for example, when Dorval had to leave Sand's home in a rush, the writer took her rapid departure personally, and was hurt to the extreme. Rather than dwelling on what she took to be an offence, Sand wrote Dorval a note.

> Why did you go off like that, you wicked creature, without so much as saying goodbye, and without giving me a program of your movements, that I might follow hard on your heels? Your leaving without a word hurt me. I was in a villainous mood. I imagined that you cared nothing about me. I cried my eyes out... I am a fool, and you must forgive me. My character is full of flaws, but my heart is ours: that I know full well. In vain do I explore the world of others – no one, not a soul comes up to you. Nowhere can I find a nature so frank, true, strong, supple, good, generous, great, odd, excellent, and in a word so complete as yours. I want to love you always: to cry with you, to laugh with you. I long to join you somewhere, to spend a few days in some place where you are staying. Where must I go? (Maurois, 162)

After the incredibly naive and self-righteous Vigny read Sand's letter, at Dorval's request, he forbade his beloved to reply to this "Lesbian." Dorval was quick to report her conversation with Vigny to Sand, causing the two many guffaws at his expense.

Although Dorval still had deep feelings for Vigny, she explained herself in a letter to Pauline Duchambge, whom she considered her friend, but who, as we know, would turn out to be anything but.

> It is impossible that we should ever come together again, but I weep for the love that is gone... I have nothing to put in its place. I do not love Sandeau, though I will try to do so. I have a feeling that I shall not succeed. I talk to him of nothing but Alfred. (Maurois, 293)

In time, however, Dorval held fast to Sandeau – and passionately so!

> Oh, how I love you! You are the joy of my eyes, the delight of my being, the sadness in my blood, the sweet magic of my heart! (Maurois, 293)

So attached were they to one another that he sometimes accompanied her on tour, and with a broad smile, commented on how she enthralled her audiences. When Sandeau, predictably, grew tired of his older lover, she was so stunned that she went directly to her one great love, her only real friend – Sand. For she alone understood her completely, accepted her as she was, listened to her words of pain in sympathetic adoration.

The author Arsène Houssaye came to label them the two *inséparables*.

> Upon returning from the theater after midnight, Dorval would find the strange woman [George Sand] waiting for her prey, while smoking cigarettes in the little blue-curtained room where a teapot steamed in front of a lively fire. A singularly amorous duo followed. The brunette loosened the blonde one's hair. The blonde one loosened the dark hair of the other. And these locks of hair were mingled amid the kisses and the bites. Never did Sappho speak so well to the beautiful Phaon. Never did Errina reply to Sappho in a more caressing voice. And thus the nighttime hours passed, more radiant than those of sunlit day. For both... were frantic for the unforeseen and insatiable for love. It was not only wantonness of the heart, but a display of Oriental, Indian, and Japanese voluptuousness. The two bacchantes would take leave of each other at the crack of dawn, still drunk on the pallor of accomplished dreams. And that day the eloquent woman had more eloquence. And that day the woman of the theater had a softer caress in her voice, more fire in her gaze, greater energy in her passion. (Cate, 227)

It is with admiration for Dorval's vigor, strength of purpose, and enormous talent as an actress, singer, and would-be dancer, that Sand wrote:

> Before reaching the heights due her, she had experienced all the vicissitudes of a nomadic existence. She had joined strolling theater troupes, whose directors suggested that a game of dominos be played during intermissions, rather than offering audiences love scenes to cheer them up. She had sung Méhul's comic opera in *Joseph's choir* during a heavy rain storm, seated on a ladder in the wings (of a former church fallen into ruin), under an umbrella large enough to protect four people, and the

choristers were obliged to stand in an opening masked by sack cloth, continuously interrupted by choruses of voices yelling to those directly above them "Animal, you are poking my eye out with your umbrella! Get rid of the umbrella!" (Ambrière, 70)

Life had suddenly changed significantly for Dorval. Her eldest daughter, Louise longed to be an actress. Of course she tried to help her by placing her in Mme Dufresnoy's company which traveled from city to city. When this did not work out, she sent her to London, placing her with the theatrical director, Pellisier, whose troupe was to perform in this city. The event never materialized and Louise returned to Paris in August, as Dorval was preparing to leave on a year-long tour. Who would care for her daughters while she was gone, she asked anxiously?

By January 1837, Dorval's arduous work schedule, the stress of her tour, in addition to her worries over her daughters, had weakened her so drastically that she fell gravely ill and was obliged to take to her bed. Only following her recovery did she learn why Vigny had attempted to delay her return to Paris – to spare her the excoriating sorrow of Gabrielle's agony and death.

Actors have little time to grieve. The show must go on! To her great relief, the five-year contract signed on July 1, 1838, with the Gymnase Theater gave her a sense of security which offered help through these difficult days. Without this long-term contract, she would have had to continue being a prey to exploitation and to the fickle fortunes of fate.

Dorval struggled on alone, performing in *Henri Hamelin* by Emile Souvestre at the Gymnase. Its plot recounted the life of a young painter who arrived in Paris, felt isolated and misunderstood by art critics, and, in time, became the target of creditors. After being serendipitously invited to the home of a kind mill owner in Normandy who encourages him to pursue his art, he takes it into his head to seduce his benefactor's wife. Her husband's undemonstrative nature encourages her to respond to the painter's charming ways. What her husband had kept hidden from her, and which accounted for his seeming lack of interest in his wife, were worries over his business and the heroic measures he was obliged to take to save it.

Thanks to the invention of a new machine and to the prudence of an uncle, everything was set back into place. The futures of both the industrialist and the painter were assured.

Some, including the perceptive Vigny, believed that *Henri Hamelin* signaled the end of Romanticism. On a personal and contrite note, he considered it to be not only an outright imitation of *Antony,* but a slur on his relationship with Dorval. Hurt to the marrow, only now had he come to realize that *she* – Dorval – was *perfidy*. His own blindness had led him into error. He had simply chosen the wrong partner to accompany him on his life-long spiritual quest.

It took Dorval more than a week to begin to recognize the loss she had suffered. Everything that had been beautiful in her world had been torn from her. She went to see Vigny on September 17, 1838, but was not received. The ensuing shock, pain, and trauma of her separation from Vigny, was to last her for the rest of her existence.

> Everything is over. I haven't separated from Mr. Vigny, but have wrenched myself from him. It's all over. I still don't believe it, despite my horrible suffering. I love no one now... Nothing consoles me... (Ambrière, 444)

On Semptember 20, Vigny and his wife moved permanently to Maine-Giraud in the Charente, the fortress estate which he had inherited.

Although Dorval continued to perform in *Henri Hamelin*, she lived her solitude and her despair. She saw no one. She had to take time out to clear her mind. She left Paris on October 10, 1838, and did not return there until February 1839. True to form, however, she was not alone as she stepped on the train, but accompanied by none other than Sandeau who claimed to be passionately in love with her. After only twelve days, he left her for greener and younger pastures. Even so, his daily letters revealed his despairing need for her. In time, however, these too became sparser, then ended.

Dorval found herself obliged to go on tour once again, responding with tears of joy to the acclamations awarded her. Honors, tributes, and rewards were hers nearly daily. At Rennes, the twenty year-old budding poet, Leconte de Lisle, described Dorval admiringly to a friend.

> Imagine a large and passionate forehead, black eyes that express what they want, a graciously brise en avant waist, a cadenced grave, austere, harmonious, and tender voice; ardent, majestic, severe expansive gestures; forceful, natural, charming intimate play... or instead, imagine nothing. What words could capture the irresistible emotion that makes the heart beat at the sight of Dorval? (Ambrière, 460)

After her successful tours, though still hounded by Parisian creditors, she returned to the Gymnase. Still adulated by her audiences, it was she who had changed. Her heart had been stilled and void following her separation from Vigny. She hurt inside. Exhausted from her travels and from her continuous performances, she suddenly became aware of the fact that the zest she had once possessed, the recuperative powers that had formerly been hers, thanks to Vigny's love and support for her, no longer existed. Fatigue, sadness, and pain absorbed her world.

On her return to Paris, she suffered an accident. Her coachman, having failed to pay attention to the traffic, smashed into an oncoming coach, nearly overturning Dorval's in the process. Although she suffered only minor bruises to the forehead, they were severe enough to necessitate a delay of several days. In Paris, the fatigued Dorval resumed her performances in *Henri Hamelin*. She yearned for better plays in which to perform, but the dearth of first class drama ruled the day. Fortunately, the remarkable actor Bocage was her stage partner. Both lamented the less than mediocre works in which they had to perform.

Hadn't Théophile Gautier, cried out in desperation: "Oh Bocage, O Madame Dorval! Why aren't you at the Saint-Martin Theater with a good solid drama...?" (Ambrière, 468).

A Parisian ménage revolved around conjugal problems. Satiated by such inanities, Dorval again sought recourse from Hugo, whose admiration for her talent earned her a five-year contract with the prestigious Renaissance Theatre, which she signed on September 11, 1840 (Ambrière, 469). Again the sense of security she would enjoy enabled her to heave a much needed sigh of relief.

Meanwhile, her beloved George Sand, although enjoying a rapturous affair with Frédéric Chopin, was always in close contact with Dorval. Aware of the paucity of worthwhile plays at the time, the big-hearted Sand responded with soothing warmth to the disenchanted Dorval. Their relationship remained indeed a blessing for Dorval.

Dorval was busy performing at the Renaissance Theatre in *Le Proscrit* (The Outlaw), a solid play by Frédéric Soulié. Its theme, designed to appeal to most audiences, revolved around a husband, whose work having taken him far from home, returns years later to find his wife, who had believed him dead, remarried. The tortuous and tortured emotions engendered at the sight of his wife's happy ménage, and her guilt feelings toward him, for having remarried, triggered the audience's compassion for the couple.

The panoplies of nuanced moods and character traits Dorval projected onto the wife, ranged from guilt, sorrow, pain, rage, anguish, joy, humility, fear, rejection, and passion. This rich combination again swept the audiences into her grasp. Théophile Gautier referred to her empathetic acting as "radiant," composed, and "sublime," for she was forever in "possession of herself." He wept during the performance, as had so many others in the audience (Ambrière, 474). Sand, who was present as well, sent her a note back stage, in which she commented on her "sublime" acting, and for the pathos it engendered in her. She confessed to having "cried like a calf" (Ambrière, 474).

Few theatrical battles engendered such acrimony at the Comédie-Française as did the maneuverings against Sand's new play *Cosima* which was to open on April 29, 1840. Even Heinrich Heine, well versed in Parisian theatrical politics, was aghast at the venom spewed by the *sociétaires* of this august theatrical house. Could such vicious condemnation of Sand's drama have resulted from her rejection of France's so-called acceptable code of ethics? Hadn't lesbianism been practised, *sub rosa,* for centuries in this holiest of holy lands? Ideas were changing. The play questioned such sacrosanct subjects as male domination in the home. The retrograde considered Sand's work a dangerous precedent, a lethal move. That *Cosima* honed in on the goings-on of a dissatisfied, bored, and unfulfilled stay-at-home wife, who came to be tempted by a Don Juan, broke all decent precedents, Paris's rear guard claimed. To even touch on the sacrosanct topic of marriage vows in the theater was still considered by France's male majority to be tantamount to defamation. Let us note that most wives at this time lived under a strict code of ethics. They were forbidden to read certain books, to see certain people, to broach certain subjects, thereby remaining enslaved in what Ibsen was to call their "doll houses." To destabilize the status quo by introducing untenable values and concepts into mainstream thinking might lead to the eventual collapse of the status quo, and with it, the end of the male's incarceration of domestic wives.

Understandably, conservative males looked upon Sand as the most depraved of women. Broadminded citizens, on the other hand, viewed her as courageous, innovative, preaching a gospel of freedom, understanding, and of love. The Comédie-Française, was, to say the least, in turmoil. Who was to prevail there, the new or the old guard?

Cosima did open at the Comédie-Française April 29, 1840. The house was packed with notables – Heinrich Heine, Mme Récamier, Mrs. Trollope, Countess Samoiloff, Marie d'Agoult, Pauline Viardot, to mention but a few. No sooner had the curtains been drawn, than screeches, poundings, and brouhahas exploded throughout the theater. Even the most regressive observers were baffled by the audience's venom and boisterousness. Nonetheless, on this fateful night, Sand had sounded the death knell of contemporary society's restrictive, regressive, and decadent customs. Henceforth, untenable relationships, bygone hypocrisies, and deceptive ways would be booted out!

Artistically speaking, *Cosima* was a less than a mediocre play. Indeed, Mérimée referred to it as a "brilliant fiasco." One may, nonetheless, question his objectivity in this matter. Might not his assessment smack of retribution for the still sharply felt remarks Dorval and Sand had directed his way a few years earlier concerning his less than stellar sexual prowess?

Perhaps, but this time, Dorval had herself had become the butt of negative criticism: her acting was below par, critics claimed. Even Sand, although complimenting Dorval on her acting, remarked that no sooner had the whistles and catcalls roared and soared, "than the actress (Dorval) lost her head," though only momentarily. Minutes later, the shock had worn off and she caught herself, reintroducing the necessary poise into her protagonist (Ambrière, 479). Nonetheless, when all was said and done, Sand admitted that it had been Dorval's genius alone that had kept audiences riveted to their seats.

On March, 9, 1840, Dorval had opened in a revival of *Chatterton*, now a virtual classic of its kind. Vigny attended, and as usual was both moved and tortured by the very sight of his Kitty Bell. Dorval's less predictable reactions were noteworthy as well. The painful emotions dredged up by the event were followed, on March 26, by a high fever which kept the actress in bed for the next two weeks. Dorval had perhaps understood how vacant her life had become, now that it was bereft of Vigny. How could anyone ever compare to her noble poet?

The sudden closing of *Cosima* increased Dorval's despair, leaving her disheartened, morose, and humiliated to the extreme. How would she ever be able to face her audiences in future productions, she wondered? How would she succeed in saving her reputation as an actress? For the first time in her life, she began to examine her feelings for Vigny, the man, his character, and his talents. Her flightiness, promiscuity, vanity, and need for sexual gratification alone had, until now, shielded her from thinking and delving into his character, his wants and talents. Who was Vigny? Did she really know him? To be sure, he had been her lover. He had been her mentor, as well. His understanding, his depth of perception, his sensitivity to pain throughout their relationship, not to speak of his genius, had finally made inroads into her psyche. Though she had lost him, at least for the present, his endearing qualities and, mostly, his capacity for pain, had remained deeply ingrained in her. She began reassessing their relationship. When first she had met him, granted, she had not understood him. How could it have been otherwise? They were poles apart. In her rough and tumble world, she had never met a man such as he. That she had tasted of him, of his work, ideas, of his code of honor, and his body, she now realized had brought her ecstatic joy along with a sense of fulfillment. These had been her best years, she admitted. To all intents and purposes, hadn't he created – or recreated – her?

In her letter of May 6 to Vigny, she confided in him her sense of humiliation at the sudden closing of *Cosima*, which had, to all intents and purposes, made her acceptance at the Comédie-Française highly doubtful. She counted not only on him to see to a revival of *La Maréchale d'Ancre,* but his reading of the play to her prior to rehearsal. His voice alone, she had told him so many times, helped her reach into the depths of her character. Six weeks later, on June 18, 1840, after Vigny had reworked his play and had read it to Dorval, it was performed at the Comédie-Française, arousing stormy bravos! Despite the dithyrambic reviews, however, Dorval's reputation had not been restored in the minds of the hardened and insensitive functionaries ruling the Comédie-Française.

Beyond the intense pain she had suffered after her break-up with Vigny, and the humiliations that had followed with *Cosima's* failure, Dorval was a fighter and a survivor – and a weeper, to be sure. Nor had her sexual urges really abated. Indeed, they seemed to have been reinvigorated by Sandeau. To be nearer her young lover, she moved from her apartment on rue Blanche to his neighborhood at 100 bis rue du Bac.

But nothing in Dorval's life had ever truly remained stable for prolonged periods of time. Not surprisingly, her path had been rocky and torment-filled for long stretches of time, only for her to reassert her ebullient nature when a new face came upon the scene. Paradoxically, the only constant in her world was the unpredictable. And so it was during the summer of 1840, when the unanchored fickleness of youth, so dazzling at times, overcame Sandeau. His jealousy of Vigny had flared, to be sure! (Ambrière, 488). Six weeks later, after having lived his intense passion with Dorval, disenchantment reared its ugly head and, after being invited to meet an eligible and wealthy bride in Paris, he summarily left his erstwhile beloved in the middle of her tour, without even accompanying her to her stagecoach. Not to worry, however, the girl in question had to delay her arrival and so the handsome Sandeau arranged to meet Dorval in Lyon. She knew he loved to be cuddled and fussed over, and she, above others, had mastered this art. Sandeau left Paris on August 24 to live his idyll with Dorval. For three blissful months the two traveled in the south of France – to Vaucluse, Avignon, Carpentras, Nîmes, Arles, and Marseille. For three months they lived their felicitous bewilderment.

Sandeau's sudden departure for Paris on November 14 broke Dorval's heart. She wrote him frantic letters. They remained unanswered. Upon her return to Paris, in January 1841, she made appointments to meet him. He chose not to appear. When reality finally took hold of her, she might have wondered whether she had not taken on the qualities of a Greek harpy from whom Sandeau fled in terror. Had she become the predator?

When he finally did write he informed her of what she herself had already understood. She took his rejection of her badly. That she was no longer loved had always been untenable to her. This time, it was excruciating. She could not survive without feeling wanted and cherished. She looked back upon her multiple kindnesses to so many in need such as Piccini. Her friends and acquaintances knew they could always count on her in time of need. Less appealing, perhaps was that other side of her nature: her insatiable and hysterical need for love, passion, and admiration. She failed, however, to take the age factor into consideration. Sandeau was thirty years old and she, forty-three: a vast difference at the time. To be abandoned by a lover brought her pain and sorrow. The very real prospect of being abandoned by Parisian audiences terrified her!

Tastes in theater were changing. Melodrama was now *passé*. A new star had been born, the exotic Rachel. Her real name was Elisa Félix. She had made her début at seventeen years of age at the Comédie-Française, on June 12, 1838, in the role of Camille in Corneille's play, *Horace*. Rachel did not declaim her lines as was customary in classical theater. She spoke them in keeping with their meaning and their melody, underscoring the beauty of their cadences. Audiences sat spellbound, as they watched her subtle and controlled gestures, her slow, measured, and sensual stage movements, her poise, and her penetrating gaze. She had already overwhelmed her audiences. Soon, she would reign in theater.

Unlike Dorval, Rachel specialized in classical theater. Dorval could not perform at the Saint-Martin Theater, where she had been for so many years, for in 1840 it declared bankruptcy. The Renaissance Theater followed suit. She wrote to Vigny asking for help. He was too busy to see her. Indeed, he was courting Countess d'Agoult. Dorval was hurt. (Ambrière, 496).

Only one option was left to Dorval, to go on tour. By mid March, 1841, she was on her way to Belgium. The young René Luguet, performing at Paris' Théâtre de la Monnaie, attempted to walk out on his commitment to be Dorval's leading man on tour. But to act so rashly could have compromised his career. So on he went with Dorval to Brussels, Anvers, Gand, Bruges, Louvain, Liège,

Amsterdam, Calais, Dunkerk, and Boulogne-sur-mer. Dorval took a boat to Dover on July 22 to visit her daughter Caroline who was teaching in a family at Preston, returning to the continent on the 30th, where she performed in Hugo's *Angelo* (Ambrière, 500).

Much admired for her mastery as an actress, for her warmth of personality, her understanding of sorrow, not to speak of her ebullience and charm, it was not uncommon to see men cluster around Dorval, particularly when she was on tour. René Luguet was, in effect, smitten with her. She, however, was still longing for Sandeau. When she learned that he was writing a book and that his landlady was threatening eviction for non- payment of his apartment, Dorval sent him 200 francs. She still nourished hopes to be loved by him. Miracle upon miracles, upon her return to Paris in 1841, a letter from her beloved awaited her. She was traumatized by what she read: he confessed that his hands trembled upon reading her letter. He thought she had found him odious. Knowing differently changed his life. He was still passionately in love with her (Ambrière, 501). Still on tour, Dorval stopped at Niort, where she was performing for a month, and visited Sandeau's mother. They took to each immediately. Dorval visited her daily. Both women wept from emotion talking about Sandeau. So close had they become that Mme Sandeau attended Dorval's performances (Ambrière, 502). It was to no avail, Dorval realized. Now launched on his writing career, and the prospect of an advantageous marriage, he must have certainly opted to not see her again (Ambrière, 504). Divested of a male partner, she now took the available and charming Luguet, grandson of Malaga, the famous tightrope dancer, to be the man in her life.

Although the tour was remunerative, theater directors no longer solicited her as they had before. Writers, however, did. One young writer in particular asked if she would perform in his still unfinished play, *Les Ressources de Quinola* at the Odéon, His name was Honoré Balzac (Ambrière, 506). Her answer, though not negative, remained vague. Once the play was completed, she affirmed, she would give her answer.

On January 14, 1842, the now forty-four year-old Dorval, had no choice but to go on another tour. Although inured to the physical strains and stresses of frequent one-night stands, of poorly heated theaters, of being at the mercy of bumpy horse-and-buggy routes, Dorval never complained. In René Luguet, she had found a considerate and warm-hearted lover. To be sure, he was no Samson. She had matured somewhat and seemingly settled on the good-natured man that he was. They seemed to go well together. Their stops in Holland, Strasbourg, Colmar, Mulhouse, proved profitable, and seemed to bode well for their intent to return shortly before Easter.

On April 10 she left alone for the Franche Comté while he returned to Paris to see to his career on the Boulevard Bonne Nouvelle. That Dorval had been detained and was unable to attend his performance on June 9 in *Edouard et Clémentine* at the Gymnase, was deeply disappointing to him, despite the favorable reviews it had elicited from the press. Unfortunately, Dorval had other pressing and painful matters to attend to now (Ambrière, 508).

CHAPTER 10

Serendipitous happenings do take place in life. They did for Dorval in a moment of need. Some months previously, during the winter of 1841, she had received a note from a stranger which must have given her pause, since she copied it and carried it with her for the rest of her life. The stranger first complimented her on her genius, then, unlike the usual obsequious letters she received, this one pointed to other, more serious, matters.

> "Why" he asked, "do you expend such effort, such talent, and all the faculties of your rich and generous nature, admirable artist and poor woman that you are? Isn't it simply to arrive at a sad exchange between you and the world, you selling pleasure and it paying you back in gold and applause, without esteem and consideration...What emptiness, Madam, must a gifted soul such as yours, find in a life sacrificed in this way... Isn't there anything better in the world than this?... Whatever one says... there exists in the world – and you are certainly capable of understanding this, for where genius lives, conscience is not dead – something infinitely superior to vainglory, fortune, the drunkenness of pleasures that sully. It is the beautiful morality realized in life...life enriched by modest and useful virtues, life purified by great thoughts and salutary sentiments of religion, which one must finally come to consider when one seeks peace of soul... and immortality that is not steeped in lies... I hope that soon you exchange your past for a future of ineffable rehabilitation in your eyes and in those of God." (Ambrière, 509)

Dorval must certainly have been troubled by these words, received at a time when she was still suffering over Sandeau's desertion. They encouraged her to think about her actions and relationships, most importantly toward her daughters, whom she had neglected for so many years, namely, the deceased Gabrielle, and Louise, now a lost soul. She had vowed that Caroline would not suffer the same fate. Not only had Dorval sent her to school, but had hired tutors to teach her English, for she knew that a second language was required for a young girl to survive in these times. Moreover Dorval had already begun to turn her life around. No longer was she the center of her world. Nor did she give her daughters short shrift. Their welfare counted for her now! Each night following her performance, upon returning to the solitude of her room, Dorval reread the anonymous letter she had received. It triggered the faith she had known as a child and which she had lost during those difficult years when fighting so diligently to make a place for herself in the theater (Ambrière, 511). She began to question her past, looking askance at the ease with which she had allowed her unbridled passions of youth to take over her world. Even her now unrequited passion for Sandeau began to wane. It all seemed so unimportant to her now. Coincidentally, on May 29, 1842, the very day of the Corpus Christi feast, she received an announcement of Sandeau's marriage. In a letter to a friend, she wrote that the news had simply "slipped gently over my heart, as gently as the undulations of the young girls in the street processions" (Ambrière, 511).

Nonetheless, the following week, on tour at Besançon, her peace of mind was suddenly shattered upon learning that Caroline was severely ill. But since God was now on her side, she believed, he was simply testing her strength. And rightly so, she reasoned. She rushed back to Paris, to find her daughter on the mend. The doctors advised Dorval, however, that Caroline could no longer tolerate the English climate, but that she had not contracted tuberculosis as had her sisters.

With this good news, the much relieved Dorval also learned that the enterprising Auguste Lireux, the Odéon's new director, was intent upon opening the fall season with a splash program. To this end, he invited Dorval to return to Paris. On July 30, she received a letter from Hugo. It was like old times, he wrote. She smiled.

> My admirable Tisbé, I have been told that you have been hired at the Odéon [for the winter]. I congratulate the Odéon. One needs a miracle to dispel this fearsome solitude, but to ask you for a miracle is to ask you to simply do what you know how to do. I hope that your reappearance there will bring us all great happiness. (Ambrière, 512)

Dorval's mood soared at the prospect of being emotionally and financially able to pay some of her outstanding bills, at least through the month of August.

Now that her relationship with Luguet had changed, she was no longer the sex-driven female of the past; she had finally become a *mother*. She likewise interpreted this change in her outlook, needs, and comportment as a sign from heaven. Her relationship with her husband Merle had also taken on a warmth and tenderness she had never before experienced. His two illegitimate children, Victor and Alexandrine, were accepted by Dorval. When Luguet was finally introduced to the Dorval household, the now twenty-two year-old Caroline, well on the road to recovery, was taken by his charm and his gentle ways. A new code of ethics had finally taken root in this once sexually promiscuous woman. Warmth, love, harmony, tenderness, truth, and good bourgeois values were now to prevail in Dorval's home on rue du Bac. Forever buried were dissension, estrangement, lies and dissimulations.

That Dorval found herself once again performing to packed houses in such revivals as *Thirty Years of a Gambler's Life* at the now reopened Porte Saint-Martin Theater with her old time partner Frédérick Lemaître went a long way towards buoying up her mood as well. She felt young, active, and full of hope. Nor did her positive attitude toward life vanish when, in November, *Antony* played to an empty house. She accepted the fact that this kind of hyperromantic focus had simply gone out of style. It was part of the life process, she reasoned. She even reconciled herself to the thought that she could no longer earn her living in Paris, and would have to keep touring those French towns and cities where modernity had not yet taken root. Never once did she complain of the hardships, the physical strain and stresses which she suffered on her extended tours. Following her nightly performances, she returned to her hotel rooms to reread that precious *sacred letter* she had received from a stranger. It and it alone had helped her cope with severe pain and disappointment. To acknowledge and then redress her sins of the past, most importantly to redress her abdication of the role of mother to her daughters, would now be her way.

Not only had Dorval's focus altered and become more measured, but Luguet's had matured as well. His talents were now appreciated. His relationship with Dorval had also eased. No longer tempestuous, it had become peaceful and positive. Sex with him did not enter into the picture. When Caroline met Luguet, she was immediately taken with him. She enjoyed listening to him talk about his painful years of privation, his difficulties finding acting jobs, the distances he traversed simply to act in bit parts. As in fairy tales, the gentle Caroline glowed listening to his happy endings as well. Dorval was delighted in Caroline's joy. *God had willed it so,* she believed.

The two would wed and she felt blessed. Nonetheless, one wonders how the naive Caroline could accommodate her mother's behavior with Vigny and Sandeau, not to speak of the other men in her life. She had led a cloistered life and had never heard of her mother's flagrant behavior. This tender and gentle girl loved and idolized her mother, but never judged her. Caroline Dorval was married to René Luguet on December 27, 1842.

The only dark cloud on the horizon was Dorval's incessant *fantasy* of being accepted at the Comédie-Française. To this end, she studied one of France's great classical female roles, that of Racine's Phèdre. Intelligent and strong-willed, she mastered the part in no time. By October of 1842, she performed it both at the Opéra-Comique and at the Odéon to frantically applauding crowds. What Dorval ignored, however, were the still powerful jealousies existing between Boulevard actors and the members of the Comédie-Française. Notorious for their deceptive ways, the latter applied them full speed in Dorval's case. That Rachel had been declared queen of classical French theater at the Comédie-Française had clearly reduced Dorval's chances of being allowed to participate in any capacity in France's state-run theater. The Rachel partisans, now in full battle gear, just like those of Mlle Mars in the past, considered Dorval's performance of *Phèdre* an unfortunate challenge!

Dorval's first performance of *Phèdre* on October 22, 1842, at the Opéra-Comique had aroused such a stir as to add fuel to the fire. Her crystal-clear voice, her punctilious enunciation, her emphasis on the right words, her murmurings and moving sighs, her tears, asides, her gesticulations – at times overt, at other moments subtle and subdued – were understandably lauded by some, but considered an affront by dyed-in-the-wool classicists. Nonetheless, to be able to perform such demanding classical works without having undergone rigorous training by the teachers at the Comédie-Française was indeed phenomenal. When Dorval played Hermione in Racine's *Andromaque,* one of Rachel's favorite roles, partisanship reigned, stirring such emotions that a fight broke out between contending parties at the Odéon. That both Dorval's and Rachel's acting stirred such violence in their audiences indicated the seriousness with which audiences of the day identified with these great artists of the stage.

It could be said that this was to be Dorval's year for successes. On December, 24, 1842, she again played opposite Bocage in Léon Gozlan's *The Right Hand and the Left Hand,* a drama about the Swedish court, winning rave reviews in the process. "Never before had Mme Dorval reached such heights." As the mother, the critic for the *Corsaire* referred to her acting as "moving, passionate, pathetic, stirring... she continuously dominated her audience... all of her gestures, movements, and words were studded with the most lively intelligence and the deepest poetic feeling" (Jan. 28, 1842, *Corsaire,* cf. Ambrière, 523).

Busy day and night performing in Racine's *Phèdre* and *Andromaque,* in Beaumarchais' the *Marriage of Figaro,* and François Ponsar's *Lucrèce,* Dorval barely had a moment to herself. She reveled in being still the great star, the talk of Paris. Gustave Flaubert, the future author of *Madame Bovary,* was so taken with her latest play that he recited entire tirades from it with gusto.

Nonetheless, the now deeply religious Dorval found herself dissatisfied. Something was missing in her life. While she had enjoyed successes in revivals of *Antony* and *La Tour de Nesle,* she rightly felt she was bathing in mediocrity when obliged to accept such feeble works as Henri Blaze's version of *Léonore.* Nor was The *Duchess of Chateauroux* by Sophie Gay anything but vacuous, replete as it was with idle chatter. Predictably, after opening on December 22, 1843, it closed after only three performances.

Fortunately, Dorval was so imbued with her new-found religious outlook that she suffered no remorse or despondency following her latest fiasco; this was understandable, since her acting was praised and the play alone was derided. Some days later, however, everything was to change. When Caroline told her mother she was pregnant, Dorval's joy knew no bounds!

CHAPTER 11

It was a boy, Georges, born on November 9, 1844. Dorval took to him instantly. She rocked and cuddled him with all the fervor of her heart. She loved tending to his every need, mood, disposition. She felt renewed, reborn, restored in him. But she worried over his health. He seemed frail. With good food, she reasoned, he would grow up to be strong and hardy. She spent days on end with him. Not that she neglected her acting. Always the realist, her financial problems obliged her to pursue her career. Nonetheless, she had changed. She smiled more readily now. Her grandson's birth had energized her. She even came to wonder whether her latest unprecedented hit, *The Right Hand and the Left Hand*, had not been an omen from heaven (Ambrière, 518). Clearly, her world had flowered anew!

Good news flowed in from other quarters as well. François Buloz, editor of the prestigious magazine, the *Revue des Deux Mondes,* which published works by Hugo, Dumas, Balzac, Sand, and Vigny to mention but a few, had succeeded the baron Taylor in 1838 as administrator of the Comédie-Française. Dorval knew him to be approachable. She, who had always longed to perform regularly at this distinguished theatrical institution, could not resist asking Buloz for help. To be a permanent member of the élite Comédie-Française would certainly lend her stature. It would also afford her security. She had performed there several times and savored the prospect of becoming a definitive part of this august institution. That she had never taken acting lessons with the great Samson, one of the pillars of the Comédie-Française, still remained a stumbling block (Ambrière, 532). Nor did the insightful Dorval forget that the directors of the Comédie-Française, including Samson, looked down on her – or anyone – who had not been trained at this institution. Nonetheless, she persevered, and requested an audition. It was granted. Her dossier would be examined, she was informed, and, those in charge *would let her know the results.* She would wait in vain!

Meanwhile, the forever debt-ridden Dorval continued to perform in such staples as *Phèdre, The Marriage of Figaro, Lucrèce,*

Antony, and *Mary Tudor,* dazzling Parisians nightly. The young Flaubert and Maxime du Camp were enthralled by her approach to theater, not to speak of those associated with Paris' Latin quarter. Critics commented on her youthful demeanor, on her endless store of energy, her understanding and sensitivity. Unlike the celebrated Mlle Mars and Mlle George, the now forty-six year old Dorval was not afraid of aging, and wisely turned down offers to play young girls. Her passion to study new roles, however, had never abated. To the contrary, she believed they gave her the opportunity to expand her repertoire and deepen her understanding of human nature.

On March 11, 1844, Dorval opened in *The Countess of Altenberg* by Alphonse Royer and Gustave Vaez. While the play itself was slight, the role of the mother who willingly sacrifices her life to preserve the honor of her sixteen year-old daughter could have been created specifically for her, so well did it suit her temperament. The writer Gérard de Nerval's (Ambrière, 544) assessment of the drama, which he saw several times, underscored the play's obvious artifices, but highlighted Dorval's "perfect" rendition of the mother. Indeed, he looked upon her as the mother *par excellence.* Nor did she perform in the exact same manner each evening. For her, acting had always been a matter of mood and emotional nuances. He noted the fluidity of her renditions. Unlike run-of-the mill actresses, Dorval was forever injecting new elements into her characters, thus constantly shifting the mood of the moment. At times she played up specific details and intonations, at other instances she focused elsewhere, on a stance, smile, or tone. She was forever creating and recreating the vital presence of her characters.

The bane of her existence was clearly her problem with money. She earned it easily, and spent it even more readily. Generous to a fault, she kept giving to the needy, recalling in so doing the poverty of her early years. She was permanently in debt and endlessly obliged to continue her habit of performing in whirlwind tours to recoup her diminishing funds. When she was young, she did not mind the long stagecoach rides, even those lasting sixteen or more hours. There were always people with whom she could chat. Furthermore, she enjoyed the change of scene. At forty-six years of age, such commuting had begun taking its toll on her. From June 10 to July 10 she toured Dôle, Châlons-sur-Marne and Macon, mustering the energy to perform in *Thirty Years in the Life of a Gambler, The Tower of Nesle, Angelo,* and *The Outlaw* (Ambrière, 548).

Although everything seemed the same, everything was different. The day religion had taken hold of Dorval, emphasis on motherhood followed. Her husband, Toussaint Merle, having lived through and accepted her years of infidelities, hardly knew what to make of this new and drastically different stay-at-home wife and mother. For the first time in his life, she treated him like a real husband, and he treated her like a real wife. Together, they celebrated the birth on December 12, 1844 of Caroline's second child, Marie.

Life seemed to have become so pleasurable to Merle that he decided to take the first vacation he had had in years. Several days following his arrival at the Austrian castle of Wildthurn in early October of 1844, he received a message informing him that his wife had suffered a *malaise.* Her performances in *The Outlaw* at the Odéon, and in Charles Duveyrier's *Lady Seymour,* at the Odéon as well, had been canceled. Not to worry was the consensus. She had suffered these spells before, most recently in March. They usually lasted only moments. Unlike the others, however, this latest one appeared to be far more severe and kept her in bed for forty-eight hours (Ambrière, 552). That she had counted on this latest play's success to pay off some of her more important debts, and found herself incapable of performing, increased her torment.

Four months later on January 5, 1845, despite her weakness, she, who had been born with a will of iron, resumed her performances of *Lady Seymour* at the Saint-Martin Theater.

While the play was mediocre, Dorval's acting was lauded by friends and critics alike. Sand considered her incarnation of Lady Seymour "gracious and natural." Jules Janin, writing for *Les Débats*, underscored her "pathos, her touching and real passion." *The Jounal des Théâtres* looked upon her Lady Seymour as one of her most brilliant creations (Ambrière, 555).

The perceptive Sand, aware of Dorval's financial problems and of her failing health, sought to rectify the former by giving her money, a gesture she could ill afford to make, by asking her publisher for an advance. No sooner had Dorval been informed of her friend's magnanimous intentions, than the deeply moved star made it clear to her that under no circumstances would she accept such a gift. Instead, she would apply to the Fund for Unemployed Actors. In this same way, surprisingly, Paris' stage star, Mlle George, once Dorval's rival, had finally come to understand the terrible lot of the actor once age and sickness begin rearing their ugly heads. With this in mind, she informed Dorval of her pledge to offer her services at a benefit performance in her honor, on May 13, 1845 (Ambrière, 556).

On that night of nights, the curtain rose at the Ventadour Theatre to a house filled to capacity. Friends such as Vigny had bought a box for the gala event; however he accepted the Countess d'Agoult's last minute invitation to sit in her box, now that she had broken off her liaison with Liszt. The evening proceeded to perfection. Mlle George performed segments of Corneille's *Rodogune,* and Dorval sequences of Vigny's *Chatterton,* to standing ovations. So impressed had Marie d'Agoult been by this gala event in general, but most particularly by Dorval's acting, that she among many others wrote her the next day, apprising her of the spell she had cast on her audiences and most notably on herself. Never, she added, had Dorval looked more beautiful.

Nonetheless, the ever-present dark side of Dorval's life had yet to be resolved. While the funds received at the gala event had been plentiful, they had not covered all of her debts. Thus she found herself yet again obliged to go on tour. Still too weak to envisage a long circuit, she accepted the actor Jeault's invitation to join the troupe he was organizing in Normandy. She met him at Elbeuf and performed in *The Outlaw and Rabelais,* which, alas, drew few people to its orbit (Ambrière, 560). Nor did the summer's torrid heat help alleviate Dorval's health problems. In fact, her stay proved to be so taxing that it caused her voice to fade at times on stage. She returned to Paris on June 24, 1845 in a state of utter exhaustion.

On the brighter side, however, her joy as a grandmother remained unbounded! She loved playing the role of baby sitter for her daughter and son-in-law. Not that it was easy, given the fact that Georges was only twenty months old and his sister less than half that.

Since nothing in life remains stable, Dorval would have to resign herself to two facts: that her popularity had waned with the passing of years, and that melodrama was now thoroughly outdated. Hard work had taken its toll on her as well. She had clearly aged before her time. Although still receiving offers to perform, these emanated for the most part from small, frequently insignificant theaters outside of Paris. She, of course, responded to them with her usual spunk, but, alas, with diminished strength. Her repertoire had also slimmed down. To her glee, however, after perusing the first few scenes of Adolphe Denery's *Marie-Jeanne*, it was clear that she had been smitten by it. How could she not be? Its scenario seemed to have been molded to her specifications. It featured a woman of the people whose debauched husband had denuded her of virtually everything. Her extreme poverty and emotional distress having caused her milk to dry up, she was forced to leave her newborn in a town hospice. Intent upon raising her child on her own, this courageous mother took a job at the home of a kind widow, whose charity and compassion for her were noteworthy. In time, Marie-Jeanne amassed the necessary funds to support her son and, with anticipated joy, returned to the hospice only to be told that her child had been kidnapped. As to be expected, following several ultra-dramatic sob-producing mishaps, everything righted itself in the end and mother and child were reunited.

Dorval's identification with her character had been so profound, that no sooner had she read the script than a broad smile crossed her face. *Marie-Jeanne* would indeed be an ideal vehicle for her on two counts: the protagonist encapsulated the wretched of the earth, and her sole *raison d'être* was her infant son.

So deeply rooted had Dorval's reading experience been, that even prior to rehearsals, the emotionally and physically spent star began fantasizing about the infant's health, his well-being, and in the process, became traumatized by the very thought of his disappearance. Nightmares started plaguing her. What if her grandchild, Georges, were to vanish, she asked herself, cringing at the very prospect of such a calamity. She grew increasingly tense. Her nerves, now continuously on edge for want of sleep, set off panic attacks. Solitude, exhaustion and extreme anxiety now governed Dorval's world.

To allay her insomnia, she had recourse to a popular sleeping medicine of the day made of poppy seeds, which are the source of opium. She was convinced that this ancient perennial herb, with its milky juice, capsular fruits, including the sleep-inducing *somniferum,* would help her through her difficulties. On August 7, readers of the *Courrier des spectacles* were shocked to learn that Dorval had almost died from an overdose of poppy seeds. Forty-eight hours later, it was announced, that this full-blooded, powerful woman, had not only risen from her bed, but had been strong enough to participate in a benefit performance organized in honor of Mlle George, one of France's most celebrated actresses.

Nonetheless, the doctors ordered her to rest. After a two-month delay, she opened on November 11, 1845 with the event of the season, the much awaited *Marie-Jeanne*. At this stage of her life, few believed Dorval still capable of galvanizing her audience. Yet once again did this great actress call upon her will of iron to breathe life into her latest role, and effected just that. Strong when need be, tearful during moments of crisis, Dorval again proved her mettle. Audiences sobbed, wailed, laughed, and reveled in each twist and turn of the plot. The critiques were overwhelmingly adulatory. Perhaps the most incisive of these were Théophile Gautier's words on the subject:

> Nothing we can say could convey the effect she produced; nor possibly measure up to the real event; never has an actress reached such heights: art no longer existed, the very essence of nature itself came into being: maternity, encapsulated in but a single woman. Torrents of tears poured from everyone's eyes... Never have hearts been touched more poignantly... From where did Dorval extract such wrenching tones, such pathetic sighs, such despairing poses... (Ambrière, 563)

Everything, nonetheless, has its price! The tremendous effort expended by Dorval during her role of this five-act play had so drained her energies, that several days after the opening, on November 16 and 17, she was obliged to cancel her performances. Two weeks later, she returned to the stage and suffered a relapse. Further rest was ordered. When she finally returned to the theater several weeks later, her doctors advised her to perform only five days a week. She acquiesced. *Marie-Jeanne* enjoyed such extraordinary success that crowds were fighting for tickets. One newspaper reported that more people were waiting in line to buy tickets than could be accommodated in the theater. Despite the fanfare and Dorval's immense popularity, creditors continued to hound her. They even brought her before a judge, who determined that one third of her salary was to be extracted to pay off her debts. But even this latest ruling failed to accomplish the desired goal. In order to increase her earnings, the determined actress spent most of her free days in a stagecoach, traveling sixteen hours to Orléans, among other relatively near-by cities, only to be disappointed by the meager crowds she had drawn.

Acting, while still Dorval's vocation, was, however, no longer her passion. Grandmotherhood had replaced it. Her beloved Georges, whom she saw daily, had become the focus of her existence. She doted on him, cared for him in every way.

By January 15, 1846, performances of *Marie-Jeanne* were suddenly canceled. This time, it was no *malaise*. Dorval had fallen gravely ill. Contrary to a younger doctor's diagnosis of a bad case of nerves, the well-known specialist Dr. Andral, called in on the case, diagnosed her illness as acute pleurisy.

To Dorval's great disappointment, a long awaited trip to Marseilles to visit some dear friends had to be canceled. Even more discouraging was the fact that she had planned on taking her beloved now two-and-a-half year-old grandson with her. Dorval, the fighter, refused to face facts (Ambrière, 560). She even kept reassuring her stage partner, the egocentric Bocage, of her return to the theater in a matter of weeks. Few people had, strangely enough, been aware of his duplicitous nature. Only upon learning that he had tried to impose Mlle Naptal as lead in François Ponsard's second play, *Agnès de Méranie,* in which Dorval was to star, did she begin to face facts. Fate, working, at times, in mysterious ways, gave her the last laugh. She learned that Ponsard had been so dissatisfied with Mlle Naptal's performance, that he demanded Dorval play the lead.

Bocage, nonetheless, pursued his insidious battle against Dorval, by allowing, or perhaps instigating, the *Courrier des spectacles* to carry articles dealing with her eroding health (Ambrière, 572). For the time being, *Agnès de Méranie* was put on hold, allowing Dorval's recuperative powers to operate. During the long months of sickness that followed, she would have time to reflect, to review her past friendships, to single out those on whom she could depend from the many false friends forever fawning about her. Uppermost on her list of true friends was George Sand. Warm, generous, understanding, and trustworthy in every sense of the word, she knew she could always be counted on in time of need. From Hugo, surprisingly, she had not received a single note. His silence could, she thought, be attributed to the fact that he had recently become a *peer of France*. Dumas, for all of his *bragadaccio*, his intrigues, his fanciful intents, had inquired about her state of health, but had never once seen fit to step into her home. That she had not received the briefest of missives from Vigny tore at her deeply. After all, they had been through so much together – *Chatterton* and *La Maréchale d'Ancre* – not to speak of their passionate love affair. She winced! She would ask her friend Olympe Chodzko to write to him, requesting he return all mementoes she had given him. That Sandeau had failed to drop her a note, was not overly vexing. She might have recalled the old adage – *take it whence it comes*.

By July, *grandma* Dorval was en route to Marseilles with her beloved two-and-a-half year-old grandson, Georges. She would have plenty of time to bask in adoration of him He was so utterly adorable, she mused. But was she quite aware of his frailty? His parents may have tried to dissuade her from taking him along, but must have acquiesced when faced by her determination. Should they have negated her intent, the child would have surely been brought to tears and, perhaps more. The doctor had warned them against provoking such emotional turmoil. Was it wise, however, to keep a child up to all hours of the night in drafty, some-times cold and damp theaters and dressing rooms? Surely not! Yet, the parents complied.

Dorval, motivated by her passion alone, never even considered an alternative.

Dorval was hopeful that her agenda – *The Two Jail Birds, The Outlaw, Marie-Jeanne,* and, her favorite tragedy, *Phèdre*, would draw crowds. Their stop in Marseilles proved to be delightful. Relatives and friends were there to entertain the child. Upon continuing on to Nîmes, Montpellier, and Sète, Georges, a normally active boy, proved not so easy to manage. He loved to roughhouse and play pranks. Dorval had to admit that she was not as strong as she thought herself to be. Twice she had to cancel performances due to ill health. Nor, for the most part, were there crowds eager to see her perform. Grandmother and child were back in Paris by early November 1846, in time for her rehearsals in *Agnès de Méranie*. By June, Dorval was diagnosed as having an inflammation of the lungs. Nor was her good old Merle in the best of health. No matter, *Agnès de Méranie* opened on December 22, at the Odéon. Although Dorval usually enjoyed playing poor and disenchanted women, she thoroughly enjoyed her new role as king Philippe Auguste's second wife in her latest theatrical venture. She commented on the joy she felt speaking elegant French and wearing such luxurious costumes. Although her acting was lauded by many, others considered it dismal. As for the play, it was less than compelling (Ambrière, 584). That Dorval's friend Gustave Planche, whom she had helped financially for many years though she could ill afford to do so, wrote a deprecating review of the play in the *Revue des Deux Mondes,* hurt her deeply. Even Ponsard, strangely enough, began maligning her. Why, she wondered? As the weeks passed, Dorval grew bitter, conceding that the few plays in which she now appeared, were mindless. Sadder still, however, was her deteriorating health. On April 13, 1847, she made her last stage appearance at the Odéon in *Le Syrien* by Latour Saint-Ybars. Her contract with the Odéon expired and would not be renewed.

By June 11, 1847, Dorval left Paris accompanied by her three year-old grandson in yet another vain attempt to forget her recent theatrical failures and to recoup her finances. In Brussels she performed only in second rate theaters and to dismal critiques, after which she and Georges wended their way southward, traveling to Toulouse, to Carpentras, to wherever a theater would have her, even if it was only a rundown barn. Her nomadic existence made her unreachable. Vigny wrote Merle to inquire about Dorval's willingness to perform in *Chatterton.* It was to no avail, since no one knew her whereabouts (Ambrière, 617). When finally reachable, Leopold Holstein, founder of the Théâtre Historique, invited her to perform in *Marie-Jeanne,* and *The Stepmother,* Balzac's, long-awaited play. Under normal circumstances she would have accepted with glee, but her beloved four year-old Georges had taken seriously ill.

CHAPTER 12

Georges, whom Dorval had adored since she first held him in her arms shortly after his birth, had always been sickly. Her love for him had moved her to take special care of him. Indeed, she had spent virtually every possible moment of day and night in his company. But had her care been the type he needed? Taking him on tour since the age of two, stopping at Nîmes, Avignon, Marseilles, to mention but a few of the cities they traversed, would have been fatiguing for even a healthy child. As for the little tot, he so adored his grandmother, that no matter her on- or off-stage antics, he responded to them with giggles, jokes and even imitations. When he heard audiences applauding her and screaming their bravos, he too applauded and hollered his approval. In time, Dorval realized that it was unwise for a child, particularly one as frail as he, to remain so late at the theater. She suggested she would put him to bed before leaving at night, and awaken him for a minute or two upon her return. So generous of heart was he, that he told his grandmother that he would awaken himself at the appropriate time. He did just that. Upon her return she would show him the bouquets of flowers she had received, then play with him for a bit, after which the deeply religious Dorval opened her Bible, said a few prayers, then, most tenderly, turned toward him, saying, "sleep, my infant Jesus," after which, Georges went back to sleep.

By day, Dorval looked for acting jobs. If she did not take him with her, Georges would patiently await her return, promising her to read the books she had given him, most of which were devoted to the lives of saints. In winter time, she admonished the docile child to stay near the open hearth but never to approach it. She looked upon her grandson as a saintly creature: tender, generous, undemanding, and loving. On those occasions when a theatrical director failed to hire her, and she returned saddened by her lot, she would smother him with hugs and kisses, compensating for the rejection weighing heavily on her heart. The extremist Dorval loved him as she had loved no other being in her life. He responded in kind, virtually anticipating her mood changes. When he thought her downcast, he would bounce up and down, pirouette about, grimace, gesture, laugh and cry at the same time, as children do. The clown in him was so pleased each time he succeeded in diverting his grandmother from her somber moods.

One evening, upon her return, as she took the child in her arms to hug him, his body suddenly went limp. At first, she thought he was playing a game. It was no game. The doctor was immediately called. Georges returned to consciousness, but only briefly. On May 16. 1848, after eleven days of utmost care on Dorval's part, the death rattle had set in, and her beloved Georges died of what the doctor diagnosed as brain fever. He was only four-and-a-half years old. In her prayers, however, the deeply religious Dorval for the first time was unable to thank her God for having taken away her beloved Georges (Ambrière, 626).

One might ask why Georges' parents had not intervened and prevented Dorval from traveling about with their sickly child? After all, he had fallen seriously ill two years earlier, in 1846, upon his return with his grandmother from a previous tour in the South of France. Hadn't his condition at that time been sufficiently serious to clue his parents in on his eroding state of health? A conscientious doctor would have also taken issue with the manner in which she traveled about with Georges, and suggested she choose other, less fatiguing alternatives. Why, one may question, had she made up her mind to leave for the South of France in September, knowing the weather to be inclement at this time?

Georges was buried in the Montparnasse cemetery, where the inconsolable Dorval visited him daily. Only he, Georges, she felt, could have redeemed her. To her ever-understanding and loving Sand, she wrote that this child had been the love of her life. She lived *paradise* with him. She believed that his birth had been God's way of recompensing her for having worked so hard and struggled so fiercely throughout her life to make a name for herself and to support her entire family and more!

After three months of horrible suffering, Dorval acquiesced to the demands from family, friends, and audiences, that she go back to the stage. Out of deference to Holstein, she agreed to do so, at the

Théâtre Historique, in *Charles VII and his great Vassals,* and would have performed in Balzac's *Step Mother,* had he not gone off to visit his beloved Mme Hanska in Wierzchownia, on September 28, 1848.

While Dorval's continuously interfering son-in-law, Duguet, kept urging her to go back to the stage, the manner in which he went about it was hardly appropriate. Merle, on the other hand, sensitive to her bereavement, hoped she would perform again, if only to distract her from her lengthy daily visits to the cemetery (Ambrière, 634). While not one of the roles offered to her was tempting, she took another theatrical matter to heart: namely, her admittance to the Comédie-Française. With this in mind, she wrote a letter to Samson on December 17, 1848, explaining her desire to return to the theater, but to perform only in certain suitable parts, most specifically those offered in Molière's plays at the Comédie-Française (Ambrière, 635). The pusillanimous actors on the membership committee revealed their true colors. Upon taking an oral, rather than a written vote, they denied her entrance to this institution. Membership committee corruption was not only tolerated, it was mandatory! Still she did not give up hope to be accepted by the Comédie-Française some day. Hugo, Scribe, Dumas, Vigny, Musset, as well as others, signed petitions in favor of her admittance. Or so they said. But it was not to be.

Although disappointed by the outcome, nothing could compare to the irreparable loss of her grandson. To try to steer her thoughts away from painful channels, Merle urged his wife to wait for a suitable part in a play she liked, rather than accepting anything that might come her way. Her son-in-law, who unfortunately had in his insidiously foolish way come to dominate his mother-in-law, convinced her otherwise. The well-known writer, Théodore de Banville, happened upon a performance of *Marie-Jeanne* at the Théâtre Saint Marcèle, playing to a group of hoodlums in a dingy and poorly lit theater on rue Mouffetard.

That she had allowed herself to be manipulated by her unthinking, unreasonable, arrogant, and dictatorial son-in-law Luguet added to Dorval's pathos. But by now performing had become rote to Dorval. Nothing mattered anymore. Neither disturbed nor disappointed by the shoddiness of the surroundings or the poor attendance, the tired, weak, and broken-hearted grandmother was sustained by Georges' memory alone. In her Bible, she wrote asking

Georges to pray to God to give her the courage to sustain her in her loss, until God saw fit to reunite them. Henceforth, Dorval spent her days in prayer besides Georges' grave, and on tour with her son-in-law, playing to ever smaller audiences the outdated works of yesteryear.

Though exhausted, she again acquiesced to Luguet's insistence that she tour Caen. This time, however, she chose to make the trip alone. Upon arrival on May 12, she attributed her great fatigue to the eighteen-hour stagecoach ride. Since she was not scheduled to perform until the 15th, she reasoned, she would have ample time to rest. She was mistaken. Her condition became worrisome. The doctor was called. He ordered complete bedrest, diagnosing her illness as a pernicious fever due to an ulcerated liver. Although in bed, Dorval's pain did not abate. She asked for pen and pencil and wrote a letter to her daughter around May 13, admonishing her to continue her mother's cult of honoring Georges. She must lock the door of his room, thus barring everyone access to it, even little Marie. Georges' bed must be placed in the center of the room and Dorval's open portrait, upon it. Flowers were to be strewn all about. "Give him the springtime he can no longer see," after which, she must spend the entire day in prayer, both in his name and in the name of his grandmother (Ambrière, 649).

Sensing that death was near, Dorval asked to be brought back to Paris. Her good and kind husband, Merle, was so saddened by his wife's condition that he was unable to write his weekly article for the *Union*. A priest was requested. One hour later, Dorval was dead. Few in Paris attended her funeral on May 22 at the Church of Saint Thomas Aquinas. The family and faithful friends, among them, Hugo, Vaquerie, Dumas, Sandeau, Mlle George, Rachel, Samson, Geffroy, Holstein, among others, accompanied the hearse to the Montparnasse cemetery. Because communication was so slow in France, Sand, Vigny, Ponsard, Lemaître, among many others, learned of her demise days after the event. The dramatist Camille Doucet spoke but a few words before tears prevented him from going on (Ambrière, 651). Dumas, not an orator, could not speak. He was, nonetheless, one of the few who accompanied her body to the grave. Vigny wrote to Charles Blanc, minister of the interior, to request sufficient funds for Dorval's burial. Hugo, recalling Dorval's kindness after the demise of his beloved daughter in 1843, requested, ironically enough, that the Comédie-Française put on a benefit performance for Dorval's grandchildren. His request was honored.

BIBLIOGRAPHY

Allevy, Marie Antoinette. *La mise en scène en France dans la première moitié du 19ème siècle.* Paris: Droz, 1938.

Almanach des spectacles de Paris, 1824.

Ambrière, Francis. *Mlle Mars et Marie Dorval.* Paris: Seuil, 1992.

Ambrière, Francis. *Marie Dorval ou la Femme Romantique.* n.p.n.d. (1937).

Aubert, Charles, *The Art of Pantomime.* Translated from the French by Edith Sears.

Baldick, Robert. *La Vie de Frédérick Lemaître.* Paris: Editions Denoel, 1961.

Banville, Théodore. *Les Pauvres Saltimbanques.* Paris: Calman-Lévy, 1895.

Bassan, Fernande. *Alfred de Vigny et la Comédie-Française.* Tubigen: Gunter Narr Verlag, 1984.

Brazier, N. *Le Boulevard du Temple,* 1832.

Brisson, Adolphe. *L'Envers de la gloire. Documents inédits.* Paris: Flammarion, 1989.

Brooks, Peter. *The Melodramatic Imagination.* New Haven: Yale University Press, 1970.

Carlson, Marvin. *Places of Performance: The Semiotics of Theatre Architecture.* Ithaca: Cornell University Press, 1989.

Cate, Curtis. *George Sand.* New York: Houghton Mifflin Company, 1975.

Coupy, Emile. *Marie Dorval,* Documents inédits, biographie, critique et bibliographie, 1868.

Croisset, Françis de. *La Vie parisienne au théâtre.* Paris: Bernard Grasset, 1929.

Davidson, Arthur Fitzwilliam. *Alexandre Dumas (père): his Life and Works.* Westminster: A. Constable & Co., Ltd., 1902.

Dorval Marie. *Lettres à Alfred de Vigny.* Paris: Gallimard, 1942.

Ducange, Victor and Dinaux (pseudonym). *Trente ans ou la vie d'un joueur.* Paris: Barba, 1827.

Dumas, Alexandre. *La dernière année de Marie Dorval.* Paris: La Librairie Nouvelle, 1855.

Dumas, Alexandre. *Mémoires.* Paris, 1888.

Dumas, Alexandre. *Mes souvenirs.* Paris: Gallimard, 1954.

Dupuy, Ernest. *Alfred de Vigny et Victor Hugo.*

Marie Dorval, *Souvenirs dramatiques*, 213.

Dunlap, William. *Ducange: False Shame and Thirty Years of a Gambler's Life.*

Dupuy, Ernest. *Alfred de Vigny La jeunesse des romantiques*. Paris: Société
Française d'Imprimerie et de Librairie, 1905.

Dupuy, Ernest. *Alfred de Vigny, la vie et l'oeuvre*. Paris: Hachette, 1913.

Durant, Will and Ariel. *The Story of Civilization*, vol. XI. The Age of Napoleon. Simon and Shuster, 1975.

Evans, David-Owen. *Le Drame moderne à l'époque romantique*. Geneva, Switzerland: Slatkine Reprints, 1974.

Flottes, Pierre. *Alfred de Vigny*. Paris: Perrin & Co., 1925

Fontaney, Antoine. *Madame Dorval*. Paris, 1831.

Fontaney, Antoine. *Journal Intime*. Les Presses françaises. Paris, 1925.

Galipaux, Félix, *Acteurs et actrices d'autrefois*. Felix Alcan, Paris, 1929.

Gaylor, Anna. *Marie Dorval: grandeur et misère d'une actrice romantique*. Paris: Flammarion, 1989.

Gautier, Théophile. *Histoire du romantisme*. Paris: Editions d'aujourd'hui, 1978.

Germain, François. *Vigny: Chatterton, Quitte pour la peur*. Paris: Flammarion, 1968.

Houssaye, Arsène. *Les Confessions*. Denty, 1891.

Hugo, Victor. *Théâtre Complet*. Préface by Roland Purnal, Notices and Notes by J.J. Thierry and Josette Mélèze. Paris: Pléiade, Gallimard, I., l963.

Janin, Jules. *Histoire de la litterature dramatique*.Vol. 3, 4. Geneva: Slatkine Reprints, volumes I, II, V, and VI, 1970.

Kozik, Francis. *The Great Debureau*. Trans. by Dora Round. New York: Farrar & Rinehart, Inc., 1940.

Lawson, Joan. Mime. *The Theory and Practice of Expressive Gesture*. Dance Horizons.

Le Hir, Marie-Pierre. *Le Romantisme aux enchères: Ducange, Pixérécourt, Hugo*. Amsterdam/Philadelphia: John Benjamin's Publishing Company, 1992.

Moser, Françoise. *Marie Dorval*. Paris: Plon, 1947.

Maurice, Charles. *Feu le Boulevard du Temple. Résurrection épistolaire.* Paris: Rue Bleue, 19, 1863.

Maurois, André. *Lélia, the Life of George Sand.* Translated from the French by Gerard Hopkins.

Palmer, Jack White (trans). Alexandre Dumas: *A Great Life in Brief.* Knopf: New York, 1955.

Maurois, André. *Les Trois Dumas.* Hachette, 1957.

Hopkins, Gerard (trans.). *The Titans: A Three Generation Biography of the Dumas's.* New York: Harper Brothers Publishers, 1957.

Nozière, F. *Marie Dorval.* Paris: Félix Alcan: Paris, 1926.

Plunkett, Jacques. *Fantômes et souvenirs de La Porte Saint-Martin.* Editions Ariane, l946.

Parigot, H. *Le Drame d'Alexandre Dumas.* Geneva: Slatkine Reprints, 1973.

Pollitzer, Marcel, *Trois reines de théâtre.* Mars, Dorval, Rachel, Paris: Editions du Vieux Colombier, 1958.

Ponsard, F. *Œuvres complètes.* Michel Levy, 1865.

Powers, Elizabeth. "From 'Empfindungsleben' to 'Erfahrungsbereich': The Creation of Experience in Goethe's Die Laune des Verliebten." *Goethe's Yearbook*, vol. viii. Columbia, South Carolina: Camden House, 1996.

Praviel, Armand, *Le Roman douloureux d'Alfred de Vigny.* Paris: Les Editions de France, n.d.

Rahill, F. *The World of Melodrama.* Pennsylvania: The Pennsylvania State University Press, 1967.

Rodmell, Graham E. *French Drama of the Revolutionary Years.* London and New York: Routledge, 1990.

Sand, George. *Correspondance inédite [de] George Sand et Marie Dorval,* published with an introduction and notes by Simone André-Maurois. Gallimard, 1953.

Sand, G. *Histoire de ma vie.* Text edited and annotated by Georges Lubin, Paris: Gallimard, 1971.

Sand, George. *Correspondance de George Sand, II (1832-1835).* Textes réunis, classés et annotés par Georges Lubin. Paris: Garnier Frères, 1966.

Sakellaridès, Emma. *Alfred de Vigny, auteur dramatique.* Paris: Edition de la Plume, 1902.

Séché, Alphonse. *La Passion romantique: Antony, Marion Delorme, Chatterton,* 1921.

Silver, M. *Jules Sandeau, l'homme et la vie.* Paris: Boisvin, 1936.

Stendhal. *Racine et Shakespeare.* Paris: Garnier-Flammarion, 1970.

Storey, Robert. *Pierrots on the Stage of Desire.* New Jersey: Princeton University Press, 1985.

Thomasseau, J. M. *Le Mélodrame.* Paris: PUF, 1984.

Touchard, P. A. *Grandes heures théâtrales à Paris.* Paris: Librairie Académique Perrin., l965.

Vacquerie, Auguste. *Profils et grimaces.* Michel Lévy, 1856.

Van Thieghem, Philippe. *Le Romantisme.* Paris: PUF, 1984.

Verve, December, 1937.

Vigny, Alfred. *Œuvre complètes, Pléiade I and II.* Paris: Gallimard, 1948.

Vigny, Alfred. *Correspondance.* Paris: Conard, 1935.

Vigny, Contesse de. *Conseils à mon fils.* Paris: Eude, 1912.

Watts, Franklin. *Alexandre Dumas Genius of Life.* Claude Schapps, trans. New York: A.J. Koch, 1988.

Whitridge, Arnold. *Alfred de Vigny.* London: Oxford University Press,1933.

Zimmermann, Daniel. *Alexandre Dumas le Grand.* Paris: Faillard, 1993.